# The Underground Railroad

# THE UNDERGROUND RAILROAD

## A REFERENCE GUIDE

Kerry Walters

Guides to Historic Events in America

ABC-CLIO

Santa Barbara, California • Denver, Colorado • Oxford, England

**Library of Congress Cataloging-in-Publication Data**

Walters, Kerry S.
  The Underground Railroad : a reference guide / Kerry Walters.
      p. cm. — (Guides to historic events in America)
  Includes bibliographical references and index.
  ISBN 978-1-59884-647-8 (hardcopy : acid-free paper) — ISBN 978-1-59884-648-5
(ebook)   1. Underground railroad.   2. Antislavery movements—United
States—History—19th century.   3. Fugitive slaves—United States—History.
4. Abolitionists—United States—History—19th century.   5. Slavery—United
States—History.   I. Title.
  E450.W323   2012
  973.7'115—dc23        2011041517

ISBN: 978-1-59884-647-8
EISBN: 978-1-59884-648-5

16  15  14  13  12        1  2  3  4  5

This book is also available on the World Wide Web as an eBook.
Visit www.abc-clio.com for details.

ABC-CLIO, LLC
130 Cremona Drive, P.O. Box 1911
Santa Barbara, California 93116-1911

This book is printed on acid-free paper ∞

Manufactured in the United States of America

# CONTENTS

# CHRONOLOGY
# OF EVENTS

1619  The first slaves in the British North American colonies arrive in Jamestown aboard a Dutch ship.

1688  Mennonites in Germantown, Pennsylvania, issue the first antislavery resolution in North America.

1775  Philadelphia Quakers found the first antislavery organization—the Pennsylvania Society for Promoting the Abolition of Slavery, the Relief of Negroes Unlawfully Held in Bondage, and for Improving the Condition of the African Race.

1777  The Vermont Republic enacts the first North American ban on slavery. The prohibition continues when Vermont becomes a state in 1791.

1787  The Northwest Ordinance allows slave owners to retrieve slaves who flee to the Northwest Territory, the 260,000-square-mile area (comprising modern-day Ohio, Indiana, Illinois, Michigan, Wisconsin, and part of Minnesota) ceded by the British to the United States after the Revolutionary War.

    Article IV, Section 2, the "fugitive slave and felon clause," is endorsed by members of the Constitutional Convention, constitutionally affirming the Northwest Ordinance slave clause.

1793  Congress passes the Fugitive Slave Act.

    The Emancipation Act of Upper Canada mandates a schedule for the full emancipation of Canadian slaves.

1800  Gabriel Prosser plans a slave insurrection in Virginia.

1804    New Jersey, the last northern state to do so, abolishes slavery, following Pennsylvania (1780), Massachusetts and New Hampshire (1783), Connecticut and Rhode Island (1784), Vermont (1791), and New York (1799).

1808    Importation of African slaves into the United States is outlawed.

1822    Denmark Vesey plans a slave insurrection in South Carolina.

1826    Secretary of State Henry Clay unsuccessfully petitions Great Britain for the return of slave fugitives in Canada.

1829    David Walker publishes *Appeal to the Colored Citizens of the World*.

        Wilberforce, the first black settlement in Canada, is founded.

1831    The term "Underground Railroad" is coined following the arrival of steam-powered locomotives in the United States.

        The New England Anti-Slavery Society is founded.

        William Lloyd Garrison publishes the first issue of the *Liberator*.

        Nat Turner's rebellion in Virginia.

1833    The American Anti-Slavery Society is founded.

1842    The U.S. Supreme Court in *Prigg v. Pennsylvania* upholds the 1793 Fugitive Slave Act but declines to oblige the states to cooperate with federal officers enforcing it.

        The Canadian black settlement of Dawn is founded.

1844    Officials in Pensacola, Florida, brand S.S., for "Slave Stealer," on Jonathan Walker's palm after his unsuccessful attempt to sail seven slaves to freedom.

        Slave abductors Calvin Fairbank and Delia Webster are sentenced to prison terms in Kentucky.

1845    *Narrative of the Life of Frederick Douglass, An American Slave* is published.

1847    The inaugural issue of *North Star*, an abolitionist paper co-edited by Frederick Douglass and Martin Delaney, is printed.

1848    Daniel Drayton, captain of the *Pearl*, tries to sail nearly 80 slaves out of Washington, D.C.

Slave Henry "Box" Brown mails himself in a wooden crate from Richmond to Philadelphia.

William and Ellen Craft disguise themselves as a white invalid and manservant and escape to Philadelphia.

Harriet Tubman escapes from slavery.

1849    *Narrative of the Life of Henry Bibb* is published.

Elgin, or the Buxton Settlement, the most successful of the Canadian black settlements, is founded.

1850    Congress passes a new Fugitive Slave Act, which mandates severe punishment for aiding and abetting fugitives.

1851    Serialization of Harriet Beecher Stowe's *Uncle Tom's Cabin* in the *National Era* begins. The novel is published as a book the following year.

Refugee Home Society, a Canadian black settlement, is founded.

The Christiana Riot erupts when slave catchers try to capture fugitives in Christiana, Pennsylvania.

William "Jerry" Henry is rescued in Syracuse, New York.

1854    An antislavery riot breaks out in Boston when fugitive Anthony Burns is arrested and returned to slavery.

True Band Societies form in Canada as relief organizations for fugitives.

Joshua Glover is rescued in Milwaukee, Wisconsin.

The Wisconsin Supreme Court declares the 1850 Fugitive Slave Act unconstitutional.

1855    Jane Johnson and her sons are rescued in Philadelphia.

1858    John Price is rescued in Oberlin-Wellington, Ohio.

1859    Charles Nalle is rescued in Troy, New York.

1861    Lucy Bagby, who will be the last fugitive rendered back to the South, is captured in Cleveland, Ohio.

South Carolina militia fire on Fort Sumter in Charleston harbor, launching the Civil War.

The first "contraband" fugitives seek asylum behind Union lines at Fortress Monroe, Virginia.

1863    The Emancipation Proclamation frees all slaves in the rebellious states.

1864    Congress repeals slave laws.

Slave abductor Calvin Fairbank is released from a Kentucky prison after 13 years and 30,000 lashes.

1865    The Thirteenth Amendment, which outlaws slavery, is ratified.

1870    The Fifteenth Amendment, granting voting privileges to black men, is ratified.

Stationmasters Levi Coffin in Cincinnati and George DeBaptiste in Detroit declare the Underground Railroad officially shut down.

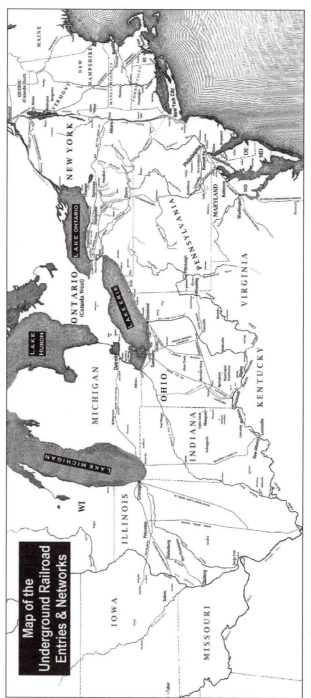

Overview of areas comprising the Underground Railroad. (Tom Calarco)

# THE UNDERGROUND RAILROAD: LEGEND AND REALITY

The only free road, the Underground Railroad, [has] tunneled under the whole breadth of the land.

—*Henry David Thoreau*

Despite its name, the Underground Railroad wasn't a subterranean passageway bored through living rock beneath the earth's surface. Instead, it was something much more extraordinary: a decades-long campaign of mainly nonviolent civil disobedience participated in by thousands of people with a burning commitment to justice. What bound all Underground Railroad workers together—women and men, black and white, rich and poor, educated and illiterate—was the shared conviction that slavery was a moral abomination and that the laws of the land that allowed some humans to own others ought to be disobeyed whenever possible by offering aid and harbor to runaway slaves.

Like all acts of civil disobedience, this one was risky. Helping a slave to escape was a crime—an act of theft, given that slaves were the legal property of their owners—punishable by fine and imprisonment. The law was unequivocal. The 1787 Northwest Ordinance and Article IV, Section 2 of the U.S. Constitution declared that slaves who escaped to Free States still remained slaves and could be seized by their owners. The Fugitive Slave Acts of 1793 and 1850 added clout to the law by mandating stiff penalties for persons abetting fugitives. Anyone convicted of helping a slave abscond—and, after 1850, even a citizen whose only offense was refusing to cooperate in a runaway slave's capture—was subject to a hefty fine, a six-month prison sentence, and "civil damages to the party injured by such

illegal conduct, the sum of one thousand dollars for each fugitive so lost."[1]
Daniel Webster, while secretary of state in Millard Fillmore's administration, upped the ante even more by calling violations of slave laws nothing
less than "distinctly treasonable."[2] And indeed, at least twice in 1851, participants in Underground Railroad actions *were* charged with treason. On
other occasions, they were jailed, imprisoned, branded, beaten, or pilloried.
At the very least, Railroad workers risked public revilement in the proslavery press, in both the North and the South.


## HIGHER LAW AND OUTLAW

Yet thousands remained undeterred. Most frequently, they justified their
willful violation of the slave laws by insisting that they were obeying a
higher, nobler law that took precedence over unjust human legislation.[3]
Rev. John Rankin, one of Ohio's leading Underground Railroad stationmasters, insisted that "disobedience to [slave laws] is obedience to God."[4]
Rankin's fellow Ohioan, Congressman Joshua R. Giddings, agreed. "Let
no man tell me there is no higher law," he declared. "We feel there is a law
of right, of justice, of freedom, implanted in the breast of every intelli-
gent human being, that bids him look with scorn upon [slave laws]."[5] The
abolitionist Theodore Parker maintained, "I owe no allegiance [to slave
laws]. Humanity, Christianity, manhood revolts against [them]. . . . For
myself, I say it solemnly, I will shelter, I will help, and I will defend the
fugitive with all my humble means and power."[6] Frederick Douglass, the
great black abolitionist, put it plainly and unmistakably. "The authority
of God," he wrote, "is greater than the authority of man."[7]

Southern response to the "higher law" justification was predictably furious. Slave owners insisted that their constitutionally guaranteed right to
hold property was violated by Railroad agents who helped fugitives, and
accused Northern officers of the law and politicians of turning a blind eye
to such violations. Stephen Hale of Alabama spoke for many of his fellow
Southerners when he warned about the threat of "Yankee fanaticism" to
their way of life. "They attack us through their literature, in their schools,
from the hustings, in their legislative halls, through the public press, and
even their courts of justice."[8] One of South Carolina's reasons for seced-
ing from the Union in 1861 was the aggrieved claim that Railroad workers and other abolitionists "have encouraged and assisted thousands of

our slaves to leave their homes."[9] And shortly after his inauguration as president of the Confederacy, Jefferson Davis had the Underground Railroad in mind when he said that "fanatical organizations [are] assiduously engaged in exciting amongst the slaves a spirit of discontent and revolt; means [are] furnished for their escape from their owners; and agents secretly employed to entice them to abscond."[10] So far as the South was concerned, Underground Railroad workers weren't following a higher law at all. They were merely outlaws, thieves of other men's property.

## SEPARATING FACT FROM FOLKLORE

Sometimes, especially north of the Free States that bordered the Mason-Dixon Line and particularly in the decade leading up to the Civil War, Underground Railroad workers were publicly defiant of slave laws and openly boastful of their deeds in newspapers. As angry opposition to slavery escalated in the 1850s, several dramatic and highly publicized rescues of fugitives at risk of being returned to the South by federal officials also took place. But for the most part, both because they were breaking the law and in order to protect the runaway slaves they were helping, Railroad workers operated as clandestinely as they could.

After the Civil War, the secrecy that surrounded the Underground Railroad tended to encourage fanciful folklore and romantic legend. As historian Larry Gara persuasively argues,[11] one reason for this is the paucity of contemporaneous written documentation about the Railroad and subsequent historians' too-uncritical reliance on anecdote and oral tradition. Railroad workers and fugitives who told their stories to reporters and chroniclers 20, 30, or 40 years after the event can hardly be faulted for imaginative embellishment, but their accounts ought to be taken with a grain of salt. Another reason is the fact that both abolitionist and proslavery journalists tended to exaggerate, for their own purposes, the scope and activities of the Railroad. A third explanation for the distortion is that most accounts of the Railroad, contemporaneous or later, were written by whites and often emphasized, even if unintentionally, white involvement at the expense of black involvement. Consequently, the understanding of the Underground Railroad that has evolved in the nation's consciousness often distorts the facts. According to popular understanding, the Railroad was a vast, highly structured, and tightly coordinated network; its hidden trails and secret safe houses penetrated deeply into the southern states; and blacks played a mostly passive role in contrast to white Railroad workers. Each of these assertions is false, or at least greatly exaggerated.

In the first place, it's more accurate to think of the Underground Railroad in terms of function rather than organization. Broadly, the work of the Railroad encompassed a wide range of activities aimed at getting slaves out of the South and protecting them once they were in the North. In some places, especially in such cities as Cincinnati and Philadelphia, the activities were relatively well coordinated. In other places, fleeing slaves were often helped by a loosely linked chain of individuals who offered a meal, a bed, and directions to the house of the next Good Samaritan up the line. Participants in the work of the Underground Railroad came and went—there were no membership lists or requirements—and this alone would have been enough to make the Railroad's organization rather fluid. But a more powerful reason for the relative absence of structure was the need for continuous adaptability. Railroad workers couldn't afford to stick to one settled route or series of safe houses, lest they be discovered by law enforcement or slave catchers. Flexibility was essential.

Given that the Railroad is better defined functionally than organizationally, it's difficult to determine a date of origin for its activities. Slaves fled bondage from the earliest days of slavery in the colonies, and many of them were assisted by sympathetic whites. Exactly when coordinated efforts to assist fugitives began remains unknown. But what is unquestionable is that the Railroad was up and running in the three decades prior to the Civil War, paralleling the emergence of the abolitionist movement, with the greatest activity taking place in the 1850s. As we'll see in later chapters, the passage in 1850 of a particularly draconian slave law was responsible for the surge in activity during that decade.

Less uncertain than the Railroad's date of origin is when it acquired the name by which it became known far and wide. Railroads weren't part of the American landscape until 1830. The earliest ones made for unpleasant riding: dust, cinders, and coal smoke flowed into the train's passenger cars, covering everyone with soot until, in the words of a contemporary traveler, everyone looked "blacker than the Ethiope"[12]—an unintentionally ironic observation, given the clientele that the later Underground Railroad would serve. But for all its discomforts, travel by rail was impressively swift, sometimes clocking in at an astounding 30 miles per hour.

It was the speed of rail transportation that seems to have inspired the term "Underground Railroad." There are several versions of how the name came about, but the most common one revolves around a fugitive named Tice Davids. In 1831, Davids, a Kentucky slave, was making for the Ohio River and freedom just ahead of his pursuing master. He leapt into the river, swam across, and disappeared so quickly that his perplexed master is supposed to have said that he must have "gone off on an underground road." In no time at all, the telling and retelling of the story turned the "underground road" into an "underground railroad," and the name stuck. Before long, well-traveled escape routes became "lines" or "tracks," fugitives were called "passengers" or sometimes "packages," volunteers became "conductors" or "agents," safe houses became "stations" or "depots" managed by "stationmasters," and citizens who contributed funds or supplies to Railroad activities without personally participating in them became "stockholders." The railroad nomenclature the movement adopted undoubtedly contributed to the legend that the Underground Railroad was centralized, nationwide, and meticulously mapped out.

It's significant that the Tice Davids story has the fugitive disappear once he hits the northern bank of the Ohio River. Underground Railroad routes and lines usually started in the free border states and blossomed northward. For the most part they didn't extend, root-like, into the southern states. There were individual Southerners who disapproved of slavery and were willing to assist the occasional fugitive who came their way, and there were even small communities, such as the North Carolina Quaker one from which future Railroad stationmaster Levi Coffin came, that collectively offered aid to runaways. It's also the case that a few agents affiliated with the Railroad ventured south to actively recruit fugitives and guide them northward. The most famous of these "abductors," as they came to be called, was the ex-slave Harriet Tubman. But proslavery sentiment was so strong in the South, and state and local laws against slave stealing were so harsh, that the Underground Railroad for the most part stayed north of the Mason-Dixon Line.

What this means is that slaves fleeing bondage generally had to rely on their own initiative, ingenuity, and courage to make it to the Free States. Once there, Underground conductors and stationmasters were available to take them farther north and help them find shelter and work. But it was up to the fugitives to plan their escape and then evade slave patrols and slave catchers, avoid illness and accident, stave off hunger and exposure to heat and cold, and find their way north, often guided by little other than the North Star. Given the odds against them, it's extraordinary that an estimated 1,000 to 2,000 slaves managed to escape each year in the three decades before the Civil War. Many others tried and failed.

Once north of the Mason-Dixon Line, fugitives were frequently assisted by white Underground workers and agents. But it's also the case that much aid came from black residents in the North, many of whom were escaped slaves themselves. Numerous Railroad conductors and stationmasters were black and worked closely with white abolitionists. In fact, the Underground Railroad was one of the first large-scale interracial collaborations in the United States. Additionally, established black communities in the North generously contributed funds and supplies to runaways. Vigilance committees, charged with seeing to the material welfare of fugitives, were often founded and operated by free blacks in such cities as New York, Boston, Philadelphia, and Cincinnati. And hundreds of ex-slaves demonstrated resolve and self-sufficiency by founding all-black settlements in Canada, a land that generously opened its doors to fugitives in the antebellum years. From first to last, blacks were active participants in the Underground Railroad, rather than mere passengers. Their engagement should come as no surprise. For generations, slaves had resisted their servitude to "ol' massa" in ways that ranged from day-to-day covert insubordination to, occasionally, overt insurrection. Indeed, given that there were no Southern Underground Railroad lines, there would have been very few passengers on the Railroad at all were it not for slaves' determination to make it to the Free States.

## A BRIGHT, SHINING MOMENT

The literature on the Underground Railroad is vast—the annotated bibliography at the end of this book gives some indication of its scope—and this volume aims to do little more than offer readers an introduction to the movement. Chapter 1 provides some background by examining the ethos of resistance in slave communities that encouraged slaves to run for freedom in the first place. Chapter 2 explores the difficulties slaves faced when they ran and the means by which they struggled to navigate their way northward. Chapter 3 takes a look at the different Underground Railroad routes available to slaves after they reached the North.

Much of the Railroad's activity was clandestine. But chapter 4 focuses on overt rescues of fugitives in danger of being returned to slavery once they reached the North. Chapter 5 examines settlements of fugitives in the "Canaan land" of Canada. In addition to the bibliography, the narrative is complemented by a timeline, a number of primary documents (including a generous selection of fugitives' narratives) pertaining to the Underground Railroad, and biographical sketches of nearly 30 key figures in the movement.

Many of the stories about the Underground Railroad that have captured the national imagination have caught on because they're the exciting stuff of dime-novel melodrama—secret hideaways in safe houses, subterranean tunnels, hair-raising night raids by slave patrols, desperate slaves fighting off bloodhounds, heroic rescues of incarcerated fugitives. Yet because it's sometimes difficult to distinguish fact from folklore in such tales, we can find ourselves uncertain about how literally to take them.

But one thing about the Underground Railroad is indisputable: the nobility of the people, fugitives and agents alike, associated with it. The Railroad era was a bright, shining moment in the history of the United States in which a relatively small number of black and white men and women made sacrifices and risked retribution to offer aid to people fleeing servitude and degradation. John Parker, an ex-slave and Railroad conductor, said it well: "The success of the fugitives was absolutely dependent upon a few conscientious men [and women] north of the [Mason-Dixon] line who received no compensation, in fact, made themselves poor serving the helpless fugitives who came to their door."[13] The story of the Underground Railroad reminds us of the heights to which human beings can reach when, aflame with a sense of justice, they dedicate themselves to undermining oppressive social structures. Surely this is what Henry David Thoreau was implying when he declared that the Underground Railroad had "tunneled under the whole breadth of the land."

## NOTES

The chapter epigraph is from Henry David Thoreau's 1853 lecture "A Plea for Captain John Brown," in *Henry David Thoreau: Collected Essays and Poems*, ed. Elizabeth Hall Witherell (New York: Library of America, 2001), 412.

1. 1850 Fugitive Slave Act, Section 7. A condensed version of the Act is included in the appendix to this book.

2. Daniel Webster, "Address to the Young Men of Albany," May 28, 1851, in *The Works of Daniel Webster* (Boston: Little, Brown, 1853), vol. 2: 277.

3. In his 1849 essay "Civil Disobedience," Henry David Thoreau spoke for many abolitionists and all Underground Railroad workers: "Must the citizen ever for a moment, or in the least degree, resign his conscience, then? I think that we should be men first, and subjects afterward. It is not desirable to cultivate a respect for the law, so much as for the right." *Collected Essays and Poems*, 204.

4. John Rankin, *National Era*, December 5, 1850.

5. Joshua R. Giddings, *Congressional Globe*, 31st Congress, quoted in Wilbur H. Siebert, *The Underground Railroad from Slavery to Freedom* (Mineola, NY: Dover, 2006), 315–16.

6. Theodore Parker, Lecture in Melodeon Hall, *The Chronotype*, October 7, 1850.

7. Quoted in Philip S. Foner, ed., *The Life and Writings of Frederick Douglass* (New York: International Publishers, 1950), vol. 2: 116.

8. Stephen Hale, Letter to Governor Beriah Magoffin of Kentucky, December 27, 1860, in Charles B. Dew, *Apostles of Disunion* (Charlottesville: University of Virginia Press, 2002), 93.

9. "Declaration of the Immediate Causes Which Induce and Justify Secession," *Journal of the Convention of the People of South Carolina* (Charleston, SC, 1861), 330.

10. Jefferson Davis, "Address to the Confederate Congress," April 29, 1861, in *A Compilation of the Messages and Papers of the Confederacy*, ed. James D. Richardson (Whitefish, MT: Kessinger, 2007), vol. 2: 67. First published in 1904.

11. Larry Gara, *The Liberty Line: The Legend of the Underground Railroad* (Lexington: University Press of Kentucky, 1996), chapters 1, 7, and 8.

12. Quoted in John Stauffer, *Giants: The Parallel Lives of Frederick Douglass and Abraham Lincoln* (New York: Twelve, 2008), 4.

13. John Parker, *His Promised Land: The Autobiography of John P. Parker*, ed. Stuart Seely Sprague (New York: W. W. Norton, 1998), 72.

# CHAPTER 1

# RESISTING OL' MASSA: MODES OF SLAVE DEFIANCE

> He is whipped oftenest who is whipped easiest, and that slave who has the courage to stand up for himself against the overseer, although he may have many hard stripes at the first, becomes in the end a freeman, even though he sustain the formal relation of a slave.
> —*Frederick Douglass*

Working for the Underground Railroad was an act of civil disobedience. But riding on it was a form of slave defiance. Fugitives who ran for freedom and eventually wound up traveling along Underground Railroad routes defied their servitude by "stealing" themselves from their owners. In doing so, they not only resisted their personal enslavement, but also challenged the entire institution and ethos of slavery.

One source of confusion about the Underground Railroad is the myth that African American slaves were so passive and submissive that they lacked the will or courage to rebel against their servitude. But this ignores several indisputable facts: overwhelmingly the slaves themselves initiated their run for freedom, ex-slaves were active in Northern abolitionist societies, and fugitives were some of the most daring and dedicated Underground Railroad agents. It also overlooks the fact that blacks who remained in slavery regularly exercised modes of resistance that defied their servitude in a number of ways.

It's undeniable that the institution of slavery created a climate of oppression that encouraged docile obedience. But it's also true that many slaves routinely defied their masters' authority. Most often, the resistance

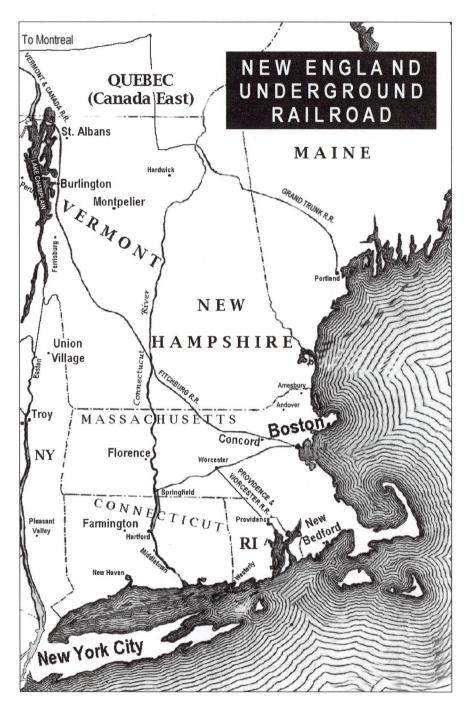

New England Underground Railroad routes generally spread out from New York City and the Massachusetts cities of New Bedford and Boston. (Tom Calarco)

was exercised undramatically in their day-to-day living. Sometimes it was more actively expressed in flight to freedom. Least often, resistance took the form of violent revolt or conspiracy to revolt. But however it revealed itself, slave resistance to "ol' massa" didn't begin with the rise of Northern abolitionism or the emergence of the Underground Railroad. It was already deeply embedded in slave culture. In its absence, the Underground Railroad would have been pointless because there would have been no northbound fugitives to aid.

In this chapter, we'll explore slave resistance and revolt to situate the Underground Railroad against its broader backdrop.

## SLAVERY AND DISSONANCE

In 1852, Harriet Beecher Stowe published *Uncle Tom's Cabin,* an antislavery novel that depicted slave owners in luridly negative ways. Two years later, partly in response to Stowe's novel, two books were published that assured readers that slaves were happy and content in their servitude. One was *A South-Side View of Slavery,* written by Nehemiah Adams of Boston, who concluded after visiting a few plantations that slaveholders were "the guardians, educators, and saviors of the African race in this country."[1] The other was George Fitzhugh's *Sociology for the South,* which claimed that the average slave, far from being the mistreated wretch portrayed by Stowe, was "as happy as a human being could be."[2]

Adams's and Fitzhugh's books may have been immediately motivated by a rising tide of antislavery sentiment in the North, but the views they defended were long-standing convictions among Southerners—and, as Adams's book suggests, some Northerners as well. Blacks, so the thinking went, were incapable of looking out for themselves. As Fitzhugh said, "The negro is improvident [and] will not lay up in summer for the wants of winter."[3] Left to his own devices, "the negro" inevitably fell into harm's way. But as a slave, he was fed, clothed, housed, and given meaningful labor. Enslaved blacks were happier and more productive, therefore, than they could ever be living in freedom. The abolition of slavery would only inflict hardship and misery upon men and women racially unsuited for freedom. Far from being immoral, slaveholders were socially responsible men who shouldered the burden of caring for those unable to fend for themselves.

Given this belief, it's not surprising that slave owners frequently fell into the sentimental delusion that their slaves were grateful and loyal to them. An antebellum lithograph nicely captures this idealized vision of the master-slave relationship. On a visit to the slave quarters, a master and his family are entertained by happily dancing slaves while an aged slave obsequiously says, "God Bless you massa! You feed and clothe us. When we are sick you nurse us, and when too old to work, you provide for us!"[4]

The conviction that their slaves were contentedly grateful was so deeply engrained that slave owners were often startled and grieved when circumstances suggested a quite different picture. Mississippi planter John Quitman, convinced as he was of his servant's absolute loyalty, was shaken when his slave John ran. As Quitman's son wrote in bewilderment, "I myself have heard [John] say, that if it were in the power of these abolitionists to give him a thousand freedoms, he would not desert us."[5] It apparently never occurred to the Quitman family that their slaves generally told them only what they wanted to hear. A similar sense of betrayal was expressed when Sarah Logue of Tennessee wrote to her runaway slave Jermain Loguen: "You know that we reared you as we reared our own children; that you was never abused, and that shortly before you ran away, when your master asked you if you would like to be sold, you said you would not leave him to go with anybody."[6] Although Loguen had escaped nearly 30 years earlier, his desertion still rankled his ex-mistress.

But alongside slave owners' deluded convictions that their own slaves were happy and loyal was their anxious and pervasive suspicion that slaves in general, as Georgia planter John Jacobus Flournoy put it, had "a natural disposition to endless riot [and] for the work of carnage and insurrection."[7] Many Southern whites also believed that blacks were unreliable. In 1815, for example, Roswell King, overseer of the huge Georgia plantation owned by Pierce Butler, wrote his employer about the loss of nearly 140 absconding slaves. He regretted the rascally ingratitude of the members of the "Ethiopian race" who fled the plantation, and he warned Butler that the remaining slaves were just as likely to betray their master's trust: "I know they would have gone off if they only had a chance."[8]

That these attitudes were inconsistent with the belief that slaves were also "naturally disposed" to be helpless without and thus endlessly grateful for their master's patronage seems to have gone largely unnoticed. Right through the end of the Civil War, these dissonant convictions—the contented loyalty of slaves on the one hand and the ever-present threat of their breaking into murderous revolt on the other—appear time and again in Southern diaries, letters, and public documents. Slave owners wanted to believe the first even while fearing the second.

The source of both beliefs was the conviction that no matter how "civilized" slaves became, they could never completely shed an "African" heritage which constantly tempted them to childish helplessness on the one hand and bloodthirsty savagery on the other. For proslavery Americans, this belief justified both the institution of slavery itself and the harshly oppressive treatment of slaves. Africans' alleged helplessness proved that blacks were destined for slavery, and their alleged savagery served as a warning that they needed to be held firmly in check.[9] As the years passed, this double conviction became the driving force behind brutally oppressive slave codes and plantation practices that aimed to stifle slave unrest. As one South Carolina planter put it, "The fear of punishment is the principle to which we must and do appeal, to keep them [slaves] in awe and order."[10]

Slave codes, enacted in every southern state, were expressly written to "keep" slaves in "awe and order"—which, of course, meant cowed submission. Although they varied in severity from state to state, the codes had several requirements in common. Slaves were prohibited from leaving their master's property without passes, practicing medicine, owning firearms, raising animals of their own, testifying against whites before a magistrate, preaching the gospel unless a white minister was present, and learning to read and write. Punishment for any slave who dared to raise a hand against a white man was predictably harsh, frequently punishable by death. The goal everywhere, as the Louisiana slave code forthrightly admitted, was to enforce absolute obedience to the master's wishes.

Slave codes also set definite limits to the behavior of free blacks. Southern freedmen were generally prohibited from assembling or meeting together in groups of more than four or five. In cities, curfews for free blacks were frequently imposed. In Washington, D.C., for example, blacks in the streets after 8:00 P.M. faced arrest and flogging. After the abolitionist movement gained strength in the North, freedmen in the South were prohibited from receiving antislavery literature through the mail or even, in some locations, from possessing it. In the spring of 1857, Sam Green, a free black in Maryland, was sentenced to 10 years in prison merely for owning a copy of *Uncle Tom's Cabin.*

Life on the plantation (or in the workplace, if the slaveholder hired his slaves out to others) also operated under the assumption that, in the words of a North Carolina planter, "there is no such thing as having an obedient and useful Slave, without the painful exercise of undue and tyrannical authority."[11] It was one thing to wax sentimental in print about the loyalty of happy slaves, but quite another when it came to the reality of supervising them. Slaves were usually overworked and underfed, and disobedience or slacking was always punished, sometimes with unrestrained fury, by masters and overseers. Slaves were expected to be deferential and cheerful. Any sign of discontent, much less independence, was seen as a threat.

Opposed to the South's romantic and utterly fictional notion of the contented and loyal family retainer were two very disturbing realities: on the one hand, the slave owners' determination, born of pervasive anxiety,

Frederick Douglass in middle age. Douglass, who escaped from slavery in 1838, became a noted abolitionist and defender of the Underground Railroad. (Library of Congress)

to break the spirit of their human chattel; on the other hand, the sim-mering discontent that their mistreatment (not to mention bondage in general) provoked in slaves. Frederick Douglass, in thinking back on his years of servitude, angrily compared his lot as a slave to that of beasts of burden. "They were property," Douglass recalled, "so was I; they were to be broken, so was I."[12] John Parker, a fugitive who became a key figure in the Ohio Underground Railroad, recalled his slave days in an equally angry tone.

> How I hated slavery as it fettered me, and beat me, and baffled me in my desires. . . . It was not the physical part of slavery that made it cruel and degrading, it was the taking away from a human being the initiative, of thinking, of doing his own ways. . . . Slavery's curse was not pain of the body, but the pain of the soul.[13]

## "TO GET OUR FREEDOM"

In the summer of 1862, Southern blueblood Mary Boykin Chesnut saw a stage play about the great Indian Rebellion of 1857, when native soldiers, or "sepoys," had revolted against their British colonial masters and fought with desperate ferocity before finally being defeated. Writing about the play in her diary, Chesnut confessed that "a thrill of terror ran through me as those yellow and black brutes came jumping over the parapets! Their faces were like so many of the same sort at home." She took some comfort in the fact that John Brown's 1859 raid on Harpers Ferry had failed to stir up slaves to "to rise and burn and murder us all." But, she anxiously wondered, "how long would they resist the seductive and irresistible call, 'only rise, kill, and be free'"?[14]

Chesnut's nightmarish fear was by no means unique to her. The pos-sibility of slave revolt was a pervasive source of anxiety throughout the South, fueled by the belief that African slaves were savages capable of un-speakable acts of vengeance against their white masters, a belief seemingly verified in the final decade of the 18th century by the bloody and suc-cessful insurrection of Haitian slaves against French colonialists. Nothing sent Southerners into a greater panic than actual or rumored slave revolts or conspiracies to revolt, and their anxiety was only escalated by the 1829 publication of black abolitionist David Walker's *Appeal to the Colored Citi-zens of the World*, which urged armed resistance of slaves to their masters.

Sometimes fear of black uprisings was deliberately provoked by Southern polemicists for the political purpose of scaring whites into a united front against abolitionists like Walker. But such tactics capitalized on already existing fears. As historian Eugene Genovese notes, "No amount of drum-beating by slaveholding extremists would have succeeded in whipping up so much panic so often if the whites had not believed that their slaves had cause to rise and might find the resources and opportunity."[15]

In reality, Southern fears about slave revolts were exaggerated. Unlike their Caribbean counterparts, blacks in the antebellum South were scattered over a vast geographical area and overwhelmingly outnumbered by whites who controlled guns, ammunition, horses, and other resources essential to a successful insurrection. But overwrought though they were about the danger of slave insurrection, white Southerners did have some cause for concern. Revolts of angry and desperate slaves took place from time to time in the effort, as one rebellious South Carolina slave wrote in 1845, "to get aur [sic] freedom."[16] Although all were quickly put down, the very fact that they occurred ratcheted up the general fear Southerners had that their slaves, given half a chance, would "rise and burn and murder us all."

The first serious slave conspiracy occurred early on, in 1663, in Virginia's Gloucester County. Discontented white indentured servants plotted and were punished alongside slaves when the conspiracy was discovered. But the first actual revolt took place not in the South but in New York City, when, in 1712, 27 slaves set fire to several houses and then murdered whites who came running to put out the flames. Nearly 20 years later, another plot by Northern slaves was uncovered and quashed in Pennsylvania.

An armed revolt even larger than the New York City one occurred in 1739, when an Angola-born slave named Cato (some sources also refer to him as "Jemmy") stirred up fellow African slaves in South Carolina. It became known as the Stono Rebellion, named for the town in which it originated, 20 miles west of Charleston. Cato and about 20 other slaves captured a small ammunition warehouse, seized its weapons, and headed for Spanish Florida, picking up other slaves on the way and killing a score or more of whites. Eventually surrounded by a South Carolina militia unit, Cato and most of his makeshift army were killed. But the fact that they got as far as they did sent a chill throughout the South.

The largest revolt in the history of American slavery occurred in the Louisiana parish of Saint John the Baptist in 1811. Led by Charles Deslondes, a freed slave who had journeyed to Haiti and been inspired by its insurrection, as many as 500 slaves deserted their masters to march toward New Orleans, burning plantation houses and crops along the way, murdering farmers, and in general terrifying white Louisianans. The state militia eventually put down the rebellion, but it took over 10 days to do so—a rather amazing fact, given that the slaves were armed mainly with such farm tools as axes, scythes, and hoes. Nearly 100 of them were subsequently executed and their bodies or severed heads put on public display as grisly warnings to other slaves contemplating insurrection.

All told, the colonies and antebellum Republic witnessed some 250 slave rebellions, both those actually carried out and the many more that were discovered by authorities before the conspirators could act. Most were in the South, and all involved 10 or more slaves. Although never successful, each one of them frightened Southern whites and encouraged even more repressive slave codes and stricter plantation supervision. But the three slave revolts that panicked the South more than any others were those led by Gabriel Prosser in 1800, Denmark Vesey in 1822, and Nat Turner in 1831.

Gabriel Prosser and his brothers Solomon and Martin were owned by tobacco planter Thomas Prosser, whose plantation was close to Richmond, Virginia. Gabriel was literate, and his brother Martin was a preacher. Inspired by the success of the Haitian insurrection, they invoked the biblical story of the Israelite exodus from Egypt to inspire other slaves to join them in an uprising. Their plan was to attack Richmond, seize arms and burn cotton warehouses, capture Virginia governor James Madison, and kill any white who resisted them. Gabriel made futile attempts to ally with local Catawba Indians and planned to march into Richmond with a flag bearing the motto "Death or Liberty."

As things turned out, it was death rather than liberty. The insurrection was planned for the night of August 30, 1800. But fierce rainfalls flooded bridges and roads, forcing Gabriel to postpone the uprising until the weather cleared. In the meantime, a couple of slaves outside the conspiracy learned of it and told their masters what Gabriel and his brothers were planning. Governor Madison called out the state militia, the Prosser brothers and 23 other conspirators were captured, and all of them were subsequently hanged. In the wake of the conspiracy, frightened Virginian legislators passed harsher slave codes that severely restricted slave movement between plantations and Richmond and obliged freed slaves to leave the state or face reenslavement.

Twenty years later, white Southerners were again reminded of their vulnerability when they learned of Denmark Vesey's attempted uprising in South Carolina. Had it succeeded, it would have been the largest slave insurrection in the United States, involving, according to some estimates, as many as 9,000 slaves and free blacks.

Vesey was an ex-slave who purchased his freedom with lottery winnings when he was 30. Like Charles Deslondes, he had spent some time in Haiti and been impressed by the black republic he found there. Settling in Charleston, he earned his living as a carpenter and became a respected and relatively wealthy member of the city's free black community. In 1817, he helped found a congregation of the African Methodist Episcopal (AME) Church there.

But even as a free and financially comfortable Charleston black, Vesey's autonomy was severely restricted. Along with other freedmen, he was not allowed in any of the city's theaters and could be stopped on the street by any white citizen demanding to see his papers. The simmering anger that these and other indignities provoked was voiced at loud and sometimes raucous meetings in his AME church, eventually prompting city authorities to close it down under the pretext that the gatherings there of "numerous black people to hear the scripture expounded by an ignorant and (too frequently) vicious person of their own color can be of no benefit either to themselves or the community."[17] Vesey, infuriated, began plotting insurrection. He was assisted in his recruiting efforts by a charismatic African-born conjurer named Gullah Jack.

Vesey's plans were meticulous and detailed. The conspiracy's core members were limited to free blacks who were mostly skilled craftsmen or sailors. Each of them in turn supervised different groups of rank-and-file co-conspirators made up of both slaves and freemen. Strict secrecy was maintained between the different groups, with no single one knowing the full insurrection plan. Vesey envisioned his rebellious army striking Charleston's arsenals, guardhouses, and powder magazines from six different points. Then he and his soldiers would slaughter as many whites as they could before commandeering ships docked in the harbor and sailing to Haiti and freedom. The uprising was scheduled for July 14, Bastille Day.

Like Gabriel Prosser's conspiracy, Vesey's was betrayed by a couple of slaves who weren't participants in the plot but somehow had gotten wind of it. Two weeks before Bastille Day, Charleston authorities arrested Vesey and 131 slaves and free blacks. Close to 80 of them, including Vesey, were hanged. Charleston's white community, reeling from what it considered a barely averted disaster, established a permanent municipal guard to keep an eye on the city's black population. Some later historians argue that the Vesey conspiracy was largely a hoax.[18] But white Carolingians at the time firmly believed in its reality.

The planned rebellions of Prosser and Vesey frightened white Southerners because of the mayhem that could have erupted had the plots not been discovered and thwarted. But Nat Turner's insurrection, which took place in southeastern Virginia in August 1831, went beyond the planning to the execution stage, and the horrible reality of it confirmed the South's deepest fears about the "savage" nature of African slaves. For years afterward, slaves who so much as mentioned Turner's name were punished, and slave parents were forbidden to christen their sons Nat.

Turner was an intensely charismatic figure, literate, moody, and prone to religious visions. His fellow slaves looked on him as a prophet, and even whites who heard him preach were impressed by his eloquence and familiarity with the Bible.

Encouraged by his visions to believe that God had anointed him to do battle against the "Serpent" of bondage, Turner gathered a number of fellow conspirators around him and waited for the right moment to strike. On witnessing a solar eclipse in mid-August 1831, Turner interpreted the phenomenon as the divine signal he'd been awaiting. One week later, at 2:00 A.M., he and his men butchered his master and his master's family while they slept. Then they roamed over the countryside to nearby farms, murdering nearly every white person they encountered and picking up additional slave recruits as they went. By the time the killing spree was over, 48 hours later, some 60 white men, women, and children had been slain.

Virginia militia quickly suppressed the revolt, but Turner managed to elude capture until the end of October. When finally caught, he was tried,

convicted, and hanged within 10 days. Fifty of his followers were also executed. His rampage so horrified the white residents of Virginia and other
southern states that dozens of blacks, slave as well as free, were murdered
in the following weeks. Some of the killings were doubtlessly motivated by
an angry spirit of retaliation. But judging from diaries, letters, and newspaper editorials of the period, most of them were sparked by panic over the
possibility that other slaves might be inspired to follow Turner's example.
The Virginia General Assembly sought to reassure the white populace by
outlawing the teaching of blacks, slave or free, to read and write and by
forbidding them to preach in religious gatherings without the presence
and supervision of a white minister. Legislators and citizens alike wanted
no more literate and charismatic visionaries arising out of Virginia's black
population.

## DAY-TO-DAY RESISTANCE

Insurrections, whether actually carried out or only planned, were extreme
expressions of slaves' hatred of their bondage. Many slaves who knew
about their planning didn't participate in or approve of them; both the
Gabriel Prosser and Denmark Vesey conspiracies were brought low by
slave informants. But in fact most slaves outside of the immediate areas in
which the revolts were suppressed had no knowledge of them beforehand
or afterward. Conspiracies by their very nature are secretive, and planters
worked hard to make sure that rumors of rebellion were silenced before
they reached the ears of their slaves. Even if news of slave rebellion did
manage to travel, so too did word of the brutal backlash against blacks
that inevitably followed every attempt. Slaves bitterly resented their
chains, but few of them were willing to cast their lots with insurrections,
which they saw as bound to fail.

This doesn't mean, however, that slaves who didn't revolt offered no
resistance to their bondage. Instead, they employed strategies of disguised
resistance that were more likely to succeed than overt rebellion because
they were incorporated into their daily life and work. Slavery was hard
and oppressive. But slaves found ways to assert some degree of independence from their masters that displayed defiance, initiative, and cunning.
They managed, as Frederick Douglass once wrote, to be slaves in form but
not in fact—not entirely in fact, anyway.[19]

Slaves were strengthened in their day-to-day resistance to bondage by two influences in particular: family life and religion. Slave families were generally close, in part because of the ever-present threat of separation, and the support system offered by such closeness gave slaves a confidence and sense of personal worth essential for the courage to resist their masters. Ironically, slave owners, in an effort to minimize running and maximize reproduction, encouraged slaves to nurture the very family ties that strengthened their resolve to resist servility.

Slave resistance was also encouraged by religion. Slaves were generally exposed to sermons by white preachers that routinely justified bondage by appealing to dubious interpretations of Christian scripture. But along the way, slaves also grew familiar with paradigmatic biblical stories of escape from slavery. Like Gabriel Prosser and Nat Turner, they identified closely with the Old Testament account of Moses leading the Israelites out of bondage and believed that God ultimately would free them from their own pharaohs. Additionally, they identified with Jesus, the suffering servant, and trusted that the same God who raised Jesus from the dead one day would likewise raise them from the living death of slavery. Their appropriation of these biblical stories of liberation was in itself a powerful act of resistance to the white culture that held them bondage. After the Civil War a similar appropriation would inspire and sustain blacks during the Jim Crow era and right up to the civil rights movement of the 1960s.

Typically, the daily resistance practiced by slaves involved a subversion of the master's interests and a furtherance of their own. Most of the time, the subversion was secretive and involved deception on the part of the slaves practicing it. Occasionally it erupted into overt physical resistance—a slave might refuse a whipping or intervene to rescue another slave from corporal punishment. Some slaves resisted their bondage by running, either for a short period of time or for good.

Perhaps the most common day-to-day form of resistance was telling the master what he wanted to hear while secretly defying his orders or disdaining his authority. John, the Quitman slave who repeatedly assured his owner that he had no desire to run away, is a good example of this kind of resistance, since apparently he was planning to desert at the first opportunity. Similar tactics might involve putting on the happy and carefree face that masters looked for in their slaves, or being so obsequious as to mock the entire culture of servitude without crossing the line into obvious and punishable impertinence. These sorts of maneuvers were particularly used by house slaves, who had more frequent contact with white masters than did field slaves. But field hands also practiced them with overseers.

Another common form of resistance practiced by both house servants and field hands was the theft of time. It was so common that one of the complaints that crops up most often in masters' letters and diaries is that their slaves have "cheated" them out of a day's work. The theft generally involved some kind of goldbricking: working slowly, taking unscheduled breaks, performing tasks sloppily or failing to complete them, pretending ignorance about how to carry out a particular chore, or feigning illness. Sometimes farm equipment such as scythes, hoes, plows, and even cotton gins was surreptitiously damaged, destroyed, or mislaid, thereby halting or delaying work. Masters and overseers often suspected that their slaves were deliberately sabotaging them, but such suspicions were hard to verify. Moreover, the standard white assumption that blacks were inferior in intelligence and initiative worked to the advantage of the slaves, who could always disguise deliberate theft of time as ineptitude or confusion about how to perform the tasks assigned them.

Time wasn't the only kind of thievery practiced by slaves. Theft of real property, especially foodstuff, was prevalent too. Many slave owners accepted as a fact of life that their slaves would steal the occasional chicken or pig to supplement their diets, and slaves in turn came to regard such purloining as something of a right. Other items regularly stolen by slaves included sheep, cattle, liquor, flour, cotton, rice—in short, as one historian puts it, "anything that was not under lock and key—and they occasionally found the key."[20]

But thievery of property didn't function merely to supplement the slave's impoverished existence. It was also an intentional act of rebellion against the master. A similar motive lay behind the acts of vandalism, such as the already-mentioned sabotaging of farm equipment, often perpetrated by slaves. To steal or damage the master's property was to harm *him*, because his property was an extension of himself. Chopping cotton or harvesting rice and sugar in a deliberately sloppy way in order to damage the harvest, injuring farm animals, pulling down fences to let livestock run loose, or setting fire to outhouses were other ways of striking back at the master—and the institution of slavery itself—by whittling away the income derived from slave labor.

Owners unwittingly encouraged defiance on the part of their slaves by hiring them out to employers. By the time the Civil War erupted, an enormous number of slaves owned by cash-poor masters were routinely hired out or leased to manufacturers, artisans, and planters willing to pay for extra help. Generally the money the slaves earned was paid directly to their masters, although some owners allowed their slaves to keep a tiny percentage of their wages or to work additional jobs in their spare time. Slaves who were hired out endured painful separation from their families and the risk of working for an employer who might mistreat them. But they generally discovered that the arrangement gave them wider latitude than they enjoyed working directly for their owners. When hired out, slaves were often less closely supervised than they were on the master's property. They could travel from place to place more easily and were often able to put aside a bit of money for themselves. The result was that they sometimes grew so accustomed to their independence that employers found them difficult to manage. When hired-out slaves returned to their masters, either because their term of employment had ended or because their frustrated employers had dismissed them, they brought back with them a taste for freedom and habits of independence that encouraged further resistance to the master's authority.

Overt resistance to masters, employers, and overseers was less common than day-to-day subversion, but it occurred often enough to be a cause of concern to the authorities. Slaves endured continuous pressure to satisfy their masters' demands while keeping their resentment safely hidden, holding their families together, and maintaining a personal sense of dignity and self-respect. So it's not surprising that the inner tension erupted occasionally. Sometimes slaves outright refused to work or disobeyed orders; at other times they stopped work—went on strike, as it were—to demand concessions from their owners.

Overt resistance was occasionally precipitated by an immediate threat such as being sold by their masters. But defiance was often a reaction to overwork. Many planters in the Lower South found that it was more cost effective to push their slaves at full throttle until they died or collapsed and replace them with new ones, than to pace and preserve them. So they worked them on cotton, sugar, and rice plantations until they were used up. During harvest season, it wasn't unusual for these slaves to be in the fields 16 hours a day. Under these kinds of conditions, especially when supervised by demanding, cruel, or inexperienced overseers, slaves could reach their breaking points quickly.

Usually overt resistance was more verbal than physical—understandable, given the harsh penalties for striking a white person prescribed by the slave codes—but violent confrontations between slaves and overseers or masters weren't unknown. Some slaves, men as well as women, fought back when threatened with a beating or whipping. Others put up a fight to defend a spouse or child at risk of physical or sexual abuse. But whatever the reason, physical confrontations between slaves and masters, unwelcome reminders as they were of the falsehood of the happy and contented slave myth, startled and enraged the white community. Predictably, Southerners reluctant to face the depth of slave resentment tended to write off slaves who physically resisted as mad-dog troublemakers.

Verbal and physical resistance usually brought brutal punishment for the offending slave. At the very least, he or she was likely to be sold quickly. But sometimes a slave who defied his master succeeded to such an extent that the confrontation transformed the slave's self-image. Frederick Douglass is a case in point. At 16, he was sold to a notorious "nigger breaker" by the name of Covey. One morning Covey tried to whip his new slave, and Douglass, who later said that "the fighting madness" had come upon him, fought back. The battle lasted for two hours and ended with a shaken and defeated master. For Douglass, the confrontation was a turning point. "I felt as I had never felt before," he wrote. "It was a glorious resurrection, from the tomb of slavery to the heaven of comparative freedom."[21] Douglass made a failed run for freedom a few months later, but succeeded two years later in 1838.

Running was a final form of noninsurrectionary slave resistance. Many slaves ran for short periods of time, hiding out in neighboring swamps or forests or in the cabins of relatives and friends on other plantations. Motives for these short-term runs included fear of punishment for some infraction, the desire to avoid a particularly grueling task such as harvesting a crop, and simply the wish for a holiday. Men as well as women, sometimes with their children in tow, disappeared for a few days or, at most, weeks. They generally had no intention of staying away permanently, much less heading for the North and freedom. Slave owners, recognizing that short-term runs were a relatively safe way of allowing slaves to blow off steam, tended to turn a blind eye to these unofficial holidays so long as they weren't taken too often or for too long.

Much rarer was a run for freedom like that undertaken by Frederick Douglass. The prospect was prohibitively daunting: leaving behind family, friends, and a familiar life to venture into the unknown. However bad slavery was, running seemed even worse to most slaves. And as we'll see in the next chapter, they had good reason to be fearful. The majority of slaves who made a run for freedom were captured, returned, punished, and frequently sold as damaged goods. Once across the Mason-Dixon Line, they might be fortunate enough to secure help on the Underground Railroad. But until then, slaves who defied their servitude by running were largely on their own and had to use all their courage and wits to make it to freedom.

## LIVING ON TWO LEVELS

The backdrop of the Underground Railroad was slave resistance to bondage. This resistance was always present, and it grew rather than diminished over time. Most slaves didn't participate in insurrections or make runs for freedom. But many of them resisted servitude in their day-to-day lives, managing to submit to the outer forms of slavery while securing for themselves some degree of real freedom. This sort of double-layered existence required initiative, discipline, and cunning, characteristics absolutely necessary for those few slaves who eventually did try to make their way northward to freedom.

As discussed, white slave owners also lived a double-layered existence: on the one hand, trying to convince themselves of the fiction that their slaves were peacefully happy; on the other, anxiously fearful of the simmering discontent they sensed in their human property. The dissonance between these two positions ate away at Southern white self-assuredness. But the tension between bondage and resistance enhanced slaves' sense of self-worth and confidence while simultaneously undermining white authority. Ongoing day-to-day resistance to ol' massa transformed slaves, in the words of Frederick Douglass, into "freemen" even if they retained "the formal relation of a slave."

## NOTES

The chapter epigraph is from Frederick Douglass, *My Bondage and My Freedom*, ed. John Stauffer (New York: Modern Library, 2003), 43. Douglass's book was first published in 1855.

1. Nehemiah Adams, *A South-Side View of Slavery; or, Three Months at the South in 1854* (Boston: T. R. Marvin & B. B. Mussey, 1854), 9.

2. George Fitzhugh, *Sociology for the South; or, The Failure of Free Society* (Richmond: A. Morris, 1854), 246.

3. Ibid., 82. In another work, Fitzhugh wrote, "The negro slaves of the South are the happiest, and, in some sense, the freest people in the world." *Cannibals All! or, Slaves without Masters* (Richmond: A. Morris, 1857), 29.

4. Quoted in James Oliver Horton and Lois E. Horton, *Slavery and the Making of America* (New York: Oxford University Press, 2005), 121.

5. Ibid.

6. "Letter from Mrs. Logue," February 20, 1860, in *Slavery in the United States: A Social, Political, and Historical Encyclopedia*, ed. Junius P. Rodriguez (Santa Barbara, CA: ABC-CLIO, 2007), vol. 2: 677–78.

7. Quoted in John W. Blassingame, *The Slave Community: Plantation Life in the Antebellum South* (New York: Oxford University Press, 1979), 231.

8. Quoted in John Hope Franklin and Loren Schweninger, *Runaway Slaves: Rebels on the Plantation* (New York: Oxford University Press, 1999), 29.

9. This attitude toward Africans wasn't shared by Spanish slaveholders in the New World. Their slave codes were based on Roman law, which considered slavery an unnatural state and legally mutable. Under the Spanish, the human rights of slaves were protected by law. Southern white American attitudes, on the other hand, were shaped by the assumption that Africans were less than fully human and that their natural state was servitude. As such, they possessed no or few legal rights and manumission was discouraged.

10. Quoted in Blassingame, *The Slave Community*, 236.

11. Quoted in Kenneth Stamp, *The Peculiar Institution: Slavery in the Antebellum South* (New York: Random House, 1956), 141.

12. Douglass, *My Bondage and My Freedom*, 118.

13. John Parker, *His Promised Land: The Autobiography of John P. Parker*, ed. Stuart Seely Sprague (New York: W. W. Norton, 1996), 25, 26.

14. C. Vann Woodward, ed., *Mary Chesnut's Civil War* (New Haven, CT: Yale University Press, 1993), 409.

15. Eugene Genovese, *Roll, Jordan, Roll: The World the Slaves Made* (New York: Vintage, 1976), 596.

16. Quoted in Franklin and Schweninger, *Runaway Slaves*, 14.

17. Quoted in David Robertson, *Denmark Vesey* (New York: Vintage, 1999), 50.

18. Robert L. Paquette offers an overview of the debate in "From Rebellion to Revisionism: The Continuing Debate about the Denmark Vesey Affair," *Journal of the Historical Society* 4, no. 3 (2004): 291–334.

19. Douglass, *My Bondage and My Freedom*, 140.

20. Franklin and Schweninger, *Runaway Slaves*, 2.

21. Douglass, *My Bondage and My Freedom*, 140.

# CHAPTER 2

# FOLLOWING THE DRINKING GOURD: FLEEING SERVITUDE

When the sun comes back and the first quail calls,
follow the Drinking Gourd.
For the old man is waiting for to carry you to freedom,
if you follow the Drinking Gourd.
> —*From the 1928 song "Follow the Drinking Gourd"*

In 1851, Dr. Samuel Cartwright, a physician recognized throughout the South as an authority on "negro diseases," alerted slaveholders to a mental disorder to which their human property was particularly susceptible. He called it "drapetomania," from the Greek for "runaway" and "madness." Its chief symptom was the obsessive desire to "abscond from service." Cartwright's assumption was that slaves who wanted to run away from their masters must be crazy, confused to the point of insanity by ill treatment on the one hand or foolish coddling on the other. His medical advice to owners was that they treat their slaves "like children," firmly but compassionately, "to prevent and cure them running away."[1]

Cartwright worried that drapetomania was in danger of going viral, and many others feared the same possibility. Slave owners everywhere were convinced that the South was bleeding slaves to the North and freedom. The fear was greater than the reality. The raw number of runaways tended to get exaggerated by both Southerners and Northerners. Southerners inflated the numbers to highlight the perfidious influence of Northern abolitionists. Northern abolitionists inflated them to underscore how unbearable it was living under the master's whip. But just as overt rebellion or revolt by slaves was an uncommon occurrence in the antebellum

South, so was successful escape to the North. Most slaves didn't run, and most of those who did never made it to freedom. The number of successful slave escapes in the half century leading up to the Civil War probably totaled no more than 135,000—this in a slave population swollen by 1860 to four million.

Still, the numbers were significant for two reasons. In the first place, the drapetomaniac flight of so many slaves was a huge financial loss to the South. Given that the average price of a slave was around $300, the total value of human capital that fled to the North in the antebellum years was a staggering $40 million. Little wonder that Missouri senator David Rice Atchison complained in 1850 that "depredations to the amount of

Slaves fleeing from the border state of Missouri sometimes traveled north to Iowa and then cut east to Canada through Wisconsin. Others fled more directly across Illinois. (Tom Calarco)

hundreds of thousands of dollars are committed upon the property of the people of the border slave states of this Union annually."[2]

Just as importantly, the fact that so many slaves ran was a disturbing moral defeat for those defenders of the peculiar institution who insisted that slaves were either too hapless or too loyal to their masters to flee (provided, of course, they weren't afflicted by drapetomania). Despite the slim prospect of making it to the North and the certain one of brutal punishment if captured and returned to their owners, each year hundreds of runaways debunked with their feet the Southern myth of the happy, contented slave.

They set out for the most part without the help of Underground Railroad conductors for the simple reason that there were nearly none south of the Mason-Dixon Line. So fugitive slaves had to rely on their own initiative and courage to get them to free soil, where Northern sympathizers could lend a helping hand. Very often, they had little more to guide them than the North Star, which they located on clear nights by searching for the Big Dipper or "Drinking Gourd." That so many of them ventured forth with no assistance was a testimonial to their resolve to be free. The Boston-based abolitionist William Lloyd Garrison promised fleeing slaves, "If you come to us, and are hungry, we will feed you."[3] But first they had to make it to the North, and they had to do it on their own. As black journalist Henry Bibb admiringly noted in 1853, "Self-emancipation is now the order of the day."[4]

## THE ABOLITIONIST MOVEMENT

Garrison was one of the pioneers in the campaign to end slavery in the United States that came to be known as abolitionism. Beginning in the early 1830s, the movement was launched by Christian reformers who sought to bring an end to slavery by appealing to the consciences of slaveholders and politicians. Their approach was nonviolent. They wielded no "carnal weapons," only "moral suasion." Their working assumption was that supporters of slavery secretly recognized the wickedness of their position, suffered guilt, and could be persuaded by word and example to mend their ways.

In 1833, 63 abolitionists (including 3 blacks) from 11 states gathered to found the American Anti-Slavery Society. They pledged "to overthrow the most execrable system of slavery that has ever been witnessed upon

By far the best-known American abolitionist, William Lloyd Garrison founded the antislavery weekly *Liberator* in 1831 and issued it until the end of the Civil War. He often published accounts of Underground Railroad escapes in his paper. (National Park Service, Frederick Douglass National Historic Site)

earth," to struggle to "secure to the colored population of the United States all the rights and privileges which belong to them as men and as Americans—come what may to our persons, our interests, or our reputations," and to do so peacefully.[5] To that end, they swore to forego "the doing of evil that good may come," tempting as that tactic may have been in light of slavery's brutality. Even civil disobedience to the laws of the land that upheld slavery was discouraged. Moral suasion, not defiant challenge, was the norm. Over the next eight years, the American Anti-Slavery Society embarked on a whirlwind campaign to spread the word, sponsoring national lecture tours, publishing pamphlets, writing petitions to Congress, and sponsoring the formation of dozens of local abolitionist groups.

Despite all this effort, abolitionism remained a frequently despised minority opinion. Hostility to it in the South was fierce and unsurprising to everyone except the abolitionists themselves. State officials there went so far as to outlaw abolitionist mailings and to approve bounties for the capture of abolitionists. But public opinion in the North was only a little less negative. By 1836, the incessant abolitionist campaign of moral suasion had become so unpalatable to Northern sensibilities that the Whigs and Democrats managed to persuade Congress to pass a gag rule prohibiting discussion of abolitionist petitions submitted by foes of slavery. Abolitionist meetings in cities across the North such as Boston, Syracuse, and Rochester were often disrupted, sometimes violently, by proslavery mobs.

There were several reasons for the hostility. A major one that influenced both Northern and Southern antiabolitionists was economic: huge amounts of wealth were tied up in the institution of slavery. In the 30 years before the 1863 Emancipation Proclamation, slaves represented the nation's second-largest capital investment, exceeded only by land. But resistance to the abolitionist message was also fueled by overt racism in both the North and the South, as well as a repugnance for what many saw as the sanctimonious "do-goodism" of abolitionist agitators.

By 1840, the abolitionist movement had splintered into several factions. The dismal track record of moral suasion had persuaded its leaders that different tactics were necessary, but there was wide disagreement about what those tactics should be.[6] One faction, led by Garrison, condemned both the government and Christian denominations for their failure to speak out against slavery. Garrisonians foreswore political lobbying, arguing that a government that protected the institution of slavery was inherently corrupt. Their repudiation of elected authority was dramatically symbolized at an 1854 Fourth of July abolitionist rally in Massachusetts where Garrison struck a match to a copy of the U.S. Constitution. As the document burned, he exclaimed, "Let the people say Amen!" The hundreds of attending abolitionists thundered back, "Amen!"

Another faction that emerged took the opposite position. Headed by Kentucky-born abolitionist James G. Birney, the members of this group believed that the only way to make headway against slavery was through the political process. According to them, the Declaration of Independence, with its insistence that all men were created equal, took both chronological and moral pride of place over the Constitution. The latter, they believed, could and should be amended to conform to the former. To pursue this goal, they founded the Liberty Party in 1840, fielding white abolitionists for political office, including five presidential elections. But the party attracted little actual support, and it eventually fizzled out shortly after Abraham Lincoln was elected president on the Republican ticket in 1860.

A third faction, led by abolitionist Lewis Tappan, was formed in shocked response to Garrison's relentless criticisms of organized religion's tolerance of slavery. Lewis and his brother Arthur were devout Calvinists who believed that a moral revival among Christians was the necessary condition for ending slavery. They also endorsed a position that proved especially offensive to the general population as well as many abolitionists: the amalgamation of the races as a solution to bigotry. Tappan believed that intermarriage would create a "copper-skinned" United States in which racial hatred would find no foothold.

In the 1840s and especially the 1850s, for reasons we'll examine in later chapters, many abolitionists became increasingly sympathetic to civil disobedience and sometimes overt violence in the struggle against slavery. Frederick Douglass was one of them, moving from a Garrisonian position of nonviolent moral suasion to allegiance with the Birney political faction and, finally, to an enthusiastic endorsement of John Brown's 1859 raid on Harpers Ferry. One of the reasons for the shift from moral suasion to overt lawbreaking was the growing impatience of black abolitionists. White abolitionists tended to object to slavery on the basis of abstract, philosophical principles. But black ones, many of whom were either exslaves or children of slaves, were all too familiar with the concrete horrors of slavery, and their opposition to it infused the movement with a practical appreciation of the need for action as well as suasion. As Frederick Douglass observed, "He who has *endured the cruel pangs of Slavery* is the [best] man to *advocate Liberty*."[7] In Northern cities, blacks formed committees to offer assistance to runaways. They funded lecture tours in which abolitionists such as Garrison and, later, fugitives such as Douglass traveled across the country, also often serving as bodyguards for the speakers. Black preachers exhorted their congregants to support the abolitionist movement by giving money and time; black writers penned antislavery pamphlets; and blacks became some of the most active stationmasters and conductors in the Underground Railroad. In time, abolitionism and the Underground Railroad became linked in the public's mind.

Still, not all abolitionists approved of the Underground Railroad's activities. Some stuck to the early Garrisonian position that moral suasion demanded obedience to laws, even unjust ones—"Resistance to the legal authorities we never hesitate to disapprove," declared Garrison in 1836,[8] although he later changed his mind when he decided that the Constitution was an unsalvageably tainted document—and consequently accepted the Southern claim that aiding slaves to escape was theft of private property. (On the other hand, other abolitionists so refused to recognize slave laws that they opposed buying slaves in order to set them free because such purchases implicitly acknowledged the legal propriety of owning humans as property.)

But most of those who expressed reservations about the Railroad did so because they believed it fell short of the drastic measures needed to end slavery. A critic in 1840 declared that abolitionists should be "for abolishing slavery itself, not by aiding [slaves] to run away, but so that slaves need not run away to get their liberty." Abolitionist Maria W. Chapman worried that "establish[ing] underground railroads" merely "[hid] from tyranny, instead of defying it." And in 1857, Thomas Wentworth Higginson, a Massachusetts clergyman turned radical abolitionist, denounced the Underground Railroad as a second-best strategy—"It may be a necessary evil, but an evil it is"—born of failure to stand up to slavery. "The Underground Railroad," Higginson declared, "makes cowards of us all. It makes us think and hesitate and look over our shoulders, and listen, and wonder, and not dare to tell the truth to the man who stands by our side."[9]

These reservations notwithstanding, the abolitionists generally applauded and often participated in the Underground Railroad's activities. Given the influential presence of blacks in the movement, it's difficult to see how things could have been otherwise. So Garrison's promise of assistance to runaways once they crossed the Mason-Dixon Line was a strong one.

## WHO RAN?

As discussed in chapter 1, most slave runs were of short duration and indulged in by single men and women, couples, and sometimes even entire families. But running northward to freedom was a different matter altogether. Such a journey required a great deal of physical strength and stamina. Women were often physically incapable of making it, and mothers were just as reluctant to expose their children to its dangers as to leave them behind. Consequently, the flight of whole families was a rare occurrence, although it did happen. In 1830, for example, Josiah Henson, the inspiration for Harriet Beecher Stowe's fictional character Uncle Tom, escaped from Maryland to Canada with his wife and four children, two of whom he carried on his back for most of the way.

Occasionally young, childless women would take off on their own, as Harriet Tubman did in 1849. Although flights of single mothers were the least common of all, they did occur. Eliza Harris, for example, fled from Kentucky across the frozen Ohio River with her two-year-old son in 1850. Levi Coffin, a Quaker convinced that "the whole system of slavery, in all its heinous forms" was "[a] sin against God and a crime against man," remembered once helping a mother and her two young daughters.[10] Fleeing from a Kentucky master, they traveled only at night, hid in woods during the day, lived off green corn, and finally managed to ford the Ohio River to freedom. By the time they landed on Coffin's doorstep, the three were in pretty bad shape. The mother was physically ill from hunger, weariness, and anxiety, and the two little girls were exhausted.

But aside from exceptions like these, typical northbound fugitives were young, single, and strong male field hands in their teens and early twenties. Ninety-five percent of them set out alone, unaccompanied by fellow travelers who might slow them down.

Field hands weren't the only slaves who fled. Those hired out by their masters to urban or rural employers as well as those skilled in crafts or trades—almost a third of all fugitives—also made runs for freedom. Slaves who worked in plantation houses rather than the fields likewise fled, and they often had advantages that field hands lacked. Owners frequently favored lighter-skinned servants for domestic work. As a result, some household slaves were so pale that they could pass for white, and a few of them picked up the demeanor and sometimes literacy while working in the plantation house to pull off forging identity papers and disguising themselves as whites. The escape of Ellen and William Craft is a case in point. William was dark, while his wife, Ellen, was light-skinned. In 1848, after months of careful planning by the pair, Ellen bobbed her hair and disguised herself as a young, sickly, white planter who was traveling north for medical treatment. William played the part of the "young master's" manservant. Together, the two traveled by train and steamer until they eventually arrived in Philadelphia. They spent the next couple of years traveling throughout the North telling the story of their escape to sellout crowds. Slave owners in the border states became so concerned about the possibility that their own light-skinned slaves might try something similar that they began seeing dark-skinned slaves as safer investments than mulattos, even though they still preferred the latter for domestic service.[11]

William and Ellen Craft's flight from slavery suggests that ingenuity was just as important a quality in potential runners as strength and stamina. Slaves who took off spontaneously or with little forethought usually didn't make it. Those who prepared carefully and thoughtfully—who demonstrated, as one commentator puts it, "self-confidence, self-assurance, self-possession, determination, and self-reliance"—had a far better chance of reaching safe haven.[12] The infrequency of slave insurrections in the South may be partly attributable to the loss through flight of those slaves with the greatest leadership potential.

Ellen Craft and her husband, William, escaped from slavery in 1848 by daringly posing as a sickly young white planter (Ellen) traveling north for medical treatment in the company of a trusty manservant (William). (William Still, *The Underground Rail Road* [Philadelphia: Porter & Coats, 1872], 368)

The Crafts' escape also points to another characteristic shared by slaves who ran: courage. In order to pull off their impersonation of a young planter and his manservant, Ellen and William needed the resolve to face down railroad officials, hotel managers, and fellow passengers, all schooled by the South to be on the lookout for runaway slaves.

But less dramatic escapes required courage as well. Slaves were programmed by their masters to be servile and dependent. As mentioned in chapter 1, most of their discontent was expressed passively by way of stealing or goldbricking rather than by overt defiance or rebellion. It took a great deal of courage to venture away from the familiar farm or plantation in search of the Free States. Most slaves had a limited grasp of their local geography, much less of the terrain that lay between them and the northern states. For many of them, fleeing for freedom was little more than a blind run.

To make matters worse, slave owners discouraged flight by frightening their slaves with tales about how difficult it was for a fugitive to reach safe haven in either the northern states or Canada. Virginia slave William Johnson was told by his master that the Detroit River, one of the boundaries between Canada and the United States, was 3,000 miles wide and that a ship starting from the American side at night would still be close to where it started when dawn broke.[13] Fugitive Henry Banks recalled, "I had heard tell of a free country—but I did not know where it was, nor how to get there."[14] Frederick Douglass noted that as great as the distance to freedom was in reality, it was even greater in a slave's imagination. "Slaveholders sought to impress their slaves with a belief in the boundlessness of slave territory, and of their own limitless power."[15] Douglass admitted that as a slave he imagined Canada a wild and desolate place, fit for geese, perhaps, but not humans.[16]

## WHY DID THEY RUN?

Slaves fled for freedom for a variety of reasons. But whatever the immediate provocation, accident of location was an important factor in making the decision to run or stay. Slaves in the border states were more likely to flee than slaves in the Lower South simply because it was easier for them to do so. Would-be fugitives from Georgia, Mississippi, Louisiana, Alabama, or Florida were hundreds of miles from the Mason-Dixon Line, and their chance of actually reaching it without getting caught or being turned back by exhaustion and hunger was slim. As one of them sadly noted, "Escape from Alabama is almost impossible—if a man escapes, it is by the skin of his teeth."[17] By contrast, border-state slaves in Maryland, Virginia, and Kentucky lived with the constantly tempting knowledge that freedom was waiting for them just across the Ohio River, Chesapeake Bay, or state line.

The prospect of being sold to the slave-hungry plantations of the Deep South was a major incentive for border-state slaves to run. As William Johnson recalled after making it safely to Canada, "The fear of being sold South had more influence in inducing me to leave than any other thing. Master used to say, that if we didn't suit him, he would put us in his pocket quick—meaning he would sell us."[18] Slaves like Johnson knew perfectly well that however bad their situations in Virginia or Kentucky were, conditions in the Lower South were much worse. The labor was hard, the weather brutal, the living accommodations primitive, and the supervision frequently harsh and unforgiving. Hearing that there was a possibility that they or their family members were headed to the auction block—and that possibility steadily increased after 1808, when it became legally impossible to import new slaves to meet the Deep South's insatiable demand for labor—was often enough to send slaves northward. For many, it was a stronger incentive to flight than even physical abuse. Virginia fugitive Anthony Blow, for example, endured beatings and floggings for years and survived no fewer than three gunshot wounds from angry masters. But the tipping point for him came when the man who was shortly to inherit him threatened to "sell him as soon as he got possession."[19]

Blow's fear of being sold south by a new master was common among slaves. The death of a slave owner often unsettled a plantation. Slaves knew they were at the mercy of legatees, many of whom were eager to sell some of their inherited property to pay off debts. Even if selling wasn't an immediate likelihood, anxiety about what sort of master a new owner would be or what kind of overseers he would appoint sometimes drove slaves to flee. To make matters worse, the danger of being sold south didn't arise only when estates were transferred from one person to another. Cash-strapped slave owners in the border states knew they could always get their hands on funds quickly by selling their slaves southward.

Another reason slaves tended to run was a change for the worse in work routine or the arrival of a new overseer more demanding than the previous one. Owners frequently changed white overseers in the hope of squeezing ever more labor from their slaves. In turn, overseers, wishing to keep their jobs by pleasing their employers, stretched work hours, tried to cut costs by reducing rations, kept a close watch on slaves to guard against laxness and stealing, and punished those judged to be remiss. Seasoned overseers knew that harsh treatment and brutal punishment of slaves were liable to backfire. But exasperation and inexperience often overrode prudence, and slaves were whipped, put in stocks for up to a week, or forced to work on Sundays and holidays. Such mistreatment encouraged flight.

A further motive for running was anger at excessive physical abuse. With some fugitives, the abuse was long-standing. Isaac, who belonged to a Delaware blacksmith, was accustomed to being beaten with a "chunk of wood" over what his master referred to as his "no feeling head." But a final beating that laid Isaac up for two weeks at last convinced him that it was time to go.[20] With other slaves, a single especially cruel beating was enough to motivate them to run. Such was the case with a 19-year-old Alabama slave named John who, having been sold to a young man "fond of drinking and carousing, and always ready for a fight or a knock-down," was so badly bullwhipped by him that he was partially paralyzed for a few days afterward.[21]

Besides anxiety about being sold south or anger over beatings, slaves headed north for a variety of other reasons. Some attributed their flight to bad or scant rations, others to their masters' failure to provide them with adequate clothing. Hired-out slaves often resented their masters' expropriation of most or all of their wages. Frederick Douglass was one of them. His master, who hired Douglass out as a ship caulker, allowed him to keep a small portion of his wages. But Douglass considered the gesture "a sort of admission of my right to the whole" and deeply resented the arrangement.[22] This kind of disgruntlement, coupled with the taste of freedom that wage-earning gave them, was sometimes enough to induce slaves to flee. Others, married to slaves from different plantations, sometimes ran because their masters refused them opportunities for regular spousal visitations. Still others fled from either the threat or actuality of sexual abuse by their masters.

After their escape to freedom, some slaves admitted that they hadn't been especially ill used by their masters. Mr. and Mrs. Isaac Riley, a slave couple who fled from Missouri and eventually settled in Canada, appear to have been two of them.[23] But the Rileys and other slaves ran nonetheless out of an unquenchable thirst for freedom. Many of the slaves who fled for the first time in their teens were chiefly motivated by a desire to be free. Regardless of whether their masters treated them relatively well or abused them, the motive that prompted them to run, no matter how often they were captured, returned, and severely punished, was the dream of freedom.

Whatever their specific reasons—physical abuse, fear of being sold, or longing for freedom—slaves ran because they were discontented with their lot. For Northern opponents of the peculiar institution (as well as for us today) the discontent was unsurprising. What person would choose to be a slave? But as discussed in chapter 1, slaveholders often expressed shock and a sense of betrayal at the disappearance of a slave.

## HOW DID THEY RUN?

When it came to running, strategies depended in large part on the fugitive's intellect, imagination, and stamina. Some escapes were thoroughly planned for months, and others were spontaneous flights with absolutely no preparation. But most fell somewhere in between. The majority of slaves traveled at night and under cover, doing their best to stay off wellused roads. Most fled on foot, but some also "borrowed" horses or wagons from their masters, especially when accompanied by children or elderly relatives. A very few, like Ellen and William Craft, disguised themselves or carried false free papers and boldly traveled by coach, rail, and steamer. Even fewer, like Henry "Box" Brown, invented novel means of escape that were emulated by other fugitives for a while until Southern authorities and slave catchers caught on to the new trick. In 1849, Brown had himself nailed inside a wooden crate and shipped from Richmond to abolitionists in Philadelphia. His nearly 300-mile journey, some of it spent riding upside down, made him an instant celebrity.[24]

Slaves fled throughout the entire year whenever opportunity arose or circumstance forced. But there were some seasons that were more promising than others. Christmas was one of them. Slaves were generally given

Eastman Johnson's 1862 painting *A Ride for Liberty—The Fugitive Slaves* captures the sense of urgency and fear felt by runaways. But most of them fled on foot rather than on horseback. (Francis G. Mayer/Corbis)

a few days off and provided with passes to visit relatives on other planta-tions, so it wasn't uncommon in the week between Christmas and New Year's Day to see them on the roads. Slaveholders were well aware that this was an especially tempting time of year for slaves to run, and many took measures to safeguard their human property. Frederick Douglass re-called that his masters discouraged Christmas flights by giving field hands generous quantities of liquor to induce in them a drunken "state of stu-pidity."[25]

Weekends were also good times to run, because slaves were generally given Saturday afternoons and Sundays off. A slave who made a run on Saturday night wasn't likely to be missed until sometime Monday, giving him a good head start on slave hunters and bloodhounds.

Running in the winter exposed fugitives to the risk of inclement weather and hunger. Spring and summer were better, but the former had the disadvantage of providing little in the way of field or garden crops for scavenging, and in the summer the days were so long that they cut down

One of the most publicized escapes from slavery occurred in 1849, when Henry "Box" Brown had himself nailed inside a small wooden crate and shipped as freight from Richmond to Philadelphia. (Library of Congress)

on night travel. Late fall was best because the weather was moderate and there was ample opportunity to glean food from harvested fields or steal from granaries and barns.

The direction in which slaves ran was more predictable, but here again there was flexibility. Border-state slaves typically headed north to the Free States, but many of them, daunted not only by the difficulty of crossing the Mason-Dixon Line but also by the utter unfamiliarity of the North, elected instead to flee to southern urban areas like Richmond where they could disappear in black communities. Other slaves, especially those in the Lower South who appreciated the near impossibility of making it to the North, either headed to New Orleans, which had the largest free black population of any city in the South, or trekked across southern Texas into Mexico.

A major problem for slaves running west or north was finding a way to cross the watery barriers that often lay between them and freedom: the Ohio River to the northwest, the Rappahannock and Potomac Rivers to the northeast, and the Mississippi River to the west. Slaves typically didn't know how to swim, and even those who did were no match for the wide and swift waters of the Ohio and Mississippi. Many slaves who successfully traveled scores or even hundreds of miles to freedom found themselves frustrated at the final stage of their flight by the rivers. As we'll see in the next chapter, it's here that fugitives often first received help from Underground Railroad agents whose business it was to ferry them to the Northern side. Less fortunate fugitives resorted to makeshift rafts or floating logs. Stationmaster Levi Coffin described the flight of a slave woman from Mississippi who, "when she came to rivers and streams of water too deep for wading, made rafts of logs or poles, tied together with grape-vines or hickory withes."[26]

A few fugitives managed to use water to their advantage. Slaves on the Atlantic seaboard or close to the Mississippi River sometimes stowed away on ships, steamers, and boats headed northward. One of them, John Jackson, ran from his master's South Carolina plantation to the Charleston docks, and there hid in the hold of a ship bound for Boston. After seven days and nights, tortured by hunger and thirst, he finally gave himself up to the vessel's captain. Jackson was lucky: the captain fed him and, when the ship docked in Boston, released him. Another fugitive, Edward "Saltwater" Davis, hid himself in a tiny space in the bow of the steamship *Keystone State*. For three days icy water swept over him as the ship made its way from Georgia to the mouth of the Delaware River. By the time he was discovered, Davis was nearly dead.

Runaways faced constant incidental dangers such as accidental injuries, snakebites, and illness. But the three primary problems that confronted most runaway slaves were navigation, food, and slave patrols. All three were formidable challenges.

As already noted, most slaves had only a limited sense of local geography and none whatsoever of the wider world except what they picked up by eavesdropping on conversations between whites or speaking to captured fugitives. So far as navigation went, they knew that they could steer a generally northern course by keeping an eye on the progress of the sun. The problem is that fugitives generally traveled in the dark of night. So to keep to the right direction, slaves oriented themselves by locating and following the North Star. The North Star (Polaris) is always seen in the northern sky but has only moderate brightness. So it's most easily located by seeking out the Big Dipper, the constellation slaves called the "Drinking Gourd." The North Star appears in a straight line with the two stars that make up the outer rim of the Big Dipper. Since the dipper is one of the easiest constellations to spot, few slaves would have had difficulty in locating and guiding themselves by the North Star.

But even with the North Star as a compass point, many fugitives quickly became disoriented, and it wasn't uncommon for them to wander in circles for several nights before finally getting their bearings. Charting a northward course on the North Star isn't a particularly easy task under the best of circumstances. Fleeing slaves were further handicapped by overcast night skies that hid the stars or by thick foliage in the forests through which they traveled to avoid the main roads. Sometimes they were forced to steer for nights on end by feeling for moss on the north side of tree trunks.

The North Star became one of the most popular symbols of freedom in abolitionist literature about the Underground Railroad. It evoked such powerful responses that Frederick Douglass named the antislavery newspaper he founded and edited the *North Star*. References to it appear in numerous fugitive narratives. William Wells Brown, an ex-slave from Kentucky, wrote that when he escaped he "welcomed the sight of my friend—truly the slave's friend—the North Star!"[27] When Daniel Fisher ran from his Virginia master, he relied on the North Star to guide him because he was "without knowledge of the country."[28]

A great deal of folklore about fugitives and the North Star sprang up in the years preceding and following the Civil War. One of the most enduring stories is that antebellum slaves taught their children a song about "following the drinking gourd" whose lyrics provided instruction for successful flights. The song was supposedly written by a free black man, a one-legged sailor named Peg Leg Joe who mapped an escape route for slaves in Kentucky. There's no historical evidence to verify the legend, and in fact "Follow the Drinking Gourd" was first published as a popular song only in 1928. (One of its stanzas is the epigraph to this chapter.) But none of this denies the importance of the North Star as a navigational tool for slaves on the run, and it's not unreasonable to suppose that slaves taught their youngsters its importance, even if they didn't do so in song.[29]

Slaves who ran knew that they had to travel swiftly and lightly, so they generally took few provisions for the journey. Instead, they counted on finding food and drink along the way. Occasionally other slaves whom they met along their route gave them something to eat, but making contact with strangers was risky business. William Wells Brown remembered that when he escaped in the winter of 1834, he suffered greatly from hunger and the cold because "I had long since made up my mind that I would not trust myself in the hands of any man, white or colored."[30] So for the most part, runaways lived off what they could scavenge or steal. Jim Bow-Legs, a slave from Virginia who made six failed escapes before finally succeeding, hid "for months in the woods, swamps and caves, subsisting mainly on parched corn and berries."[31] When Harry Grimes fled his North Carolina master, he took with him a little bread and a few "roasting ears and 'taters," but he soon "suffered mighty bad with the cold and for something to eat."[32] At one point in his flight to freedom, Charles Peyton Lucas went three days with nothing to eat or drink but some green corn he stole from the fields, sucking the juice and gnawing on the unripe kernels. A few nights later he was able to break into a farmer's spring house and steal a "good pan" of milk. But at other times he was forced to drink muddy water from horse tracks.[33] It's not surprising that Underground Railroad stationmasters north of the Mason-Dixon Line nearly always found that the fugitives who came to them were half-dead of starvation.

Formidable as problems of navigation and sustenance were, fugitives especially dreaded running into slave patrols or professional slave catchers. One of the ways proponents defended slavery was by appealing to the sanctity of property rights: slaves were property, pure and simple, and property owners had a right to hold on to what was theirs. Even if an owner might have been secretly glad to see an especially troublesome slave flee, the runaway had to be pursued and captured lest the Southern insistence that slaves were property be undermined.

To that end, communities in every state in the South organized militia-like slave patrols, usually manned by local farmers and planters assigned military-style ranks who regularly watched roads and byways for runaways. Typically, the patrols were boisterously amateurish, too focused on hard drinking and joyriding to focus well on finding runaways. Even if they'd been more conscientious than they usually were, their job was difficult. Fugitive slaves were likely to stay away from roads and keep to forests and swamps. Despite their general ineffectiveness, what made the patrols a

Ex-slave William Wells Brown, author of *Clotel,* the first novel written by an African American, was also an Underground Railroad conductor. Working on Lake Erie steamboats in the 1830s and 1840s, he ferried dozens of fugitives to Canada. (Hulton Archive/Getty Images)

danger to fugitives is that they had the legal right to stop and question any black they encountered, to ride onto private property and search buildings, and to shoot on sight any black declared an outlaw. "The patrols go out in companies at about dark and ride nearly all night," reported one fugitive from Alabama. "If they meet a colored man without a pass, it is thirty-nine lashes. . . . If there is a party assembled at the quarters, they rush in half drunk, and thrash round with their sticks, perhaps before they look at a pass . . . I can't paint so bad as 'tis."[34]

More of a threat to runaways than the slave patrols were professional slave catchers. These were men who made a living from hunting down runaways. They would follow a fugitive's trail for miles, often accompanied by "nigger dogs" especially trained to track down blacks. The dogs were brutal creatures bred to corner and savage runaways, and they had such ferocious reputations that several states legislated penalties against slave catchers who let them maul fugitives. Georgia's penal code, for example,

declared such behavior a misdemeanor, not because of the suffering in-
flicted on the runaway so much as the damage caused to human property.
Occasionally, though, owners who accompanied slave catchers in pursuit of fugitives were willing to sacrifice property for pleasure. Louisiana
planter David Barrow confessed that he had a "zest" for the "sport" of
fugitive-chasing. Once, after trailing a slave for about a mile, Barrow's
dogs treed the runaway, pulled him off its branches, and bit him badly.
"Think he will stay at home a while," Barrow smugly observed.[35]

Runaways knew about the dogs and were terrified of them. To throw
the hounds off their scent, whenever possible they waded through creeks
and marshes. They also rubbed the soles of their feet or shoes with animal

# $200 Reward.

RANAWAY from the subscriber, on the night of Thursday, the 30th of Sepember,

# FIVE NEGRO SLAVES,

To-wit : one Negro man, his wife, and three children.

The man is a black negro, full height, very erect, his face a little thin.   He is about forty years of age, and calls himself *Washington Reed*, and is known by the name of Washington.   He is probably well dressed, possibly takes with him an ivory headed cane, and is of  good  address.   Several  of his teeth are gone.

*Mary*, his wife, is about thirty years of age, a bright mulatto woman, and quite stout and strong.

The oldest of the children is a boy, of the name of FIELDING, twelve years of age, a dark mulatto, with heavy eyelids.   He probably wore a new cloth cap.

MATILDA, the second child, is a girl, six years of age, rather  a dark mulatto, but a bright and smart looking child.

MALCOLM, the youngest,  is a boy, four years old, a lighter mulatto  than the last, and about equally as bright.  He probably also wore a cloth cap.   If  examined, he will be found to have a swelling at the navel.

Washington and Mary have lived at or near St. Louis, with the subscriber, for about 15 years.

It is supposed that they are making their way to Chicago, and that a white man accompanies them, that they will travel chiefly at night, and most probably in a covered wagon.

A reward of $150 will be paid for their apprehension, so that I can get them, if taken within one hundred miles of St. Louis, and $200 if taken beyond that, and secured so that I can get them, and other reasonable additional charges, if delivered to the subscriber, or to THOMAS ALLEN, Esq., at St. Louis, Mo.  The above negroes, for the last few years, have been in possession of Thomas Allen, Esq., of St. Louis.

# WM. RUSSELL.

ST. LOUIS, Oct. 1, 1847.

An 1847 poster offering a reward of $200 for the return of five fugitive slaves.
Slaves who managed to escape in the antebellum years probably numbered no
more than 135,000, but their total market value was a staggering $40 million.
(Library of Congress)

fat to mask their own scent or threw pepper behind them to inflame the dogs' nostrils and hamper their ability to track. The Southern cornmeal balls known as "hush puppies" may have derived their name from fleeing slaves' tossing them in their wake to distract the hungry dogs pursuing them.

Slave catchers charged hefty prices, usually calculated in terms of the length of time and the distance covered in tracking down runaways. Having to pay to recover "self-stolen" property increased the odds that angry owners, already intending to punish captured fugitives as a deterrent to other would-be runaways, would deal even more severely with them. It wasn't unusual for apprehended slaves who feared what awaited them if they were returned to their owners to refuse to identify themselves to their captors. In such cases, their physical descriptions were advertised in newspapers and posters while the fugitives were held in the local jail. If left unclaimed for a year, they were sold to the highest bidder, usually a planter in the Lower South looking for field hands. Few other whites wanted to risk buying a slave who was a known runaway.

## THE NEW ORDER OF THE DAY

One of the enduring myths about the Underground Railroad is that black fugitives, cowed by years of slavery into a near-helpless passivity, simply couldn't have made their way north to freedom without the aid of white agents and stationmasters. But even a quick examination of runaways in the antebellum South puts the lie to this stereotype. The initiative for running was the slave's, and it was taken in full knowledge that the chance of success was low and the penalty for failure severe.

Moreover, even if fugitive slaves occasionally relied on the kindness of other slaves or freedmen they met along the way, they were for the most part entirely on their own when it came to finding their way to the Mason-Dixon Line, keeping body and soul together during their flight, and avoiding slave patrols and slave catchers. It was only after they escaped from the South under their own steam that they might run across abolitionists and Underground Railroad agents, themselves often black, who could give them a helping hand.

Acknowledging this isn't to downplay the very real aid white abolitionists extended to escaping slaves, but only to point out that Henry

Bibb was absolutely correct when he wrote in 1853 that self-emancipation was the new order of the day. In the inaugural issue of the *North Star*, Frederick Douglass declared to his readers that blacks "must be [their] own representatives and advocates."[36] He was referring in particular to abolitionist and Underground Railroad activities. But he could just as easily have been speaking of the brave and ingenious souls who ran from their masters with little more than the North Star to guide them and a longing for freedom to sustain them.

## NOTES

The chapter epigraph is a stanza taken from the song "Follow the Drinking Gourd." The first line suggests that the would-be fugitive should look for signs of spring before running.

1. Samuel Cartwright, "Diseases and Peculiarities of the Negro Race," *De Bow's Southern and Western Review* (September 1851): 331–33.

2. *Congressional Globe*, 31st Congress, 1st Session, Appendix, p. 1601. Quoted in Wilbur H. Siebert, *The Underground Railroad from Slavery to Freedom* (Mineola, NY: Dover, 2006), 341.

3. Quoted in Wilbur H. Siebert, *The Underground Railroad*, 310.

4. Quoted in Larry Gara, *The Liberty Line: The Legend of the Underground Railroad* (Lexington: University Press of Kentucky, 1996), 149.

5. Claudine L. Ferrell, *The Abolitionist Movement* (Westport, CT: Greenwood Press, 2006), 152.

6. Another splintering disagreement among abolitionists was the extent to which women should be involved in the leadership of the movement. Garrison was in favor of including them.

7. *North Star*, December 3, 1847.

8. *Liberator*, August 6, 1836.

9. All three quotations are from Larry Gara, *The Liberty Line*, 74, 76, 77.

10. Levi Coffin, *Reminiscences* (Cincinnati: Western Tract Society, 1876), 592.

11. An account of the Crafts' escape may be found in the appendix to this book.

12. John Hope Franklin and Loren Schweninger, *Runaway Slaves: Rebels on the Plantation* (New York: Oxford University Press, 1999), 224.

13. Siebert, *The Underground Railroad*, 197.

14. Benjamin Drew, *The Refugee: A North-side View of Slavery* (Reading, MA: Addison-Wesley, 1969), 51. Drew's book was first published in 1855.

15. Frederick Douglass, *The Life and Times of Frederick Douglass* (Mineola, NY: Dover, 2003), 199. Douglass's *Life and Times* was first published in 1881.

16. Ibid.

17. Drew, *The Refugee*, 175.

18. Ibid., 19.

19. William Still, *The Underground Railroad* (Philadelphia: Porter & Coates, 1872), 46.

20. Ibid., 504.

21. Ibid., 96.

22. Frederick Douglass, *Narrative of the Life of Frederick Douglass* (London: H.G. Collins, 1851), 92.

23. The story of the Rileys' escape may be found in the appendix to this book.

24. The story of Brown's escape may be found in the appendix to this book.

25. John W. Blassingame, ed., *The Frederick Douglass Papers* (New Haven: Yale University Press, 1979), series I, vol. 1: 208.

26. Coffin, *Reminiscences*, 256.

27. William Wells Brown, *Narrative of William W. Brown, An American Slave* (London: Charles Gilpin, 1849), 95. The story of Wells's escape may be found in the appendix to this book.

28. Quoted in Charles L. Blockson, *The Underground Railroad* (New York: Berkeley Books, 1987), 58.

29. Another bit of folklore that has been mistaken for fact is the claim that slaves stitched escape routes on patterned quilts. Although widely accepted, especially after the publication of Jacqueline Tobin and Raymond Dobard's *Hidden in Plain View: A Secret Story of Quilts and the Underground Railroad* (New York: Anchor, 2000), there's little hard evidence for the claim.

30. William Wells Brown, *Narrative of William W. Brown*, 94.

31. Still, *The Underground Railroad*, 246.

32. Ibid., 441.

33. Drew, *The Refugee*, 75.

34. Ibid., 174.

35. Quoted in Franklin and Schweninger, *Runaway Slaves*, 161.

36. *North Star*, December 3, 1847.

# CHAPTER 3

# RIDING THE LIBERTY LINE: UNDERGROUND RAILROAD ROUTES

Ho! the car Emancipation
Rides majestic thro' our nation,
Bearing on its train the story,
Liberty! a nation's glory.
Roll it along, thro' the nation,
Freedom's car, Emancipation!
            —*From the 1844 song "Get Off the Track!"*

Runaway slaves had to rely for the most part on their own wits and stamina while still south of the Mason-Dixon Line. Once north of it, however, they had a decent chance of encountering people, black and white alike, willing to help them on their way. Many times these Good Samaritans acted solely on their own initiative in providing fugitives with a meal and a hayloft for the night. But often they were intentional collaborators—or, in the eyes of the law, co-conspirators—with the Underground Railroad, serving as hosts and guides on dozens of routes, or "liberty lines."

As noted in the introduction, the Underground Railroad was never as systematically organized as folklore then or now claims. But that doesn't mean we should conclude, as historian Wilbur Siebert does, that "the work was everywhere spontaneous, and its character was such that organization could have added little or no efficiency."[1] There were more or less clearly defined regular and alternative routes used by Underground Railroad conductors, designated depots or stations along them, and a number of organizations that openly or clandestinely funded the Railroad and helped its passengers settle in the North. It's true that routes were better organized in some parts of the country than others. It's also the case that, given the nature of the work, there was a great deal of flexibility in most Underground Railroad activities. Stationmasters, conductors, and safe houses came and went, and modes of transportation and specific routes were often chosen to fit the circumstances. Consequently, much of the work was necessarily opportunistic or, as Siebert says, "spontaneous." But what all Railroad activity had in common was a more or less stable network of routes, a shared range of tactics, and a reliably steady core of black and white supporters bound together by their opposition to slavery.

## THE ROUTES

Tracing the origins of specific Underground Railroad routes is difficult, as is precise tracking of all but the most heavily traveled ones. The obvious reason for this is that much of the Railroad's work, because it was illegal, was clandestine. As a general rule, the closer to the border states, the more secretive things were. Details about fugitives and specific routes were often not recorded in writing; if they were, frequently such documents were destroyed for fear of their being discovered. The only systematic contemporaneous record to be kept was compiled by William Still, a Philadelphian who helped oversee one of the most competent liberty lines in the nation. Consequently, the vast majority of reports about Underground Railroad routes are from sometimes questionable anecdotal reports often recorded years after the end of the Civil War.

In states farther north of the Mason-Dixon Line, the operations of the Underground Railroad were less clandestine and the routes more publicly known. The presumption, of course, was that the farther north the lines ran, the safer fugitives were from pursuit and capture (although this ceased to be the case with the passage of the draconian 1850 Fugitive Slave Act). Agents boasted of their connection with the Railroad, and newspapers with abolitionist sympathies wrote glowingly of the routes in their locales. In July 1844, for example, the Chicago-based *Western Star* ran an ad announcing that the Underground Railroad was booking seats for "Libertyville, Upper Canada." Ladies and gentlemen wishing "to improve their health or circumstances by a northern tour" were invited to ride on one of the Railroad's "regular trips." But proslavery "Police Offi-

The Kentucky-Ohio border was a bustling center of Underground Railroad activity. Cincinnati to the west and Ripley to the east were important depots. (Tom Calarco)

cers" trying to catch a ride on the train, the ad warned, would be shipped as dead freight to Texas.

At times, secrecy was also broken by Railroad workers jubilantly crowing about extraordinary escapes, such as Henry "Box" Brown's imaginative shipment of himself from Richmond to Philadelphia or the Crafts' daring masquerade as master and manservant. On the one hand, publicizing these episodes heartened abolitionists and others who deplored slavery, and they also testified, contrary to the Southern myth of the contented slave, to the fugitive's longing for freedom. But on the other hand, trumpeting them tended to make the work of the Underground Railroad more difficult. As Frederick Douglass complained, "The practice of publishing every new invention by which a slave is known to have escaped from slavery has neither wisdom nor necessity to sustain it. Had not Henry Box Brown and his friends attracted slave-holding attention to the manner of his escape, we might have had a thousand Box Browns per annum. The singularly original plan adopted by William and Ellen Crafts [sic], perished with the first using, because every slaveholder in the land was apprised of it." In short, Douglass worried, the "very public manner" in which some locales advertised their liberty lines transformed the "*Under*-ground Railroad" into the "*Upper*-ground Railroad," disclosing its stations, routes, and safe houses to more slave owners than slaves.[2]

Douglass was undeniably correct in his fear that too much publicity was bad for the Underground Railroad. But he overestimated the effects of the publicity. Most routes remained so clandestine that they're still difficult to trace today.

The dates of origin for specific liberty lines are also, in most cases, hard to pin down. Besides the lack of documentation, the chief difficulty is distinguishing between the aid to fugitives offered by individual Good Samaritans or church congregations and aid offered by Railroad workers and Railroad stations. President George Washington complained in a couple of 1786 letters, for example, that two runaway slaves, one belonging to him, were apparently aided in their bids for freedom by "gentlemen" who would "rather facilitate the escape of slaves than apprehend them."[3] Since the fugitives disappeared into Philadelphia, it's reasonable to suppose that they were aided by Quakers or perhaps even a Quaker congregation. But there's no evidence of an actual liberty line or organized series of depots at play in their flight. Similarly, escaping slaves found haven as early as 1819 in the home of North Carolina Quaker Vestal Coffin. It's too much, however, to think of Coffin's refuge as an Underground Railroad station. He seems to have offered hospitality to runaways and then pointed them in a northerly direction. There was no established chain of stations or depots north of Coffin's home to which fugitives were transported.

What's likely is that many liberty lines and depots gradually emerged along those routes that were natural geographical conduits to the North, pioneered by Good Samaritans who, initially working alone, eventually became connected with other folks in their area willing to aid and abet fugitives. The Underground Railroad, in other words, was truly a grassroots movement. Later, local and regional vigilance committees, organizations established to coordinate the movement of runaways along the liberty lines, formalized ad hoc routes and safe houses. The first committees emerged in the 1830s. New York City's vigilance committee was formed in 1835, Philadelphia's in 1838, and Boston's in 1846. Similar committees in Cleveland, Detroit, Cincinnati, Beloit, Syracuse, and points west followed in the 1850s.

Broadly speaking, there were two main land routes, one east and one west of the Appalachian Mountains, with dozens of auxiliary lines branching off from them. The eastern route, originating in Pennsylvania and New Jersey and forking northward through New England or New York, especially served fugitives from the border states of Maryland, Delaware, and Virginia. Stations along its New York line included Frederick Douglass's Rochester home, through which some 400 fugitives passed, and Rev. Jermain Loguen's Syracuse home and church. The western route began in Indiana, Illinois, and Ohio and mainly served fugitives from the border states of Kentucky to the south and Missouri to the west.[4] Western liberty lines ran north of Missouri through Iowa—Grinnell and its new college were important Underground Railroad stations—before veering eastward through Wisconsin. Lines running through Indiana, Illinois, and Ohio tended to converge first in Cincinnati and eventually Detroit, a favorite final American destination because of its proximity to Canada.

## Eastern Lines

The earliest Underground Railroad routes were in the east, dating probably to the 19th century's first decade. Philadelphia quickly became one of the most active stations in the country, funneling fugitives from slave-heavy Virginia and Maryland to parts northern. One of the busiest lines leading into Philadelphia ran through Washington, D.C. Jacob R. Gibbs, a printer who lived in Washington, kept a file of "free papers"—documents attesting to the bearer's manumission—which had belonged to deceased freedmen. He regularly dispensed them to runaways who passed through the District. By the time the Civil War broke out, Gibbs estimated that he'd supplied as many as 2,000 fugitives with false papers. Thomas Garrett, stationmaster on an equally busy line running into Philadelphia from Wilmington, Delaware, estimated that he also aided around 2,000 refugees. William Still recalled sheltering more than 600 fugitives in his Philadelphia home and otherwise helping nearly 3,000 others.

Still and Garrett were undoubtedly the two most important station-masters on the entire eastern route, partly because of accident of place: they served as the first points of contact for fugitives on the eastern seaboard and were responsible for channeling them northward. They worked well with one another for many years, holding each other in high esteem. Their partnership exemplified the cooperation and mutual respect between black and white Underground Railroad agents that made the enterprise so successful.

Still, the freeborn son of ex-slave parents, moved to Philadelphia from his home state of New Jersey in 1847, when he was in his mid-twenties. He was immediately taken on by the Pennsylvania Anti-Slavery Society as a clerk. Three years later, he threw in his lot with a revitalized vigilance committee formed in response to the passage of the oppressive Fugitive Slave Act. (The original Philadelphia vigilance committee, founded in 1838, was pretty much inactive by then.) He soon became its executive secretary, and under his leadership the committee organized an impressive network of safe houses and Railroad branches, conductors, and station-masters. Still was also adept at soliciting funds from churches, abolitionist societies, philanthropic groups, and wealthy individuals for the relief of fugitives.

Impressively, Still kept a record of the fugitives who passed through his hands, recording in meticulous detail the particulars of their stories and escapes. At one point, fearing that this document would fall into the hands of slave catchers and compromise both fugitives and agents, he hid it in an old cemetery building. Fortunately, his record survived. After the Civil War, in 1872, he retrieved it and published it as a book. It's one of the period's few accounts of the Underground Railroad written by an African American, and it offers invaluable testimony to the courage and initiative displayed by slaves who ran as well as the dedication of the Railroad agents who aided them.

One of the most extraordinary cases recorded by Still is the story of an ex-slave who called himself Peter Freedman. Freedman told Still that he had been born to free parents in Philadelphia but kidnapped by slave catchers at the age of six and sold south, first in Kentucky and then in Alabama. After years of backbreaking servitude, he had managed to save enough money to buy his freedom. Determined to reunite with his family, he had made his way back to Philadelphia, where an Underground Rail-

Underground Railroad stationmaster in Philadelphia William Still was one of the most important figures on the eastern route. His meticulous records of the fugitives he aided were published after the Civil War. (Library of Congress)

road worker had brought him to Still on the chance that Still could help him to find them.

On hearing Freedman's story, Still asked him whether he remembered the names of his parents. Freedman did: their names were Sidney and Levin. Still, surprised, mentioned that his own father's name was also Levin. Looking more closely at Freedman, he noticed a resemblance between this man and his own mother, and eventually the two realized to their astonishment that in fact they were brothers. It turned out Freedman had misremembered the events of his childhood: he had been born to Sidney and Levin when they were slaves. Levin later purchased his own freedom and arranged for Sidney and their four children (Peter, another boy, and two girls) to ride the Underground Railroad to join him in New Jersey. Soon afterward, however, Sidney and the children—not just Peter—were captured and returned to their master. Several months later, Sidney ran again, taking the two girls but leaving the boys behind (the other brother died in captivity some years later). Upon rejoining her husband, she changed her name for safety's sake to Charity. William, who was born after Sidney and Levin were reunited, never knew he had a brother in bondage.

Still's close collaborator in Underground Railroad work, Thomas Garrett, was a Quaker from Wilmington, Delaware. Three decades older than Still, Garrett began helping slaves escape from slavery as early as 1814 and continued giving them shelter and sending them on to the Free States of Pennsylvania and New Jersey for over 40 years. He was fearless in standing up to slave catchers on the prowl for fugitives. As his friend Still described him, "He seems to have scarcely known what fear was, and though irate slave-holders often called on him to learn the whereabouts of their slaves, he met them placidly, never denied having helped the fugitives, positively refused to give them any information, and when they flourished pistols, or bowie-knives to enforce their demands, he calmly pushed the weapons aside, and told them that none but cowards resorted to such means to carry their ends."[5]

Garrett was as fearless in facing down the law as he was in defying slave catchers. In 1848, when he was 60 years old, Garrett was sued by a number of Maryland slaveholders for aiding their "property" to escape. The presiding judge at his trial (in federal circuit court) was Roger B. Taney, the Supreme Court chief justice who nine years later wrote the Dred Scott decision, which found that since slaves weren't citizens, they had no constitutionally guaranteed rights. Predictably, Taney ruled against the defendant and imposed such a large fine on Garrett that it bankrupted him. But after sentence was passed, Garrett calmly vowed to redouble his efforts on behalf of the Underground Railroad. When Taney admonished him to take the verdict to heart and refrain from future civil disobedience, Garrett is supposed to have responded, "Judge, thou hast not left me a dollar, but I wish to say to thee, and to all in this court-room, that if anyone knows of a fugitive who wants a shelter and a friend, send him to Thomas Garrett and he will befriend him."[6]

### Western Lines

Philadelphia was probably the single busiest station on the Underground Railroad, but an estimated half of all fugitives fled to freedom at

Underground stationmaster in Wilmington, Delaware, Thomas Garrett worked closely with William Still and Harriet Tubman. When convicted of "slave stealing" and fined into bankruptcy, Garrett said he hoped the publicity from his trial would lead more fugitives to his door. (Library of Congress)

the Ohio-Kentucky border crossing farther west. Western Railroad conductors were kept especially busy ferrying runaways safely across the watery divide: the deep and wide Ohio River.

John Parker, an ex-slave who lived in the town of Ripley on the Ohio side, nightly rowed across to Kentucky to meet fugitives looking for a way to cross over. He estimated that he ferried at least one runaway a week, occasionally venturing inland to guide fugitives to the river. On one such expedition, Parker and a band of fugitives made it to the Ohio River just ahead of the pursuing bloodhounds to find that the boat couldn't handle so many passengers. Two of the men were left standing on the riverbank; as the boat started to pull away, a passenger cried out that one of them was her husband. Then, remembered Parker: "I witnessed an example of heroism and self-sacrifice that made me proud of my race. For one of the single men safely in the boat, hearing the cry of the woman for her husband, arose without a word [and] walked quietly to the [river] bank. The husband sprang into the boat as I pushed off."[7]

The runaways whom Parker aided, as well as hundreds more who made it across the river on their own, usually found their way to the home of Rev. John Rankin, another Ripley resident. A native of Tennessee who left proslavery congregations in Kentucky to settle in a Free State, Rankin bought a house on a high bluff overlooking the Ohio River and every night for nearly 40 years hung a lantern on a pole as a beacon for runaways. The light could be seen for miles. In 1826 he published *Letters on American Slavery*, a tract in which he argued that neither reason nor religion justifies slavery, and addressed the book specifically to his own brother, a slaveholding merchant in Virginia. During his time on the Underground Railroad, Rankin offered refuge to over 2,000 fugitives, hiding them away in his barn or house and feeding, clothing, and sometimes nursing them before sending them on to the next station. On two occasions outraged Kentucky slave owners, who had already put a bounty on his head, tried to burn down his house. Each time, Rankin and his sons managed to drive them off.

The house of Rev. John Rankin in Ripley, Ohio, perched atop a high bluff overlooking the Ohio River. Every night for over 20 years, Rankin hoisted a lit lantern on a pole as a beacon for runaway slaves crossing over from the Kentucky side of the river. (Library of Congress)

Western Underground Railroad lines were established in southern Illinois and Indiana by the late 1820s. One of the region's most important stationmasters was the Quaker Levi Coffin, who estimated that he aided an average of 100 fugitives a year for over 30 years. Levi, born and raised in North Carolina, was cousin to the same Vestal Coffin who offered refuge to fugitives in the early years of the 19th century. Moving to Indiana in 1826 to devote himself to the assistance of runaways, Levi relocated 20 years later to Cincinnati. When he arrived there, he discovered that aid to runaways was haphazard and disorganized. Working closely with the local black community, he began coordinating and systematizing Underground Railroad activities throughout the entire lower Ohio River Valley. He was so successful that Cincinnati became known as the "Grand Central Station" of the Underground Railroad. It was the first major station for most slaves coming into Ohio from Kentucky.

Quaker abolitionist and businessman Levi Coffin was the leading Underground Railroad stationmaster on the western line. Based first in Indiana and then Cincinnati, he and his wife Catherine aided hundreds of fugitives. (Library of Congress)

### Water Routes

In addition to the two main land routes east and west of the Appalachian Mountains, there were also a number of water routes for fleeing slaves to follow. Slaves from the Deep South occasionally made their way to freedom by following the Mississippi River northward, either by stowing aboard northbound cargo or passenger steamers or, more commonly, by accompanying their masters on northerly journeys and jumping ship when the opportunity arose. The latter was so common that it provoked Sen. Jefferson Davis to complain about the number of fugitives escaping in this way from his state of Mississippi. In 1840 the *St. Louis Gazette* advised steamboats to cease hiring freedmen as crew members because they encouraged slaves at river ports to flee. Other major river routes included the Ohio, Missouri, and Illinois Rivers. Even if fleeing slaves didn't journey upriver, many of them were forced to cross rivers that served as borders between slave states and Free States. To do so, they often relied on skiffs hidden by Underground Railroad conductors, stole boats, or floated across as best they could on makeshift rafts.

Well-traveled as rivers were, the two major Underground Railroad water routes were the Atlantic seaboard on the one hand and the Great Lakes region between Detroit in the west and Niagara in the east on the other. Fugitives fleeing to Canada along either the eastern or western land route commonly made the last leg of their journey over one of the Great Lakes, usually Erie or Ontario, but sometimes Huron. Runaways heading for Canada by way of Wisconsin often veered eastward over Lake Michigan to Detroit, where they then ferried across the Detroit River to freedom. Steam and sailing vessels regularly journeyed over the Lakes to the Canadian side from ports at Racine, Chicago, Detroit, Sandusky, Cleveland, Toledo, and Buffalo. Friendly captains like J. W. Keith of the Sandusky-based steamer *Arrow* could always be found to ferry fugitives to Canada, either out of compassion or for a price. Many crew members of the Great Lakes vessels were black—working on boats, steamers, and sailing vessels was one of the most common occupations for freedmen in the years before the Civil War—and they weren't hesitant about secreting fugitives aboard if their white captains refused steerage.

As in the case of land routes, many conductors on water liberty lines were ex-slaves. One of them, William Wells Brown, worked on Lake Erie steamships out of Detroit and Buffalo.[8] "While on the lakes," he recalled, "I always made arrangement to carry [fugitives] on the boat to Buffalo or Detroit and thus effect their escape to the 'promised land.' The friends of the slave, knowing that I would transport them without charge, never failed to have a delegation when the boat arrived at Cleveland. I have sometimes had four or five on board at one time."[9] In the latter half of 1842 alone, Brown claimed to have transported 69 fugitives across Lake Erie to the Canadian shore.

The second major water route was northward up the Atlantic coast. Stowaways from southern ports such as Baltimore, Norfolk,[10] Wilmington, Charleston, and Savannah headed for the northern ones of New Haven, New Bedford, Boston, and Portland. New Bedford in particular was an important port of refuge. So many fugitives escaped there, and so determined were the white residents to protect them, that the town became known as the "Fugitive's Gibraltar." Frederick Douglass, who made his escape from Maryland across the "waters of the noble Chesapeake," that "broad road of destruction to slavery," was one of the ex-slaves who found refuge there.[11]

Although nearly all maritime Railroad conductors took their passengers northward, one notorious case from 1844 went in the opposite direction. Capt. Jonathan Walker, a Massachusetts-born seaman who relocated to Florida in mid-life, tried to sail seven fugitive slaves in an open boat from Pensacola to the Bahamas. The attempt was a disaster. Walker fell ill in the boat, the fugitives knew nothing about navigation, and all were ultimately captured and returned in manacles to Key West. Walker was jailed in Pensacola, chained to the floor of his cell, and poorly treated until his trial, which became a showcase event for both defenders and opponents of slavery. To no one's surprise, Walker was found guilty of kidnapping slaves. He was fined and pilloried, the letters "S.S."—for "Slave Stealer"—were branded onto his right hand, and he languished in prison until the fines were finally paid off four years later by friends and supporters. Walker became an overnight hero of the Underground Railroad. The Quaker poet John Greenleaf Whittier announced that the "S.S." brand really stood for "Slave Savior," and he wrote a widely circulated and enthusiastically received poem extolling Walker:

> Then lift that manly right hand, bold ploughman of the wave!
> Its branded palm shall prophecy, "SALVATION TO THE SLAVE!"[12]

In 1844, the North was outraged when Capt. Jonathan Walker was pilloried, imprisoned, and branded on the hand for attempting to rescue slaves in Florida. The brand, "S.S.," stood for "Slave Stealer." Quaker abolitionist poet John Greenleaf Whittier declared that it should stand for "Slave Savior." (Library of Congress)

The most dramatic flight along a maritime route—and the largest single passenger load in any Underground Railroad operation—occurred in the year Walker was released from prison. In mid-April 1848, while Washington, D.C., was celebrating the recent overthrow of King Louis Philippe and the reestablishment of a French republic, 77 slaves took advantage of the distracting festivities to board the *Pearl*, a schooner captained by Daniel Drayton. Drayton had a history of sailing runaways to freedom, but this was by far his boldest venture.

Drayton planned to sail down the Potomac into Chesapeake Bay, cut around Maryland and Delaware, and unload his human cargo in the Free State of New Jersey. But bad weather made it too dangerous to enter the bay, and the schooner was quickly overtaken by a posse of 35 armed men aboard a steamship. The *Pearl* was towed back to the capital and Drayton was charged with slave stealing. Predictably convicted, he was sentenced to 20 years in prison. Most of the slaves he'd tried to lead to freedom on

Image from an 1837 anti-slavery broadsheet. The broadsheet also included Quaker abolitionist John Greenleaf Whittier's poem "Our Countrymen in Chains" and a scriptural warning (Exodus 21:16) about the sin of slavery. (Library of Congress)

the *Pearl* were sold south by their angry masters. Drayton's fate was less brutal. President Millard Fillmore commuted the sentence after Drayton had served four years behind bars. In a memoir published after his release, Drayton confessed that his philosophical objections to slavery prior to his arrest and imprisonment had subsequently taken on a very personal feel. "If a man wishes to realize the agony which our American slave trade inflicts in the separation of families, let him personally feel that separation, as I did; let him pass four years in the Washington jail."[13]

Prior to 1850, when the new Fugitive Slave Act made it dangerous for escaped slaves to settle even in northern Free States, most fugitives who traveled on the Underground Railroad integrated as best they could into white urban and rural communities. But a few exclusively black settlements sprang up in the north—Snow Hill and Timbuctoo in New Jersey, Pokepatch in southern Ohio, Lick Creek in Indiana, and New Philadelphia in Illinois—and while they lasted, they served as important stations

Daniel Drayton, captain of the schooner *Pearl*, tried to pull off the largest single escape in the history of U.S. slavery. He sailed out of Washington, D.C., with nearly 80 fugitives bound for the North. Bad weather fouled the rescue attempt, and Drayton and his passengers were captured. Sentenced to 20 years, Drayton was eventually pardoned by President Millard Fillmore. (Library of Congress)

on the Underground Railroad and havens for fugitives hoping to find a new home among their own people. After 1850, as I'll discuss in chapter 5, all-black settlements migrated northward across the Canadian border, and Underground Railroad routes stretched to accommodate them.

## THE METHODS

The immediate goal of Underground Railroad conductors was to convey their passengers to some northern point safe from slave catchers or local whites who might be tempted to turn them in for bounties. This involved finding means of transportation as well as safe houses or depots along the way that could offer fugitives temporary refuge. Adaptability was the order of the day. Conductors and stationmasters alike needed to be flexible enough to adapt to challenges at the last minute. So in addition to major routes, crooked and less obvious substitute ones that could be taken to throw off pursuing slave catchers were mapped. Potential hiding places also had to be improvised. Contrary to Underground Railroad lore, most safe houses didn't have escape tunnels or secret rooms and closets for fugitives to hide in. The Tullman house in Jonesville, Wisconsin, had an underground tunnel leading up from a nearby river, and Josiah Grinnell built a secret "liberty room" for runaways in his Iowa home. But more typically, weary runaways slept on kitchen or parlor floors or in barn lofts. If they needed to be hidden, they were stashed away in whatever was at hand: hayricks, woodpiles, or smoke houses. Some hiding places were more imaginative. Rev. J. Porter of Green Bay, Wisconsin, regularly hid fugitives in the belfry of his Congregational church.

Stations along routes were ideally spaced 10 to 20 miles apart, the distance an able-bodied fugitive could comfortably travel during one night. But, particularly in the west, they could be separated by as much as 25 or 30 miles. In the early days of the Underground Railroad, most fugitives were single men who were able to make long, uninterrupted treks on foot. But in later years, with more women and children riding the liberty lines, transportation became increasingly necessary. Conductors used horses, covered wagons, closed carriages, and farm wagons to convey their passengers. Double-bedded wagons with false bottoms to conceal supine fugitives were also used. Occasionally conductors put fugitives on actual railroads, sometimes called "surface lines," for part of their journey. But this method required false identification papers and sometimes even disguises. To be on the safe side, Delaware's Thomas Garrett often disguised the fugitives he transported in open farm wagons. His favorite ruse was to have them hold garden tools as they sat in the wagon to give observers the impression that the blacks were laborers headed for a job. When they arrived at the next station, their tools were retrieved for the next batch of fugitives.

A variety of signals, many of them unique to specific locales, was invented to clue conductors and their passengers as to whether a particular station was safe or to assure station masters that wayfarers traveling without conductors had indeed been sent by the station just down the track. Lanterns were placed in windows or suspended from porch ceilings or poles and ribbons were tied around tree trunks and branches to serve as beacons for fugitives. Very occasionally, hitching posts in the shapes of slave boys or quilts hung from windows signaled a safe house.[14] For their part, visitors were taught patterns of rhythmic knocks on doors or windows to announce their arrival. Passwords were also used. In York, Pennsylvania, for example, a favorite was "William Penn." Bird calls such as owl screeches were also frequently exchanged to test and assure the safety of a stretch of route or a depot.

Friendly whites associated with the Underground Railroad who encountered blacks they suspected of being fugitives sometimes used hand signals to identify themselves as friends. A tug on an earlobe, for example, meant "follow me to a safe house." Conductors also frequently wrote in code to stationmasters to alert them of impending arrivals. In 1843, for example, John Stone of Ohio notified fellow Railroad agent David Putnam that "Business is aranged [sic] for Saturday night be on the lookout and if practicable let a cariage [sic] come." A few months before the Civil War, G. W. Weston of Iowa wrote to C. B. Campbell: "By tomorrow evening's mail, you will receive two volumes of the 'Irrepressible Conflict' bound in black. After perusal, please forward."[15] In hindsight, such coded messages seem transparent enough. But the very fact that conductors and stationmasters felt obliged to use them suggests the riskiness of the work they were engaged in. They were, after all, breaking the law.

The risk wasn't just from federal marshals, slave catchers, and hostile Northern whites. Bamboozle artists sometimes tried to catch rides on the Underground Railroad. Free blacks posed as fugitives to solicit free meals, clothing, and money from unsuspecting stationmasters. There were also white con men (as well as some black ones) who, masquerading as Railroad agents, charged fugitives enormous sums to guide them to safety. Some actually followed through on their promises. But more often, they took their fees up front and then abandoned their unsuspecting clients. Even worse, sometimes they simply resold their hapless passengers to available buyers. Ex-slave Henry Bibb, who settled in Canada and edited the *Voice of the Fugitive*, advised readers in 1854 to be cautious: "If any professed friend refuses to aid you or your friends in making their escape from Slavery unless they are paid an extravagant price for it, they are not to be trusted: no matter whether they are white or black."[16]

## ABDUCTIONS

Typically, blacks and whites working on the Underground Railroad waited for fugitives to come to them rather than venturing below the Mason-Dixon Line to gather and lead slaves to freedom. There were three main reasons for this reticence. The most obvious was the realization that slave abduction, as the act came to be known, was dangerous business. If caught by authorities, white abductors risked heavy prison sentences—or worse, at the hands of furious mobs—and black ones would immediately be sold back into slavery. Abductions were also censured by some abolitionists out of concern that sorties into the South to rescue slaves only increased vigilance on the part of slaveholders, thus making it more difficult for slaves to run. Finally, a few foes of slavery saw a significant difference between giving assistance to fugitive slaves and physically snatching them away from their masters. The first was considered a legitimate violation of an unjust law. But in the minds of some abolitionists, the second was a species of thievery that crossed a moral line and thereby risked undermining the authority of law in general, not simply unjust individual ones.

Despite these reservations, a few Underground Railroad workers traveled to slave states with the intention of leading slaves to freedom. Some, like John Parker, preferred to stay relatively close to the border, primarily offering runaways a helping hand with the final river crossing. But others ventured farther south to pass on navigational directions to slaves they met along the way or actually to collect and guide slaves to the North. Abductors didn't always rescue slaves solely out of principle; sometimes they did so for pecuniary gain. Many were commissioned by fugitives in the North who had left family members in slavery and wanted desperately to reunite with their loved ones. The pain of separation from spouse, parents, and children was bitter. As one fugitive who settled in Toronto put it, "I can say I once was happy, but never will be again, until I see [my wife]; because what is freedom to me, when I know that my wife is in slavery?"[17] Some runaway slaves even ventured back below the Mason-Dixon Line themselves to rescue those they had left behind.

One fugitive who returned south for relatives still in slavery was Harriet Tubman, the best-known of all abductors. Escaping from her Maryland owner in 1849, she ventured southward 19 times between 1850 and 1860 to lead family members, acquaintances, and strangers to freedom.

Reflecting late in life on her more than 300 rescues, she proudly and accurately boasted, "I never ran my train off the track and I never lost a customer."[18] She worked closely with stationmasters William Still and Thomas Garrett, both of whom were unstinting in their praise of her. John Brown so admired Tubman's fearlessness that he called her "General Tubman" and often referred to her using masculine pronouns. Awestruck blacks in both slave states and Free States called her "Moses," after the great Old Testament liberator. But perhaps the greatest tribute to her daring came from Maryland slave holders who eventually offered $40,000 for her capture.

Tubman's abductions all had happy endings. But abductions attempted by others weren't always as successful. In 1844, Rev. Calvin Fairbank, a white graduate of Oberlin College, engineered the escape of an entire Lexington slave family. Although the fugitives were safely delivered to John Rankin on the Northern side of the Ohio River, Fairbank and his

Known as the "Moses of her people," ex-slave Harriet Tubman traveled south 19 times to "abduct" fellow slaves and lead them to freedom on the Underground Railroad. "I never went off track and I never lost a passenger," she boasted. (Library of Congress)

collaborator, a white schoolteacher named Delia Webster, were arrested by Kentucky authorities, charged with slave stealing, and sentenced to prison terms. Webster was pardoned shortly afterward, but Fairbank served five years of hard labor. Upon his release he toured the North speaking to antislavery groups; in 1851 he was once again arrested, this time for trying to rescue a young mulatto girl. Sentenced to prison again, he served nearly 15 years behind bars. After his release in 1864, Fairbank estimated that he had suffered more than 30,000 lashes from prison guards.

Rev. Charles Torrey, a Rhode Island Congregational minister, and the young Quaker Richard Dillingham were two more martyred abductors. Torrey, who resigned his pulpit to devote himself to full-time Underground Railroad work, was arrested by Virginia authorities while trying to reunite a slave family with a fugitive husband and father. While awaiting trial Torrey confessed to a friend, "If I am a guilty man, I am a very guilty

American abolitionist Calvin Fairbank spent nearly two decades in prison for abducting slaves from the South and leading them to freedom. He later reported that he had received more than 30,000 lashes while imprisoned. (Calvin Fairbank, *Reverend Calvin Fairbank during Slavery Times* . . . [Chicago: R.R. McCabe & Co., 1890], frontispiece)

one: for I have aided nearly four hundred slaves to escape to freedom."[19] Virginia jurors sentenced him to six years' imprisonment. Torrey barely made it through two before dying.

For his part, Dillingham was approached in 1848 by a family of fugitives in Cincinnati who asked him to rescue enslaved family members in Tennessee. A young man deeply committed to abolitionism, Dillingham readily agreed. But he had neither skill nor cunning to match his enthusiasm, and he was handily caught by authorities. Charged with slave stealing, he asked for clemency for the sake of his elderly parents but also forthrightly admitted that he'd willingly defied a law he considered unjust. His youth as well as his apparent physical frailty swayed the judge to give him only three years instead of a much longer sentence. But even this was too much, and Dillingham was dead in just a few months.

Obviously, the risks of venturing into the South to lead slaves to freedom were daunting. But for opponents of slavery impatient with merely helping fugitives once they crossed over into the Free States, the opportunity to actually go "behind enemy lines" outweighed the danger. Their adventures, successful or not, captured the imagination of both Northerners and Southerners. Whenever an abduction attempt came to light, Southerners saw it as another Northern-sanctioned assault on their property rights and settled even more firmly into a state-of-siege mentality. Most opponents of slavery, on the other hand, extolled abductions as valiantly high-minded resistance to an evil institution that was corrupting the nation's heart and soul. Even abolitionists who expressed reservations about the propriety or practicality of abduction couldn't help but admire the daring of a Tubman or sympathize with the heroic failure of a Dillingham.

## A HALF-HIDDEN GRID

We'll never be able to map with final certainty the scores of liberty lines along which fugitives trudged or were transported in their flights to freedom. As already noted, the grid of Underground Railroad routes remains somewhat obscure for many reasons. These include the dearth of contemporaneous documentation, the lack of centralized organization, the frequently ad hoc nature of the aid extended to fugitives by private citizens, the need for flexibility, the fact that agents often undertook Underground

Railroad work for short periods or intermittently, and the unreliability of reminiscences recorded years later.

But despite the forgetfulness, distortion, and exaggeration that often obscures the locations of actual liberty lines, the basic contours of the Underground Railroad grid are clear enough. It's not surprising that the various routes were fluid and that their maintenance was primarily local rather than centralized. The Underground Railroad was, after all, an illegal movement whose success depended on keeping under the radar and adapting to unexpected bumps in the road. What *is* astounding is that there were so many routes, that fugitives traveling along them were aided by hundreds of people from all walks of life, and that despite the absence of overall supervision, traffic flowed from one branch of the liberty line to the next with more efficiency than might have been expected from such a loose structure.

---

## NOTES

The chapter epigraph is the first stanza in Jesse Hutchinson's "Get Off the Track!," a popular abolitionist song written in the 1830s and sung to the tune of "Old Dan Tucker." The song was printed hundreds of times, including in the April 19, 1844, issue of William Lloyd Garrison's *Liberator*, from which the quotation is taken.

1. Wilbur H. Siebert, *The Underground Railroad from Slavery to Freedom* (Mineola, NY: Dover, 2006), 69.

2. Frederick Douglass, *My Bondage and My Freedom*, ed. John Stauffer (New York: Modern Library, 2003), 188.

3. Quoted in Siebert, *The Underground Railroad*, 33.

4. Slaves escaping from Tennessee also typically followed the western liberty lines. Slaves from the states south of Tennessee had much less chance of successfully reaching the North to make use of Underground Railroad routes, east or west.

5. William Still, *The Underground Rail Road* (Philadelphia: Porter & Coates, 1872), 625.

6. Quoted in Siebert, *The Underground Railroad*, 110.

7. John Parker, *His Promised Land: The Autobiography of John P. Parker*, ed. Stuart Seely Sprague (New York: W.W. Norton, 1996), 103.

8. Brown, a prolific author, wrote *Clotel; or, The President's Daughter* (1854), the first novel published by an African American. The plot centered on a mulatto child of Thomas Jefferson.

9. William Wells Brown, *The Travels of William Wells Brown*, ed. Paul Jefferson (New York: Markus Wiener, 1991), 68. Brown's book was originally published in 1847 as *The Narrative of William W. Brown, Fugitive Slave*.

10. An estimated 14 percent of all fugitives from Virginia in the 18th century left by way of water routes such as the one at Norfolk. See Gerald R. Mullin, *Flight and Rebellion: Slave Resistance in Eighteenth Century Virginia* (New York: Oxford University Press, 1972), 95.

11. Douglass, *My Bondage and My Freedom*, 177.

12. John Greenleaf Whittier, "The Branded Hand," in *Poems* (Boston: Sanborn, Carter, & Bazin, 1856), 200.

13. Daniel Drayton, *Personal Memoir of Daniel Drayton, for Four Years and Four Months a Prisoner (for Charity's Sake) in Washington Jail, Including a Narrative of the Voyage and Capture of the Schooner Pearl* (Boston: Bela Marsh, 1855), 119.

14. On the other hand, there's no real evidence for the recent claim that quilts with African-derived symbols were used in the Carolinas to guide fugitives. The strongest brief for the quilt thesis is Jacqueline L. Tobin and Raymond G. Dobard, *Hidden in Plain View: A Secret Story of Quilts and the Underground Railroad* (New York: Doubleday, 1999). Xenia E. Cord offers an alternative view in "The Underground Railroad," *Popular Patchwork* 14, no. 3 (March 2006), http://www.popularpatchwork.com/news/article.asp?a=115.

15. Quoted in Siebert, *The Underground Railroad*, 57, 58.

16. Quoted in Larry Gara, *The Liberty Line: The Legend of the Underground Railroad* (Lexington: University Press of Kentucky, 1996), 53.

17. Letter from Isaac Forman to William Still, February 20, 1854, in Still, *The Underground Rail Road*, 65.

18. Quoted in Catherine Clinton, *Harriet Tubman: The Road to Freedom* (New York: Little, Brown, 2005), 192.

19. Quoted in Siebert, *The Underground Railroad*, 169.

# CHAPTER 4

# LAYING THE TRACK ABOVE GROUND: OVERT DEFIANCE AND RESCUES

The only way to make the Fugitive Slave Law a dead letter is to make half a dozen more dead kidnappers. . . . Slaveholders ought not only forfeit their right to liberty, but to life itself.

*—Frederick Douglass*

L ate in 1850, John Brown, who would later lead the famous raid on Harpers Ferry, met with 44 free black men and women in Springfield, Massachusetts, to form a secret organization called the League of Gileadites. Its purpose was to protect runaways from slave catchers who, since the passage of the Fugitive Slave Act in September of that year, had been crossing the Mason-Dixon Line in record numbers. According to the League's "Agreement and Rules," members pledged to use whatever physical force was needed to rescue fugitives and make "clean work" of slave catchers. "Hold on to your weapons," the document encouraged members, "and never be persuaded to leave them, part with them, or have them far away from you."[1]

In the 1830s and 1840s, agents and supporters of the Underground Railroad carried out their mission of aiding fugitives more or less clandestinely and, inspired by William Lloyd Garrison, nonviolently. Occasionally, however, the anger of some slavery opponents erupted in strong rhetoric that called for violence. David Walker's 1829 *Appeal to the Colored Citizens of the World* urged armed slave resistance. In 1841, New York Underground Railroad agent David Ruggles took up Walker's call, insisting

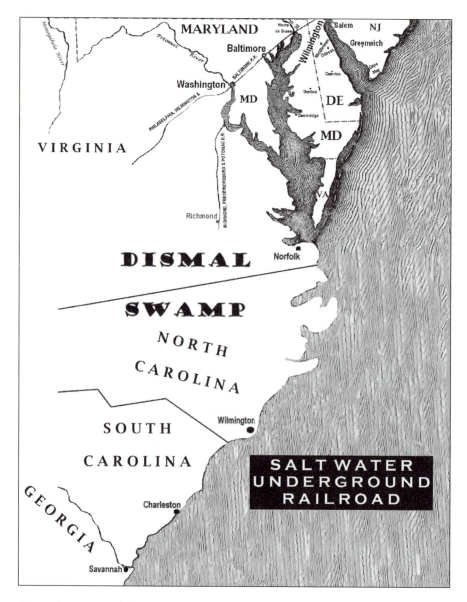

Some slaves stowed aboard ships bound to northern ports from southern ones in the Carolinas and Georgia. Many Maryland fugitives fled by sailing across the Chesapeake Bay. (Tom Calarco)

that the time for words had ended and the time for action begun. Two years later, a former fugitive named Henry Highland Garnet dramatically repudiated nonviolence at the National Negro Convention held in Buffalo, New York. "There is not much hope of Redemption without the shedding of blood," he thundered. "Rather die freemen than live to be slaves."[2] But such eruptions were notable for being exceptionable. The tide of opinion among abolitionists and Underground Railroad workers ran against them.

Still, the tide came in less calmly in the decade leading up to the Civil War. The Underground Railroad continued its clandestine work of welcoming fugitives and transporting them to safety in northern U.S. cities or over the Canadian border. But active and overt resistance, typically led by free blacks in collaboration with whites, became increasingly common in the 1850s. Frederick Douglass broke with his earlier pacifism to declare slavery a "state of war," urged slaves to adopt Virginia's state motto, "Death to Tyrants," as their own, and at the 1852 national convention of the Free Soil Party gave the sanguinary bit of advice that serves as this chapter's epigraph.[3] A Convention of Fugitive Slaves held in Cazenovia, New York, in the summer of 1850 pledged to protect fugitives and urged slaves to rise up against their masters. Just a few months later, a public meeting of free blacks held at a Philadelphia African Methodist Episcopal (AME) church called the forceful rescue of captured fugitives a "sacred duty" owed to "ourselves, our wives, our children, [our] common nature, [and] the panting fugitive from oppression."[4] Over the next 10 years, there were more than 80 documented rescues or attempted rescues of captured runaway slaves. The Underground Railroad had opened a new line, this one above ground and in full view of defenders as well as foes of slavery.

## THE FUGITIVE SLAVE ACT OF 1850

What sparked the change in tone and tactic? Anger had been building for a long time, but the immediate cause was the congressional passage of the Fugitive Slave Act, part of a larger legislative package that came to be known as the Compromise of 1850. The Compromise, brokered by Henry Clay, Daniel Webster, and John Calhoun, aimed to address Southern discontent while at the same time limiting the spread of slavery. Southern states threatened secession over two points. The first centered on the impending admission of California to the union as a Free State, which the South saw as a threat to the parity between slave states and Free States in the U.S. Senate. To mollify this worry, the Compromise allowed for the possibility of popular sovereignty when it came to slavery in the territories of New Mexico and Utah, recently ceded to the United States by Mexico. Many Southerners saw this as scant compensation, since the climate of the two territories was unsuited to the large-scale plantation planting system that required slaves.

The second point of Southern discontent was the perceived refusal on the part of northern states to respect the legality of slavery. As public opinion north of the Mason-Dixon Line soured against the South, the federal law known as the Fugitive Slave Act of 1793, which mandated the return of fugitive slaves to their masters, became increasingly un-

An 1850 illustration provoked by the passage of the Fugitive Slave Act, a federal law intended to crack down on Northerners who aided or harbored runaway slaves. Blacks accused of being fugitives were denied habeas corpus and the right to testify on their own behalf. Whites could be impressed by federal marshals and civilian slave catchers to aid in the capture of fugitives. (Library of Congress)

enforceable. Moreover, the way in which the law was written actually encouraged noncompliance. It allowed slave owners or their agents to pursue and capture runaways, and it prescribed penalties for anyone who harbored them, but it didn't oblige northern state officials to assist in apprehending fugitives. An 1842 Supreme Court decision, *Prigg v. Pennsylvania*, which upheld the Act's penalties for assisting slaves but refused to rule on the question of whether Northern citizens were required to assist in their capture, was a further blow to slave owners who already felt, with some justification, that their constitutionally guaranteed right to own human property was being flouted in the North. Seizing the moment, antislavery legislators in Massachusetts, Vermont, Connecticut, New Hampshire, Pennsylvania, and Rhode Island quickly passed "personal liberty laws" that actively forbade state officials from cooperating in the capture of fugitives. Slave owners were outraged and demanded stiffer federal protection of their legal rights.

They got what they wanted in the 1850 Fugitive Slave Act, and the threat of secession receded for a few more years. The Act sustained all the provisions of the 1793 law while adding several more. It created special federal commissioners who were authorized to act independently of local or state liberty laws; it mandated severe penalties for local officers of the court who refused to cooperate in the apprehension of runaways; it denied captured fugitives the rights of trial by jury and habeas corpus; it established a system of bounties for the arrest and return of fugitives; and it obliged, under threat of harsh penalties, "all good citizens" to "aid and assist in the prompt and efficient execution of this law, whenever their services may be required."[5]

The free black community and white abolitionists responded with alarm. President Millard Fillmore had scarcely put his signature to the law when angry denunciations of it filled the press and public protests condemned it in cities and towns throughout the North. Martin Delaney, a black abolitionist, author, and leading exponent of black immigration from the United States, warned that if a slave catcher came to his door, "one of us must perish."[6] Rev. Jermain Loguen of Syracuse proclaimed the law "a tyranny" that blacks must either "crush by force, or be crushed by."[7] Frederick Douglass agreed. In his eyes, the Act was so blatantly unconstitutional that it left blacks with the uneasy feeling of living in enemy territory. "There is no valley so deep, no mountain so high, no plain so extensive, no spot so sacred to God and liberty in all this extended country, where the black man may not fall prey to the remorseless cupidity of his white brethren."[8] A public meeting of free blacks in Philadelphia angrily pledged to "resist this law at any cost and at all hazards," a resolve echoed by blacks in Boston, Syracuse, Cleveland, New Bedford, New York, and elsewhere.[9]

Nor was the opposition to the Fugitive Slave Act merely verbal. In city after city, new vigilance committees that aimed at defying the law by aiding runaways were formed. The first, formed in Syracuse a mere eight days after Fillmore signed the Act, immediately broadcast a scathing censure of the new law. Already-established committees in New York City, Philadelphia, Boston, Detroit, and Cincinnati quickly followed suit.

In many ways, local vigilance committees were the most effective arms of the Underground Railroad. Overwhelmingly organized and operated by free black men and women, the committees offered newly arrived fugitives immediate assistance by providing them with shelter, food, and medical attention and offered long-term aid by helping them find work in various towns and cities throughout the North. They also worked to shape public opinion against the Fugitive Slave Act while mounting legal challenges to its constitutionality. Just as importantly, vigilance committees tried to protect fugitives from being kidnapped by slave catchers or arrested by local officials. The New York City committee, founded in 1835 by David Ruggles, actually compiled a "Slaveholders Directory" that published the names of police, judges, and other city officials who cooperated with federal commissioners in the apprehension of fugitives. The directory's aim was to expose the collaborators to public calumny as well as to alert Underground Railroad agents to their identities.

In some towns, vigilance committee members tolled church or courthouse bells to signal the arrival of slave catchers. Others posted placards and flyers with physical descriptions of slave catchers warning citizens to be on the lookout. Given the illegal activities of vigilance committees, much of their work and operational methods were necessarily clandestine. But the swiftness with which members publicly rallied around fugitives when slave catchers came to town suggests that the committees were well organized in many locales. Moreover, many vigilance committee members weren't reluctant about arming themselves with knives and guns when confronting slave catchers. Both their organizational efficiency and their resolute determination to protect fugitives was demonstrated again and again throughout the 1850s.

## SLAVE CATCHERS

As discussed in chapter 2, slaves who fled their masters had to be on the lookout south of the Mason-Dixon Line for volunteer slave patrols and professional slave hunters. But once they were north of the Line, their worries weren't over. Fugitives who made it to the North as well as legally free blacks already settled there, especially ones in the border states, were in danger of being snatched by gangs of men either commissioned by slave owners or working independently. These slave catchers occasionally traveled up from the South, but more often they were Northerners hired by Southerners either directly or through the services of a broker. Many Maryland and Delaware slave owners in search of runaways went straight to the "Gap Gang," a notorious crew of slave catchers that operated in southeastern Pennsylvania. Some also called upon the services of Lucretia Hanley Cannon and her husband, heads of a cold-blooded kidnapping ring on the Maryland/Delaware border. More scrupulous Southerners made use of brokers such as F. H. Pettes, a New York City–based lawyer who advertised in 1840 that he would arrange for the recovery of runaways if owners sent him a detailed physical description of the fugitives and a power of attorney. His fee was $20 up front, with an additional $100 for each slave caught.

As can be seen from attorney Pettes's advertisement, slave catching, which defenders justified as the recovery of stolen property but opponents believed to be nothing less than kidnapping, was a threat to Northern blacks long before the 1850 Fugitive Slave Act. The 1808 outlawing of the importation of new slaves to the United States, the cotton boom in the Lower South, and the opening of Texas as a slave market all served as incentives for slave catchers to ply their trade. Sometimes they went through legal channels, conforming to the guidelines prescribed by the 1793 Fugitive Slave Act: apprehended fugitives were hauled before "any magistrate of a county, city or town," as the Act required, affidavits were sworn, and the slaves were returned to their owners. But often blacks were simply seized by slave catchers, taken to the South, and sold on the open market. In 1849, slave catchers burst into Mrs. Ann Sprigg's Washington, D.C., boarding house and snatched away a black waiter while he was serving guests, one of whom was an Illinois congressman named Abraham Lincoln. In the summer of 1835 and again in 1837, gangs rounded up a number of black children in New York City and sold them in Mississippi. Because they were no match in physical strength for burly men, children were a favorite target of slave catchers.

Probably the most notorious case of a Northern free black who was snatched by slave catchers and sold into slavery was that of Solomon Northup. Born in 1808, Northup was a musician who entertained white vacationers with violin and song at resort hotels in Saratoga Springs, New York. In 1841, he fell in with a couple of white performers who offered him a job in their traveling stage show. Northup accepted and accompanied the men as they worked their way southward. But when they arrived in Washington, D.C., the two drugged Northup and sold him to a slave dealer who beat him cruelly and repeatedly, swearing, as Northup later wrote, "that he would either conquer or kill me."[10] Eventually sold to a Louisiana planter, he remained a slave for the next 12 years until authorities in New York finally managed to secure his freedom. His best-selling memoir of the ordeal, *Twelve Years a Slave*, appeared in 1853 and ratcheted up antislavery sentiment considerably among Northern readers.

The liberty laws enacted in several middle Atlantic and New England states after the 1842 *Prigg v. Pennsylvania* decision, as well as the rising tide of antislavery opinion, created a chilly climate for slave catchers. On more than one occasion in the 1840s, their attempts to apprehend fugitives were met with forceful and successful resistance in such cities as Utica, Chicago, Pittsburg, Buffalo, and Boston. Women frequently took part in fending them off. In 1848, angry black women in Cincinnati armed with nothing more than washboards and rolling pins chased off a gang of slave catchers on the prowl for fugitives from Kentucky.

But the 1850 Fugitive Slave Act gave slave catchers new encouragement by sweeping aside liberty laws and obliging local citizens and officials to assist them in their capture of runaways. Consequently, the pursuit and apprehension of fugitives (and free blacks, whom the new law forbade to testify in their own defense) became even more common in the decade prior to the Civil War. Slave catchers frequently staked out suspected Underground Railroad stations and routes. They were known to stop wagons and coaches on the roads in order to search them. Sometimes they actually forced their way into private homes they suspected of harboring runaways, using as a legal pretext Section 6 of the Fugitive Slave Act, which authorized them to "seize and arrest" fugitives.

They took the seizure and arrest clause very seriously indeed. In August 1850, even before the Act was signed by President Fillmore, slave catchers, emboldened by the knowledge that the new law was just around the corner, tried to snatch Henry "Box" Brown off the streets of Providence, Rhode Island, in broad daylight. He managed to escape them and subsequently fled to England. A few days later, the first arrest under the new law was made in New York City. James Hamlet, a fugitive from Maryland, was seized and returned to his master in Baltimore. Black churches in the city eventually raised enough money to purchase his freedom. Ellen and William Craft, the married couple who escaped slavery in 1848 by disguising themselves as a young planter and manservant, were targeted by slave catchers a month later. Like Brown, they fled to England.

These attempted enforcements of the Fugitive Slave Act ended happily for the intended victims. But other fugitives weren't as lucky. In 1856, Margaret Garner and her four children fled across the frozen Ohio River and sought refuge in an Underground Railroad house in Cincinnati. They were pursued by a posse of slave catchers who surrounded the house, smashed open the door, and burst through it. What they saw horrified them. Maddened by desperation and fear, Margaret, determined that her children wouldn't be returned to slavery, had stabbed one of them to death and had started to slash another when she was prevented by the slave catchers.[11] Margaret Garner's tragedy was the inspiration for American Nobel laureate Toni Morrison's 1987 novel *Beloved*.

The Fugitive Slave Act of 1850 undeniably invigorated the activity of slave catchers north of the Mason-Dixon Line. But it also strengthened the resolve of vigilance committee members as well as average citizens unassociated with the Underground Railroad to resist them. Noncooperation with slave catchers and rescues of captured fugitives, often instigated by free blacks, occurred in states from Massachusetts to Ohio. When it came to slavery, the 1850s was the decade of open defiance of the law of the land.

## RESCUES AND ATTEMPTED RESCUES

### The Christiana Riot

Almost a year to the day that Congress passed the Fugitive Slave Act, a violent clash between fugitives and Underground Railroad agents on one side and slave catchers and officers of the law on the other made national headlines. The open and forceful defiance with which the law was flouted inspired similar acts of resistance across the country.

The showdown occurred in the early morning of September 11, 1851, in the southeastern Pennsylvania village of Christiana. Because of its proximity to the Maryland border, Christiana was a stop on a busy Underground Railroad route and also had a sizeable population of free blacks and fugitives. But its closeness to the Mason-Dixon Line made it a favorite target of slave catchers. Local blacks led by ex-slave William Parker organized a vigilance committee charged with resisting slave catchers and kidnappers.

One year after the 1850 Fugitive Slave Act became law, slave catchers and runaway slaves came to blows in Christiana, Pennsylvania. One white man was killed and several others wounded. The fugitive slaves were tried for treason but acquitted by a Philadelphia jury. (Library of Congress)

Maryland slave owner Edwin Gorsuch, whose plantation was only 40 miles south of Christiana, had gotten word that four of his slaves who had fled a year earlier were hiding in the house that William Parker shared with his wife and their children. Accompanied by an armed posse that included his son, a nephew, a cousin, and Deputy Marshal Henry Kline, a lawman notorious in the area for his sympathy with slave catchers, Gorsuch marched up to the Parker house and demanded his "property." Parker didn't deny that the fugitives were upstairs, but he refused to give them up. In the meantime, his wife, Eliza, climbed to the roof of the house and blew a horn, a prearranged signal of distress that summoned between 30 and 40 armed vigilance committee members to the Parker residence. But the alarm also attracted a number of curious local whites whom Kline deputized on the spot. Two of them, Quakers and opponents of slavery, refused to cooperate but insisted on remaining as witnesses.

The standoff lasted about an hour, Gorsuch loudly demanding that his legal right to the fugitives be honored and Parker retorting that he would die before he gave them up. At one point, Parker challenged Gorsuch on religious grounds. "Where do you see it in Scripture," he demanded, "that a man should traffic in his brother's blood?" Gorsuch furiously retorted, "Do you call a nigger my brother?" Parker just as angrily shouted back, "Yes!"[12]

The exchange between the two served only to further inflame the situation, and before long the verbal volley was replaced by gunfire. It's not clear where the first shot came from, but by the time the firing stopped, Gorsuch was dead and his son severely wounded. Two other whites and two blacks were also injured in the fracas. The rest of the white posse, including Marshal Kline, made a quick and undignified retreat, pursued for some distance by the Christiana blacks who had responded to Eliza Parker's horn blast. Parker later boasted that the "slavocrats" were "driven off in every direction."[13]

The very next day, Marshal Kline filed charges against 15 blacks as well as the two white Quakers who had refused deputation. Rumors spread throughout northern Maryland that Gorsuch had been murdered in a black uprising, and it was reported that a gang of Maryland whites was on its way to Christiana to capture and punish the perpetrators. Parker fled to Canada, and President Fillmore ordered out a platoon of U.S. Marines to apprehend him and other blacks involved in the riot.

By the time the dust settled, five white men, including the two Quakers, and 36 blacks were jailed and charged, rather incredibly, with treason. Free blacks from across the North held meetings to raise funds for their defense. Three years after the confrontation, the trial finally took place at Philadelphia's venerable Independence Hall. The defendants were represented by a legal team that included the abolitionist congressman Thaddeus Stevens. On December 11, 1854, the jury deliberated for only 20 minutes before acquitting them. Philadelphia Railroad agent William Still claimed that the verdict, demolishing as it did the federal government's claim that resistance to the Fugitive Slave Act was treasonous, was the "most important [one] that ever took place in this country relative to the Underground Railroad."[14]

### The Jerry Rescue

Less than a month after the Christiana incident, another public action against the enforcement of the Fugitive Slave Act erupted in Syracuse. It was sparked by the October 1 arrest of William "Jerry" Henry (some sources refer to him as "McHenry"), a runaway from Missouri who had lived in Syracuse since the late 1840s. It was common knowledge that Jerry, as he was called, was a fugitive. But he was a peaceful member of Syracuse's black community and a skilled cooper.

After being seized by federal marshals, Jerry was manacled and marched to the federal commissioner's office for indictment. As word of his arrest spread, a large crowd of blacks and whites, many of them delegates to a convention of the abolitionist Liberty Party, which happened to be meeting in the city, surrounded the building. Slipping his guard, Jerry made a run into the crowd. He managed to get a block or so before he was caught, beaten, and transferred to the city jail, where another large crowd promptly gathered. Stones and bricks smashed through the building's windows, and Samuel Ringgold Ward, himself an ex-slave who had escaped 30 years earlier to become an influential Christian minister, rousingly addressed the assembly. "Fellow citizens," he shouted, "upon us, the voters of New York State, to a very great extent, rests the responsibility of this Fugitive Slave Law. It is for us to say whether this enactment shall continue to stain our statute books, or be swept away into merited oblivion."[15] Inspired by his challenge, a group of 40 or 50 blacks and whites broke into the building, wounded a couple of deputy marshals, tore down the door of Jerry's cell, and hurried him into a waiting coach, which started him on his way to Canada. Samuel Ward kept the chains that had been filed off of Jerry, put them in a finely crafted mahogany box, and defiantly mailed them to President Fillmore.

Coming as it did on the heels of the Christiana riot, Jerry's rescue infuriated federal authorities. Secretary of State Daniel Webster insisted that arrests be made and those apprehended be charged with treason, just as the Christiana defendants had been. For their part, most of the Syracuse rescuers welcomed a public showdown with the federal government. As abolitionist Samuel J. May wrote, "it was necessary to bring people into direct conflict with the Government—that the Government may be made to understand that it has transcended its limits—and must recede."[16]

Twelve black and 14 white rescuers were indicted by the federal government. Eventually, however, only one of them, a black man named Enoch Reed, was convicted. Even then, Reed never spent a day in jail; he died while his conviction was under appeal. The acquittal of the other defendants heartened abolitionists and Underground Railroad workers across the North, encouraged further defiance of the Fugitive Slave Act, and fueled the angry suspicion of Southern planters and politicians that the North lacked the will to enforce the law.

## Joshua Glover and the Wisconsin Supreme Court

A rescue in 1854 confirmed the South's fear that neither Northern lawmakers nor Northern citizens could be counted on when it came to returning runaways. On March 11 of that year, Joshua Glover, another fugitive from Missouri, was arrested in Racine, Wisconsin, where he'd lived as a free man for two years. Thrown into a Milwaukee jail cell until he could be rendered back to Missouri, Glover was rescued the next day by an angry group of blacks and whites who broke down the jail doors and bundled the prisoner onto a Canada-bound wagon. The rescue was organized by a local vigilance committee under the leadership of Sherman Booth, editor of the antislavery newspaper the *Milwaukee Free Democrat*. Afterward, Booth and several others were predictably arrested and eventually just as predictably released. But what made their case unique is the manner of their release. They weren't acquitted by a sympathetic jury of their peers. Instead, two months after their arrest, the charges against them were dropped by Wisconsin Supreme Court judge Abraham Smith on the grounds that the Fugitive Slave Act's denial of jury trials to captured runaways was unconstitutional. The U.S. Supreme Court reversed the ruling five years later. But Smith's decision was viewed by foes of slavery as a great legal victory, and it was cited as precedent in numerous litigations before being overturned in 1859.

### Anthony Burns and Black Crepe

Not all rescue attempts ended as happily as the ones in Christiana, Syracuse, and Milwaukee. The most famous failure occurred in Boston in May 1854, the same month that the Wisconsin Supreme Court handed down its decision in the Glover case. Anthony Burns, a young Virginia slave who had escaped to Boston by stowing away on a northbound ship, was arrested by federal commissioners and held in the city courthouse until he could be returned to his master. Antislavery sentiment was strong in Massachusetts, and Boston's vigilance committee was a particularly energetic one. So it took only two days from Burns's arrest for its members to organize a massive protest meeting in Faneuil Hall. Orators whipped up the huge crowd with one fiery speech after another denouncing the Fugitive Slave Act and the arrest of Burns. Eventually a dozen or so men led by abolitionist Thomas Wentworth Higginson left the hall to make a rush on the nearby courthouse where Burns was held. They managed to force their way into the building's front hall before being pushed back by police. Unfortunately, a deputy marshal was killed during the scuffle. To forestall further violence, Boston's mayor, with the approval of President Franklin Pierce, called up four companies of marines and artillery stationed at nearby Fort Independence. The courthouse yard was also encircled by huge harbor chains to hold back angry protesters. The irony of enchaining a courthouse to guard against the liberation of a manacled slave was not lost on the citizens of Boston.

Burns was remanded back to slavery, as everyone knew he would be. On the day he was marched down to the docks to board a Virginia-bound ship, church bells pealed throughout the city and black crepe hung from shop windows and doorways. An estimated 10,000 people came out to mourn his departure and hiss at the hundreds of federal troops, state militia, and city police flanking him. All told, authorities spent at least $20,000 to return a slave who was subsequently sold by his master for $962.00.[17]

## Jane Johnson and Her Sons

Northern opponents of slavery frequently referred to the capture of runaways as kidnapping. In a highly publicized 1855 rescue, North Carolina slave owner William Wheeler turned the tables by insisting that three of his slaves had been kidnapped by Underground Railroad agent William Still. In July of that year, Wheeler, U.S. minister to Nicaragua, had stopped in Philadelphia on his way to New York. He was accompanied by a slave, Jane Johnson, and her two young sons, Isaiah and Daniel. Still and a white abolitionist named Passmore Williamson confronted Wheeler and Jane while they were on the docks. They informed Jane that, according to Pennsylvania law, any slave brought into the state by a master had the right to claim freedom. Moreover, they pointed out, her bid for freedom couldn't be contested by the Fugitive Slave Act because she wasn't technically a runaway.

Still and Williamson apparently didn't rely on verbal arguments only. According to a local newspaper account, the two men were accompanied by "some dozen or twenty negroes, who by muscular strength carried the slaves to the adjoining pier" and threatened to cut Wheeler's throat if he resisted.[18] Wheeler naturally *did* resist, protesting that his slaves were perfectly happy and had no desire to be free. Still later testified that Jane interrupted Wheeler by saying "distinctly and firmly, 'I am not free, but I want my freedom—always wanted to be free! But he holds me.'"[19] She and her two sons immediately left their master and departed with their rescuers.

Wheeler swore out complaints against Still, Williamson, and five others involved in the rescue, including two men he claimed had threatened him. During the trial, Wheeler repeated his insistence that Jane, Isaiah, and Daniel had been carried off against their will. But on hearing him, Jane rose from her seat in the courtroom and dramatically denied Wheeler's claim, protesting as she had on the docks that she wanted to be free and had willingly left her master. The jury acquitted all the defendants except the two men who had threatened Wheeler. They each received

Jane Johnson and her two children were rescued from their North Carolina owner John Wheeler upon their arrival in Philadelphia. When Wheeler protested, Johnson cried out, "I am not free, but I want my freedom—ALWAYS wanted to be free! But he holds me!" Johnson and her children remained in the North. (William Still, *The Underground Railroad* [Philadelphia: Porter & Coats, 1872], 89)

one week of jail time. But Wheeler's insistence that his slaves had been kidnapped rather than rescued was thoroughly discredited, Jane and her sons remained free, and abolitionists declared the verdict a victory.

### The Oberlin-Wellington Rescue

The 1854 Glover rescue in Milwaukee raised questions about the constitutionality of the Fugitive Slave Act. Another legal battle erupted four years later, prompted by an episode that came to be known as the Oberlin-Wellington Rescue. Oberlin, Ohio, was a major station on the western Underground Railroad. Both the townspeople and students and professors at Oberlin College held strong antislavery convictions, as two Kentucky slave catchers and a U.S. marshal discovered in mid-September 1858. They seized John Price (or Pryce), an 18-year-old fugitive who had been living in Oberlin for a couple of years, and quickly transported him to the nearby village of Wellington, where they awaited the arrival of a southbound train to take him back to slavery. When news of the arrest spread, an armed contingent of 200 black and white Oberlin men traveled to Wellington, surrounded the hotel where Price was being kept, and freed him. He then rode the Underground Railroad to Canada.

Legal prosecution followed quickly. Thirty-seven of Price's rescuers were arrested and indicted. But before a federal judge in Cleveland could even set a trial date, vigilance committees across eastern Ohio organized public demonstrations that stirred up sympathy for the rescuers and contempt for the federal court. One of the larger meetings, held in Cleveland, passed a resolution that condemned the Fugitive Slave Act as an improper usurpation of power by the federal government and collected a "Fund of Liberty" to cover the rescuers' legal expenses. Back in Oberlin, a grand jury, citing a personal liberty law passed in Ohio two years earlier, indicted the slave catchers who had seized Price. This led to some rather frantic negotiating between federal and local authorities, and a quid pro quo agreement was eventually reached in which charges on both sides were dropped. The rescuers, who had refused bail, returned triumphantly to Oberlin, and the *Cleveland Plain Dealer* proclaimed that the federal government, despite all its "law, justice, and facts," had been soundly trounced by antislavery's "rebellious Higher law creed."[20]

## Charles Nalle and "African Fury"

Less than a year before the outbreak of the Civil War, a rescue took place in Troy, New York, whose intensity and ferocity well exemplified the strong feelings that the Fugitive Slave Act evoked. In April 1859, a Virginia fugitive named Charles Nalle was seized by a slave catcher who, astoundingly, was his own brother, a freedman employed by Nalle's master. A large crowd gathered outside the building where Nalle's case was being heard by a federal commissioner. When judgment was pronounced against him, the desperate Nalle tried to jump out of a second-story window but was restrained by bailiffs. He was then manacled and marched outside, where a boat was waiting to take him back south.

One of the angry people outside the building where Nalle was remanded was Harriet Tubman, who was in Troy visiting a cousin. As soon as the guards appeared with Nalle, she snatched him away from them and dragged him into the crowd, even though she was severely beaten on the head and shoulders with police clubs. Despite her efforts, Nalle was again seized by authorities and hurried to another building. Tubman rallied the crowd, and men and women threw themselves against the building's barricaded door. "At last," wrote a reporter, "the door was pulled open by an immense Negro and in a moment he was felled by the hatchet in the hands of [a] Deputy Sheriff; but the body of the fallen man blocked up the door so that it could not be shut."[21] Tubman and a number of other women leapt over the man's body, grabbed Nalle, pulled him outside, and got him out of Troy and into Canada. According to a newspaper account, the "rank and file" of the rescuers were black, providing a sobering example of the power of "African fury" when directed against slavery.[22]

### Lucy Bagby: The Last Rendition

Despite a heroic rescue attempt, 28-year-old Lucy Bagby earned the sad distinction of being the last runaway returned to the South under the Fugitive Slave Act. In January 1861, while working as a maid in Cleveland and pregnant with her first child, Lucy was apprehended by her former master, William Goshorn, a wealthy Virginia planter.

Her capture wasn't motivated by financial considerations. Goshorn was so rich that he could easily afford to lose a slave. Instead, his seizure of Lucy was a deliberate testing of the political waters. The antislavery Republican Abraham Lincoln had just been elected president, and several states in the Lower South had already left the Union in protest. Goshorn had come to Cleveland with the intention of seeing whether the post-election North would respect the Fugitive Slave Law by allowing him to recover his human property. The outcome was eagerly awaited by Virginian lawmakers, who hadn't yet made up their minds about secession.

Cleveland was an important hub of the Underground Railroad and had a long history of opposition to the Fugitive Slave Act. But this time her leading citizens, hoping to keep the Union together, reluctantly decided that they had no choice but to abide by the Act and allow Goshorn to take Lucy back to Virginia. The city's blacks tried on two separate occasions to free her, first when she was led from her jail cell to the courthouse and again as she was put on a train for her southbound journey. Each time, however, they were beaten away by city police. Lucy, sacrificed for the sake of keeping the Union together, was returned to slavery. But the sacrifice proved futile. War broke out less than three months later.[23]

## A LAW THAT BACKFIRED

There's no doubt that the architects of the 1850 Fugitive Slave Act believed that it would safeguard the property rights of slaveholders and thereby ease sectional tensions that threatened to split the nation in two. There's also no doubt that the Act in fact resulted in the forced rendition of many fugitive slaves back to their masters or the auction block. As we'll see in the next chapter, it posed such a threat to runaways that many of them, fearing to stay in the northern towns in which they had settled, departed for Canada.

But it's also true that the Act backfired in at least two ways. Its uncompromising denial of basic legal rights for fugitives, not to mention its harsh penalties for noncooperation on the part of free citizens, gave abolitionists and Underground Railroad defenders a potent weapon in the propaganda battle against slavery. During the 10 years the Act was the law of the land, public sentiment against slavery increased in the northern states. Denunciations of slavery by abolitionists who in earlier years had been viewed by the general public with dislike and suspicion were heeded more attentively. The amazing popularity of Harriet Beecher Stowe's *Uncle Tom's Cabin*, a novel Stowe claimed was provoked by the Fugitive Act, attested to the breadth of antislavery sentiment, even though racism remained alive and well in the North. This shift in public opinion encouraged Underground Railroad workers to supplement their clandestine operations with open rescues of runaways threatened with rendition.

The Act backfired in another way as well: it inflamed rather than mollified the South's distrust and dislike of the North. Time after time Southerners saw the Fugitive Slave Act blatantly violated by private citizens as well as public figures. For abolitionists, defiance of the Act was a sacred moral obligation. But for Southerners, disobedience of it was a threat to their personal fortunes and a high-handed disregard of their constitutional rights to own private property and to have that property protected by the courts. When the Act was under debate in Congress,

Mississippi senator Jefferson Davis opposed it, sadly noting that it would prove ineffective because the North's antipathy to slavery would make it unenforceable. Just how correct he was would be demonstrated 10 years later at Fort Sumter.

## NOTES

The chapter epigraph is from a speech Douglass delivered at the 1852 Free Soil Party national convention. Quoted in John Stauffer, *Giants: The Parallel Lives of Frederick Douglass and Abraham Lincoln* (New York: Twelve, 2008), 149.

1. The League of Gileadites' Agreement and Rules is reproduced in F. B. Sanborn, ed., *The Life and Letters of John Brown* (Boston: Roberts Brothers, 1891), 125.

2. C. Peter Ripley, Roy E. Finkenbine, Michael F. Hembree, and Donald Yacovone, eds., *The Black Abolitionist Papers* (Chapel Hill: University of North Carolina Press, 1991), vol. 3: 408, 410.

3. Quoted in John Stauffer, *Giants*, 133, 148.

4. Ripley et al., *Black Abolitionist Papers*, vol. 4: 69.

5. Section 5 of the Fugitive Slave Act of 1850. A condensed version of the Act is included in the appendix to this book.

6. Frank A. Rollin, *Life and Public Services of Martin R. Delaney* (New York: Arno Press, 1969), 76. Rollin's book was originally published in 1883.

7. Jermain Loguen, *The Rev. Jermain Loguen as a Slave and a Freeman: A Narrative of Real Life* (New York: Arno Press, 1968), 393. This book was originally published in 1859.

8. John Blassingame, ed., *The Frederick Douglass Papers* (New Haven, CT: Yale University Press, 1982), series 1, vol. 2: 295.

9. *Pennsylvania Freeman*, October 31, 1850.

10. Solomon Northup, *Twelve Years a Slave*, in *Puttin' On Ole Massa: The Slave Narratives of Henry Bibb, William Wells Brown, and Solomon Northup*, ed. Gilbert Osofsky (New York: Harper & Row, 1969), 243.

11. Underground Railroad stationmaster Levi Coffin's account of the Garner story is excerpted in the appendix to this book. Margaret and her two surviving children were returned south to slavery. On the way, the steamboat carrying them collided with another vessel. Margaret and her youngest child, an infant, were thrown overboard, and the child drowned. Margaret is reported to have been grateful for the child's death.

12. William Parker, "The Freedman's Story: In Two Parts," *Atlantic Monthly* XVII (February and March, 1866), Part II: 285. Part of Parker's memoir is included in the appendix to this book.

13. Ibid., 287. Parker darkly claims (p. 288) that Gorsuch, wounded in the fray, was finished off by the women of the house.

14. William Still, *The Underground Rail Road* (Philadelphia: Porter & Coates, 1872), 381.

15. Samuel Ringgold Ward, *Autobiography of a Fugitive Negro* (Chicago: Johnson, 1970). Ward's memoir was originally published in London in 1855.

16. Samuel J. May, "Letter to William Lloyd Garrison, 23 November 1851." Quoted in Larry Mara, *The Liberty Line: The Legend of the Underground Railroad* (Lexington: University Press of Kentucky, 1996), 112.

17. Thanks largely to the work of Rev. Leonard Grimes, a free black who was pastor of Boston's 12th Street Baptist Church, Burns's freedom was later purchased. Burns settled in Canada, was ordained, and died in 1862. Grimes's congregants were so active in the Underground Railroad that the 12th Street Church was known as the "Fugitive Slave Church."

18. *Philadelphia Bulletin*, July 27, 1855.

19. Still, *The Underground Rail Road*, 76.

20. *Cleveland Plain Dealer*, July 6, 1859. Quoted in Wilbur H. Siebert, *The Underground Railroad from Slavery to Freedom* (Mineola, NY: Dover, 2006), 337.

21. *Troy Whig*, April 27, 1860.

22. Quoted in Catherine Clinton, *Harriet Tubman: The Road to Freedom* (New York: Little, Brown, 2005), 138.

23. I'm grateful to Robin Jarrell for bringing the Lucy Bagby case to my attention. Fortunately, her story has a happier ending than beginning. Lucy managed to make her way to Union lines in June 1861 as a "contraband of war." She returned to Cleveland two years later, where she lived until her death in 1906.

# CHAPTER 5

# CROSSING INTO CANAAN: THE UNDERGROUND RAILROAD'S CANADIAN TERMINUS

I'm on my way to Canada,
That cold and dreary land;
The dire effects of slavery
I can no longer stand.
My soul is vexed within me so,
To think that I'm a slave,
I've now resolved to strike the blow,
For Freedom or the grave.

—*Martin Delaney*

In 1793, three events occurred that greatly influenced the course of slavery in the United States.

The first was President George Washington's signing the Fugitive Slave Act into law, making it a crime to harbor runaway slaves and authorizing owners or their agents to pursue and seize fugitives. The new law was an indication that the flight of slaves was already becoming a political and economic issue, that there were white Northern citizens prepared to shelter them, and that slaveholders, mainly in the South, were impatiently demanding federal protection of their human property.

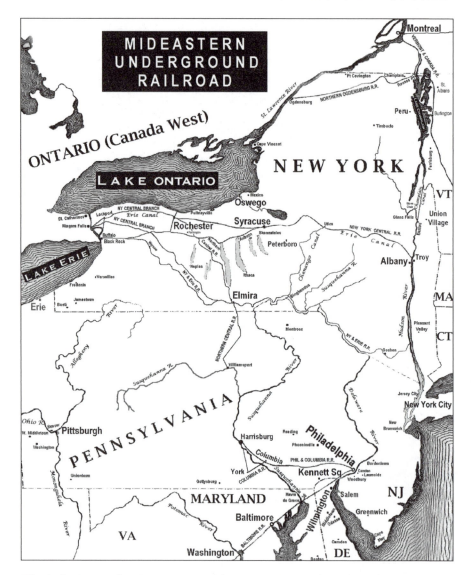

The Lake Erie-Lake Ontario region between New York and Michigan was the biggest hub of fugitive immigration into Canada. (Tom Calarco)

The second was the young New Englander Eli Whitney's invention of the cotton gin, a contraption that mechanically separated cotton fibers from seed, which up till then had been a laborious manual task. The gin revolutionized the cotton industry. Because cotton could now be processed more quickly and efficiently, more of it could be grown on huge plantations in the Lower South. But the growth of King Cotton meant that the South became increasingly dependent on slave labor to plant, tend, and harvest the crops, and this in turn swelled the number of slaves in the South.

The third event was this: the legislature of Upper Canada[1] (which comprised the southern portion of the present-day province of Ontario) enacted an antislavery bill, the 1793 Emancipation Act, which for all practical purposes banned slavery in the vast territory north of the United States. Upper Canada's lieutenant governor, John Graves Simcoe, had made it known upon taking office a year earlier that he deplored slavery and wished to see it abolished. But slaveholding American Loyalists who'd fled to Canada during the Revolution adamantly defended the institution and resisted Simcoe.

The tipping point was the highly publicized fate of a slave girl named Chloe Cooley, the property of one William Vrooman, a Loyalist New Yorker who had settled in the small village of Queenston just north of Niagara Falls. Perhaps sensing that slavery's days in Canada were numbered, in March 1793 Vrooman bound Chloe, hauled her down to a boat, rowed her across the Niagara River, and sold her to an American. Chloe, screaming the whole time, attracted a crowd of sympathetic onlookers. Several of them recounted the sorry affair to government authorities, and Simcoe, horrified by the story, set the wheels in motion for the Emancipation Act. The Act forbade the importation of new slaves into Upper Canada and mandated that the children of current slaves be freed when they reached the age of 25. Lower Canada (the southern portion of present-day Quebec and Labrador) passed a similar measure seven years later.

The United Kingdom didn't abolish slavery until 1833. But the unhappy fate of Chloe signaled its doom in Canada long before that date. After 1793, Canadian policy was to welcome fugitive slaves and refuse to extradite them when their American owners demanded their return. Attorneys representing slaveholders insisted that the runaways were criminals guilty of theft—of themselves, their masters' property—rather than refugees seeking asylum. But Canadian authorities found this charge of self-theft less than convincing. As Lt. Gov. Sir Francis Bond Head remarked in 1837, "surely a slave breaking *out* of his master's house is not guilty of the burglary which a thief would commit who should force the same locks and bolts in order to break *in*."[2]

## LIBERTY LINE.
### NEW ARRANGEMENT---NIGHT AND DAY.

The improved and splendid Locomotives, Clarkson and Lundy, with their trains fitted up in the best style of accommodation for passengers, will run their regular trips during the present season, between the borders of the Patriarchal Dominion and Libertyville, Upper Canada. Gentlemen and Ladies, who may wish to improve their health or circumstances, by a northern tour; are respect-fully invited to give us their patronage.
SEATS FREE, *irrespective of color.*
Necessary Clothing furnished gratuitously to such as have *"fallen among thieves."*

"Hide the outcasts—let the oppressed go free."—*Bible.*
☞For seats apply at any of the trap doors, or to the conductor of the train.

J. CROSS, *Proprietor.*
N. B. For the special benefit of Pro-Slavery Police Officers, an extra heavy wagon for Texas, will be fur-nished, whenever it may be necessary, in which they will be forwarded as dead freight, to the "Valley of Ras-cals," always at the risk of the owners.
☞Extra Overcoats provided for such of them as are afflicted with protracted *chilly-phobia.*

*FAC-SIMILE OF UNDERGROUND RAILWAY ADVERTISEMENT*
*(From "The Western Citizen," July 13, 1844)*

The notion of an "underground railroad" is taken literally in this 1844 adver-tisement from the *Chicago Western Citizen*. Passengers on the "Liberty Line" are promised a destination of "Libertyville, Upper Canada." (Norman D. Harris, *The History of Negro Servitude in Illinois, and the Slavery Agitation in the State, 1719–1864*, ca. 1904, 16)

Canada's position infuriated slaveholders in the American South. In 1821, Kentucky sponsored a general resolution in the U.S. Con-gress protesting Canadian protection of slave fugitives. Five years later, U.S. Secretary of State Henry Clay, under pressure from the South, petitioned the British government to rein in Canada. Slyly, he tried to make the case that the runaways were troublemakers. "They are gener-ally the most worthless of their class and far, therefore, from being an acquisition which the British government can be anxious to make. The sooner, we should think, they are gotten rid of the better for Canada."[3] The British foreign secretary, unimpressed by Clay's argument, refused to interfere.

American slave owners may have fulminated against Canada's open arms policy in regard to fugitives, but enslaved and free blacks celebrated it and, invoking the biblical story of the promised land, called Canada the new Canaan. Fugitive slave laws and an ever-increasing demand for slaves made the United States a bleak Egypt of servitude for black men and women. Canada, on the other hand, became the promised land of freedom from servitude.

During the first half of the 19th century, and especially in the decade before the Civil War, blacks fled to Canada on the Underground Railroad in impressive numbers. The most reliable estimate is that 40,000 blacks, three-quarters of them fugitives, lived in Canada by 1860. The refugees settled where they could. Many found employment as laborers in rural areas. Others, especially those with skills, headed for Canadian cities and assimilated into their largely white populations. Others gravitated to a number of all-black settlements that became showcase communities closely monitored by proponents and foes of slavery alike. Along the way, black fugitives encountered many of the same racial prejudices they had endured in the United States. But the saving difference was that in the Canadian Canaan, blacks had the same standing as whites under the law. As one refugee put it, "Among some [white] people here, there is as much prejudice as in the States, but they cannot carry it out as they do in the States; the law makes the difference."[4]

## "A DARK TRAIN"

Prior to 1830, black immigration to Canada was sporadic and unorganized. Fugitives coming up from the South on the Underground Railroad usually settled in the northern Free States. They encountered social and legal discrimination there and lived with the possibility of capture and return to slavery—but for the most part, that risk was relatively low. As discussed in chapter 4, many northern states resisted federal fugitive laws.

Everything changed in the wake of the 1850 Fugitive Slave Act. Faced with severe penalties for noncompliance, state officials became more cooperative when it came to the capture and rendition of escaped slaves. Moreover, forcible kidnappings of free blacks by freelance gangs also picked up speed. All this made refuge in northern states especially risky for both fugitive slaves and freedmen, and hundreds of blacks already settled in the North headed for Canada. It took only two days after the Act became law before black churches in Boston lost sizeable percentages of their congregations. Half the black population of Columbia, Pennsylvania, left for Canada in the five years following the Act's passage. Similarly dramatic exoduses occurred in Buffalo, Rochester, and Pittsburgh. Moreover, Underground Railroad agents who previously had found home and work for fugitives in northern states now started sending them all the way to the Canadian border. So many blacks fled to safety in the Canadian Canaan that Frederick Douglass described the exodus as "a dark train going out of the land, as if fleeing from death."[5] According to one historian, black flight to Canada in the decade preceding the Civil War was the "largest expatriate movement in American history."[6]

The most heavily traveled Underground Railroad routes to Canada tended to converge on Detroit in the west and through the New England states or, less commonly, along the Atlantic coast, in the east. The Lake Erie–Lake Ontario region between New York and Michigan was the biggest hub of fugitive immigration into Canada. Refugees from the border states of Missouri and Kentucky crossed over the Detroit River to the Canadian town of Amherstburg in such numbers—an average of 30 per day by the mid-1850s—that Levi Coffin called the Canadian town the "principal terminus of the Underground Railroad in the West."[7] Runaways traversing western Pennsylvania and New York often crossed over at Niagara, near Buffalo. Fugitives from Virginia, Maryland, and Delaware favored the eastern routes but frequently veered west to cross over in the Great Lakes region.

Canadian cities and towns bordering the two Great Lakes were natural destinations for runaway slaves, even though some fugitives preferred to settle farther from the U.S. border. Besides Amherstburg, towns with sizeable refugee populations included Chatham, Dresden, and Windsor near Detroit and Saint Catharines, Hamilton, and Toronto in the Niagara area.

In 1855, one local resident described Chatham as a place where "fugitives are as thick as blackbirds in a corn-field."[8] Out of a population of 5,000, nearly 1,000 were refugees. For the most part they maintained separate churches and schools, but there seems to have been little tension between white and black Chathamites. Eliza Harris, whose dramatic escape across ice floes in the Ohio River inspired an equally dramatic scene in Harriet Beecher Stowe's *Uncle Tom's Cabin*, settled there. So did Martin Delaney, physician, separatist, and advocate of black immigration who came to be known as the Father of Black Nationalism. In 1858, Delaney was instrumental in arranging a congress of black abolitionists in which John Brown and some 70 delegates met to discuss Brown's vision of a rerouted Underground Railroad—what he called a "Subterranean Passage Way"—that would terminate in Kansas rather than Canada. It was at this meeting that Brown also revealed plans for his raid on Harpers Ferry. (When this came to light during Brown's later trial, an indignant Henry Wise, governor of Virginia, blasted the "predatory war of the abolitionists" that had been hatched "from Canada itself."[9])

Farther east, in the Saint Catharines, Hamilton, and Toronto area, ex-slaves also settled and began adjusting to their newly acquired freedom. A journalist who visited Saint Catharines' black community of nearly 1,000 effused that the city offered "Refuge! Refuge for the oppressed! Refuge for Americans escaping from abuse and cruel bondage in their native land! . . . Rest for the hunted slave! Rest for the travel-soiled and foot-sore fugitive!"[10] Harriet Tubman took rest and refuge in the city between 1851 and 1857. Anthony Burns, the fugitive whose 1854 rendition to slavery enraged Boston, also settled there after abolitionists purchased his freedom. He served as minister to the black congregation of Zion Baptist Church until his premature death in 1862.

Toronto was the city in which refugees made the most profound impact. Two years before the eruption of the Civil War, the New York *Tribune* reported that more blacks lived there than in any other town in Canada. In fact, American blacks had been settling in Toronto long before the 1850 Fugitive Slave Act and by the 1830s had built a solid middle class of barbers, dry-goods sellers, and tailors. Hundreds more blacks worked as laborers, dockworkers, porters, housekeepers, and laundresses. Most of them lived in the northwestern section of the city, and there were at least three all-black churches. But Toronto schools were open equally to black and white students, and many of the city's churches had mixed congregations. By 1840, Toronto's black population had become such a fixture that it successfully protested the arrival of a traveling blackface minstrel show.

Many leading black abolitionists also settled in the city, and as a consequence antislavery sentiment as well as Underground Railroad depots were well in place in Toronto by the 1850s. The Anti-Slavery Society of Canada was launched there in 1851, and that same year the city hosted the first North American Convention of Colored People, a gathering that drew more than 50 delegates and lasted three days.

Most fugitives arrived in Canada with nothing but the clothes on their back. The luckier ones carried a bundle of provisions or a couple of dollars given them by Underground Railroad agents. All were in immediate need of clothing, shelter, food, and employment. The problem was that most of them lacked marketable skills. Even fugitives who had been field hands frequently knew next to nothing about farming techniques. As slaves they had merely carried out backbreaking labor without learning the basics of agronomy. Those slaves who did know something about agriculture were often limited in knowledge and experience to cash crops like cotton and tobacco, neither of which fared particularly well in Canadian soil. Ex-slaves with such skills as barbering or tailoring were more likely to land on their feet once across the border, but they constituted a small percentage of refugees.

Additionally, many fugitives, unaccustomed as they were to either the responsibilities of freedom or the perils of a market economy, stumbled in their first months as refugees. As one ex-slave observed, "the mere delight the slaves took in their freedom, rendered them at first, contented with a lot far inferior to that to which they might have attained." Moreover, he noted, "their ignorance often led them to make unprofitable bargains." For example, "they would often hire wild land on short terms, and bind themselves to clear a certain number of acres. But by the time they were cleared and fitted for cultivation, and the lease was out, the landlords would take possession of the cleared land and raise a splendid crop on it."[11]

The precarious situation of newly arrived fugitives clearly meant that they needed relief aid, and this in turn made them dependent on the generosity of abolitionists and Underground Railroad supporters back in the United States. Black and white abolitionists frequently toured the northern states to solicit funds for improvident Canadian refugees. Churches were regularly canvassed for money and clothing. On their end, most all-black settlements in Canada routinely sent emissaries to the United States to beg for help from private individuals, congregations, and abolitionist societies. Ex-slave Josiah Henson, who lived in the Canadian black settlement of Dawn, traveled regularly throughout New York, Massachusetts, and Connecticut asking for monies and supplies. On one such trip, he raised over $14,000 from Boston businessmen to build a sawmill at the settlement.

The practice of soliciting funds for ex-slaves who crossed the Canadian border stirred up a battle of words between two expatriates who held quite different views of what black settlement in Canada ought to look like. Ex-slave Henry Bibb, founder and editor of *Voice of the Fugitive*, the first black newspaper in Canada, defended the solicitation of funds from white philanthropists as a necessary first step in the successful entry of fugitives into Canadian culture. Mary Ann Shadd, born into a free black Delaware family and founder and editor of the rival *Provincial Freeman*, disapproved of soliciting funds from white benefactors on the grounds that doing so both perpetuated black servility and fed into the bias that blacks were incapable of taking care of themselves. The two debated the issue in their own newspapers as well as in a series of exchanges in Frederick Douglass's *North Star* until Bibb's death in 1854.

Ex-slave Henry Bibb fled the United States for Canada where in 1851 he founded the *Voice of the Fugitive*, the first Canadian abolitionist newspaper. He urged fugitive slaves to immigrate to Canada and settle in all-black communities. (Library of Congress)

Help from largely white relief agencies and individual philanthropists was certainly useful and at times absolutely necessary, but Shadd's opinion was the predominant one among black fugitives in Canada. Their conviction was that ex-slaves needed to attain self-sufficiency as soon as possible and that whatever relief they received until then was best received from fellow blacks. This policy, they believed, would both enhance the self-respect of refugees and appease the hostility with which many white Canadians viewed the influx of blacks into their communities. This way of thinking was endorsed by the Canada Anti-Slavery Society as early as 1853, when it announced, "The true principle is now to assume that every man, unless disabled by sickness, can support himself and his family after he has obtained steady employment. All that able-bodied men and women require is a fair chance, friendly advice and a little encouragement, perhaps a little assistance at first."[12]

In keeping with the spirit of blacks helping blacks, several refugees formed a relief agency that they called the True Band Society in 1854. Originating in Amherstburg, the society aimed to provide emergency funds to incoming refugees, assist them in finding jobs and educational opportunities for their children, arbitrate disputes between them, and ease their integration into Canadian society. Membership fees, which were modest enough to be affordable to a wide range of black supporters, were used to fund the society's projects. The first True Band Society proved so successful that 14 sister societies sprang up in West Canada (as Upper Canada was called after 1841) within two years. Additionally, black citizens of Toronto founded several aid organizations to help refugees secure housing and jobs without having to rely on white handouts. Many of these organizations—for example, the Society for the Protection of Refugees, the Ladies Colored Fugitive Association, the Queen Victoria Benevolent Society, and the Ladies Freedman's Aid Society—were organized and run by black women.

True Band Societies aimed at offering relief to individual refugees and their families. But other relief agencies, largely funded by white philanthropists from the United States, financed the establishment of all-black settlements in Canada that sought to be truly self-sufficient communities. The corporations that supervised the communities typically offered land to refugees at rock-bottom prices payable over a number of years. Most fugitives who rode the Underground Railroad to the new Canaan wound up assimilating into the white population instead of joining the all-black communities, and none of these settlements survived long. Moreover, their emergence sparked another heated debate between Henry Bibb and Mary Ann Shadd, he publicly defending them and she insisting that black refugees needed to integrate. But the settlements were bold experiments in black initiative and self-reliance that confounded slave owners and gratified abolitionists.

## THE SETTLEMENTS

### Wilberforce

The first black settlement in Canada, established long before the 1850 Fugitive Slave Act, was the result of an equally oppressive set of laws directed against runaway slaves and freedmen in Cincinnati. Situated on the Ohio River just across from the slave state of Kentucky, Cincinnati was a major station on the Underground Railroad. Hundreds of fugitives passed through it on their way north, and hundreds more opted to remain in the city. In 1820, a mere 2 percent of the population was black. Just a decade later, the figure had jumped to 10 percent, with a lively community of more than 2,000 men, women, and children.

As the city's black population swelled, so did racial tension. Whites claimed that the growing black population was stealing jobs from able-bodied white men. To stem the tide of black migration into the city, Cincinnati authorities announced that the state's Black Codes, enacted in 1804 and 1807 but rarely enforced, henceforth would be taken seriously.

In the years before the Civil War, most Free States enacted Black Codes, laws that severely restricted the rights, liberties, and numbers of black residents. Ohio, although it had abolished slavery in 1802, passed especially draconian ones. Black residents were prohibited from serving on juries, enlisting in the state militia, or owning firearms. Newly arrived blacks were required to register with local officials, present written affidavits testifying to their free status, and post bonds of $500 within 60 days. They were forbidden to harbor runaways or to aid fugitives in leaving the state—which effectively made black participation in the Underground Railroad, already illegal at the federal level, an offense against the state of Ohio as well.

White rancor against blacks simmered in Cincinnati until it exploded in the hot summer of 1829. In mid-August, white mobs attacked black neighborhoods, burning homes and stores and beating residents. The riots lasted for three days. By the time they ended, some 1,500 blacks, two-thirds of the black population, had fled the city.

The blacks fleeing Cincinnati scattered to different locales. But five families, under the leadership of ex-slave James C. Brown, headed for Upper Canada to settle on 800 acres that Brown and other blacks had purchased a couple of months earlier, after it had become apparent that Cincinnati wasn't safe. The land was bought from the Canada Company, a corporation authorized by the British government to promote settlement in the western frontiers by offering cheap land to pioneers, and underwritten by philanthropic Quakers in Ohio and Indiana. When Brown wrote a letter to the lieutenant governor of Upper Canada asking for asylum for the families leaving Cincinnati, the reply was more than reassuring. "We Royalists do not know men by their color. Should you come to us you will be entitled to all the privileges of the rest of His Majesty's subjects."[13]

The settlement founded by Brown and the five fugitive families was eventually named Wilberforce, after the "Liberator" William Wilberforce, the parliamentarian whose two-decade-long battle ended slavery in the British Empire. At its height, the settlement boasted some 200 residents, a couple of churches, a gristmill and sawmill, and a school with 20 to 30 students, some of them white children from neighboring communities.

But despite strong endorsements and widespread publicity by American abolitionists such as William Lloyd Garrison, Wilberforce failed to flourish. Part of the reason was the harsh living conditions the black settlers faced. The thickly forested land was difficult to clear, and many of the original refugees had little experience in either timbering or farming. Another reason for the community's decline was the Canada Company's refusal, largely motivated by the antagonism of newly arriving Irish immigrants, to sell blacks any more land. By 1836, most of the black families in the area had given way to the Irish—founder James C. Brown himself relocated to Toronto—and the settlement known as Wilberforce was eventually incorporated as the town of Lucan.

Even though it failed, Wilberforce inspired the founding of subsequent black settlements in Canada. These intentional communities, populated primarily by ex-slaves seeking a foothold in the new Canaan, enjoyed varying degrees of success. But all of them attested to the same longing for freedom that fueled the Underground Railroad.

## Dawn

Racial tension in Cincinnati not only helped birth the black settlement of Wilberforce, but also sparked the founding of the optimistically named settlement of Dawn. Just five years after the race riots of 1829, the trustees of Cincinnati's Presbyterian Lane Seminary instructed faculty and students to cease participating in Underground Railroad activities and publicly expressing abolitionist sentiments. (Lane's president, Lyman Beecher, was the father of Harriet Beecher Stowe, author of *Uncle Tom's Cabin*.) Several members of the seminary, who came to be called the Lane Rebels, refused to abide by the seminary's prohibition and departed for Oberlin College, an institution that was both racially integrated and thoroughly committed to the work of the Underground Railroad.

One of the Rebels, a student by the name of Hiram Wilson who was convinced that fugitives could truly be free only in Canada, launched a campaign to fund a series of schools for black children in Canada. One of them, the British-American Institute located near Chatham in Canada West and established for the "Education, Mental Moral and physical, of the Colored inhabitants of Canada, not excluding white persons and Indians," became the nucleus of Dawn, a black settlement formally organized in 1842.[14]

The British-American Institute was in many ways the heart of the community. It trained students in the mechanical and domestic arts, requiring them to work part-time to support the school, and many refugee families gravitated to Dawn so that their children could benefit from the training offered by the institute. By 1845, more than 70 students were enrolled in the school. One of their teachers was Hannah Wilson, Hiram Wilson's wife.

Unlike Wilberforce, which never quite managed to get off the ground, Dawn grew rapidly to a population of 500. The institute owned upward of 300 acres, the black settlers another 1,500, and almost all the cleared land was planted in such crops as wheat, oats, corn, and tobacco. Because Dawn was surrounded by thick forests of black walnut, settlers negotiated for timber rights, built a sawmill, and began selling finished lumber. Dawn's fame as a producer of fine lumber earned it an invitation to send a delegation to the 1851 World's Fair in London's Crystal Palace. When the delegation arrived to set up its display of walnut boards, the authorities in charge of the U.S. exhibit insisted that the boards be displayed as an American rather than a Canadian display. The delegation reluctantly complied but painted a huge, bold-lettered sign to display with the lumber:

THIS IS THE PRODUCT OF THE INDUSTRY OF A FUGITIVE SLAVE FROM THE UNITED STATES, WHOSE RESIDENCE IS DAWN, CANADA.

The fugitive slave and Dawn resident who had the sign painted was Josiah Henson, a man so famous that Queen Victoria insisted on meeting him during his London visit. His reputation rested in large part on Harriet Beecher Stowe's public announcement that he had served as the inspiration for her famous character Uncle Tom. But the details of his own life, as well as his tireless efforts on behalf of Dawn, made him fascinating in his own right.

Henson was born a slave in Maryland in 1789 and belonged to three different masters before fleeing to freedom with his wife and four children, two of whom he carried in a knapsack on his back, in 1830. Their journey to Canada along Underground Railroad routes took six weeks, and when they arrived the only place they could afford to live was a farm shack, from which Henson evicted a herd of pigs. Although severe beatings as a young slave had left him unable to raise his hands above his head (the result of a broken arm and two broken shoulder blades), Henson threw himself into a number of physically demanding jobs, eventually saved enough money to buy livestock and land, and made sure that his children were educated. For the rest of his life, Henson remained convinced that the keys to black independence were land ownership and education, both central to the spirit of Dawn. After settling in Canada, Henson also became a Methodist preacher, even though he was barely literate, and he made two secret journeys to Kentucky to lead slaves to freedom on the Underground Railroad.[15]

Dawn was an embodiment of everything Mary Ann Shadd disliked about black settlements. Except for the presence of a few white children in the British-American Institute, Dawn made no effort to integrate with the neighboring white community. Moreover, the settlement's leaders, especially Henson, frequently solicited abolitionist groups in the United States for material and financial support. But even large contributions from outside couldn't save Dawn from the poor management practices, for which Henson was partly responsible, that brought one financial crisis after another to the settlement. Moreover, internal squabbling over religion and between original settlers and subsequent arrivals was common. Eventually, internal dissention among the black residents and external cooling-off of white benefactors led to the 1872 closing of the British-American Institute. The black community that had clustered around the school disintegrated, land was sold off, and what was left of the settlement was absorbed by the town of Dresden.

The reaction to Dawn's failure was generally dismal. Racists in both the North and the South saw its collapse as a testimony to the inability of blacks to prosper without white supervision. Others less willing to dismiss the idea of black self-reliance concluded that the settlement's demise underscored the fatal weakness of self-segregated communities, which inevitably relied on external financial support. Refugee blacks, they insisted, needed to enter into white mainstream culture if they hoped to thrive. Even observers sympathetic to black settlements were disheartened by the mismanagement of the community's leaders and the low morale that sapped the energy of its residents. Ex-slave and Underground Railroad conductor William Wells Brown pulled no punches in his assessment of Dawn. No other settlement, he stated, "has excited more interest, or received a greater share of substantial aid, than [Dawn], and no place has proved itself less deserving."[16]

For the most part, however, these evaluations are too harsh. Dawn may have been mismanaged by well-intentioned but administratively incompetent leaders, and it certainly relied too heavily on external financial support from white benefactors. But its collapse didn't at all suggest, as some critics insisted, that fugitive slaves were incapable of making it on their own. In its heyday, Dawn was a thriving community with locally based industries, a respected school, and a reputation that stretched all the way across the Atlantic. Its failure, although disappointing, in no way confirmed Brown's harsh judgment that no place was "less deserving."

### The Refugee Home Society

A black settlement more deserving of censure than either Wilberforce or Dawn was the Refugee Home Society, founded in 1851 and located just a few miles from the Canadian township of Sandwich. Start-up funding came largely from two abolitionist organizations: the Fugitive Union Society and the Michigan Anti-Slavery Society. But the Refugee Home Society was really the brainchild of Henry Bibb, editor of the *Voice of the Fugitive*.

Like all the black settlements in Canada, the Refugee Home Society began with laudable intentions. Its mission statement declared that it was organized for the purpose of helping poor, uneducated, and frightened refugees who, although willing to work, were unable to support themselves through lack of employment opportunity or land to farm. To that end, the society purchased 2,000 acres with the understanding that it would be resold cheaply to black settlers. Each family received 25 acres at $2 per acre. If five acres were cleared and planted within the first three years, they were given to the homesteader free of charge. Houses had to contain at least two rooms, and neither land nor house could be sold for 15 years or willed to anyone other than blood relatives. Moreover, only fugitive slaves were eligible for land from the society. Free blacks searching for cheap land had to look elsewhere.

The experiment was a disaster from the very beginning. The chief obstacle to success was the fact that the lots sold by the society were scattered about. The absence of contiguity destroyed the possibility of building any spirit of community and cooperation among the 150 blacks who purchased lots. Another difficulty was the settlers' lack of capital. Because the society sold only to impoverished ex-slaves who were often unable to keep up with the payments for their lots, many of them wound up losing their land.

A major source of discontent among settlers was their perception that the society placed too many restrictions on what they could and couldn't do with their property. Settler Thomas Jones chafed, for example, at the rules against reselling property or willing it to anyone but wife and children. He thought it ironic that he and his fellow settlers, who had escaped to Canada in order to be free, were now once again bound by authority. Speaking for them all, he said, "They [fugitives] want to do as they please.

If they want to exchange and get a bigger place, they want to do it without being cramped."[17]

But probably the single biggest cause of the Refugee Home Society's collapse was the relentless public attacks against it by Mary Ann Shadd. It's difficult to determine whether her primary motive for the campaign against the society was her principled opposition to segregated black communities that relied on external financial support or her personal animosity toward Henry Bibb. But whatever her reasons, her vociferous criticism of the society demoralized its members and alienated potential white backers. When Bibb died in 1854, the society lost its public voice and chief source of resistance to Shadd's attacks. By the time the Civil War erupted, the Refugee Home Society was on its last legs.

## Elgin

The largest and most successful refugee settlement in Canada was built in 1849 near the town of Chatham, just a couple of miles from Lake Erie. Named the Elgin Association in honor of the reigning governor general, Lord Elgin, it was also often referred to as Buxton or the Buxton Mission because of its association with the Presbyterian Church of Canada mission and school in the local community of Buxton.

Elgin was the child of Rev. William King, an Irish Presbyterian minister who immigrated to the United States and married the daughter of a Louisiana planter. When his wife died, he inherited 15 slaves from her. Plagued by an uneasy conscience, and also censured by the elders of his church because of his ownership of humans, King took his slaves north to Canada, freed them, and successfully raised funds to purchase an initial 200 acres of land on which to settle them and other fugitives. Moreover, King built himself a house within the settlement, living and working alongside his former slaves and forming the nucleus of what became the Elgin settlement.

Unlike the other three black communities in Canada, Elgin was well-planned and competently administered from the very beginning. Financial accountability was guaranteed by a stock company and a 24-member board of directors made up of successful businessmen. Meticulous bookkeeping and carefully prepared annual reports were the orders of the day.

Elgin's physical layout was also the product of thoughtful foresight. Land was divided into 50-acre lots at $2.50 an acre. All lots faced a thoroughfare, and the houses built on them had to be no smaller than 18 feet by 24 feet by 12 feet, stand 33 feet from the road, have a 2-foot drainage ditch running alongside the road, and have a picket fence–enclosed garden in front of the house. King and his fellow planners clearly wanted Elgin to be a model community. In some ways, its uniform design anticipated the layout of 20th-century suburban developments.

The community supported itself by farming and lumbering the oaks, hickory trees, and maples that grew abundantly in the area. There was a "downtown" center complete with post office, general store, two-story hotel, and the Buxton Mission church and school. The settlement also boasted a sawmill, a gristmill, and the only brick factory for miles around. From the very beginning, Elgin distinguished itself from other settlements by refusing to accept monetary donations from the outside world. The community's goal was to be entirely self-reliant, and this ambition reflected King's own "full faith," as one journalist put it, "in the natural powers, capacity, and capabilities of the African race."[18] King wanted to show the world that black homesteaders were just as able to make it on their own as white ones. As one public letter released by Elgin authorities put it, "We wish the people of the United States to know that there is one portion of Canada West where the colored people are self-supporting."[19]

The sole exception to Elgin's "no-begging" policy was the Buxton school. King regularly solicited books and maps for the use of its students. Unlike the schools in other settlements, which focused primarily on vocational training, the Buxton school offered its students a classical education. The sons and daughters of ex-slaves, taught from the same curriculum that schoolchildren in white academies followed, studied Latin and Greek, mathematics, history, geography, and theology. The school quickly earned such a reputation for excellence that many white Canadians who lived nearby pulled their children out of public institutions to send them to Buxton. King's commitment to teaching black children the classics underscored his conviction that blacks were the intellectual and moral equals of whites. It also attested to his concern that teaching blacks nothing but manual skills was a tacit admission that they were good only for physical labor.

At its peak, Elgin's population numbered more than 2,000, and the settlement was warmly praised by most observers. Even Frederick Douglass, who initially had criticized King for his one-time slaveholding, lauded Elgin as living proof that slaves could live independently of whites. When the black citizens of Pittsburgh sent Elgin the congratulatory gift of a "Liberty" bell, their accompanying expressions of admiration for the settlement's achievements were richly deserved.

## LEAVING NEW CANAAN

When the Union Army finally started recruiting black soldiers in 1862, close to a hundred of Elgin's settlers returned to the United States to join up. Their departure signaled the slow decline of Elgin as well as the end of Underground Railroad–conveyed refugees to Canada. With the coming of war, and especially after the Northern victory, movement across the border reversed its earlier flow of south to north. Many ex-slaves who had escaped to Canada chose to remain there, but many more returned to rejoin family and friends they had left behind.

The black migration to Canada was a fitting capstone to antebellum slave resistance in the United States. As discussed in chapter 1, the backdrop against which the Underground Railroad developed was the day-to-day resistance, punctuated by occasional insurrections, of slaves. Such resistance demonstrated resolve, initiative, and independence in slaves and gave the lie to the Southern myth of the happy, contented "darkie." That same resolve was exhibited when slaves made a run for freedom, when they made contact with the Underground Railroad north of the Mason-Dixon Line, or when they in turn served as conductors on Railroad routes, offered shelter to other fugitives, and resisted the forcible southward rendition of ex-slaves. Relocating to a strange country, even when it was seen as a Canaan-like land of promise compared to the slaveholding United States, required perhaps the greatest degree of courageous resolve of all. Once there, blacks who settled in Canadian cities and villages, as well as those who participated in the communal experiments of Wilberforce, Dawn, the Refugee Home Society, and Elgin, demonstrated that they were prepared to make a life for themselves as free people. From first to last, the resolute hunger for freedom that lay behind the resolve was the same spirit that had built the Underground Railroad.

An 1838 print from the American Anti-Slavery Society captures the fact that most runaway slaves fled with next to no provisions for their journey. (Library of Congress)

## NOTES

The chapter epigraph is from Martin Delaney, *Blake; or, The Huts of America*, ed. Floyd J. Miller (Boston: Beacon Press, 1970), 143. Delaney (1812–1885), an ex-slave who became an abolitionist, physician, and advocate of black migration from the United States, published *Blake*, a novel about a West Indian slave who leads a slave insurrection in Cuba, on the eve of the Civil War.

1. Canadian geographical divisions in the 18th and 19th centuries can be confusing. Between 1791 and 1841, the territory was divided into "Upper" and "Lower" Canada, designations reflecting proximity to the headwaters of the Lawrence River. After 1841, Upper Canada became Canada West, and Lower Canada was renamed Canada East.

2. Quoted in Robin W. Winks, *The Blacks in Canada: A History*, 2nd ed. (Montreal and Kingston: McGill-Queen's University Press, 2008), 170.

3. Quoted in Wilbur H. Siebert, *The Underground Railroad from Slavery to Freedom* (Mineola, NY: Dover, 2006), 201.

4. Benjamin Drew, *The Refugee: A North-side View of Slavery* (Reading, MA: Addison-Wesley, 1969), 214. Drew's book was first published in 1855.

5. Quoted in R. J. M. Blackett, "'Freemen to the Rescue!': Resistance to the Fugitive Slave Law of 1850," in *Passages to Freedom: The Underground Railroad in History and Memory*, ed. David W. Blight (New York: HarperCollins, 2004), 138.

6. Donald Yacovone, *Samuel Joseph May and the Dilemmas of the Liberal Persuasion 1797–1871* (Philadelphia: Temple University Press, 1991), 139.

7. Levi Coffin, *Reminiscences* (Cincinnati: Western Tract Society, 1876), 250.

8. Drew, *The Refugee*, 164.

9. Quoted in Jacqueline L. Tobin, *From Midnight to Dawn: The Last Tracks of the Underground Railroad* (New York: Anchor, 2008), 58.

10. Drew, *The Refugee*, 11.

11. Josiah Henson, *Autobiography of Josiah Henson* (Mineola, NY: Dover, 1969), 89. Henson's memoirs were first published in 1849.

12. Quoted in Siebert, *The Underground Railroad*, 204.

13. Quoted in Tobin, *From Midnight to Dawn*, 13.

14. Quoted in William H. Pease and Jane H. Pease, *Black Utopia: Negro Communal Experiments in America* (Madison: Wisconsin State Historical Society, 1964), 64.

15. See the appendix to this book for Henson's account of his second journey.

16. Quoted in Winks, *The Blacks in Canada*, 204.

17. Drew, *The Refugee*, 230. See the appendix to this book for Jones's full discussion of the Refugee Home Society.

18. Ibid., 208.

19. Quoted in Tobin, *From Midnight to Dawn*, 128.

# THE END OF THE LINE

We need not always weep and mourn,
Or wear these slavery chains forlorn,
So let us all from slavery flee,
And soon may all the earth be free!

*—From the spiritual "Go Down, Moses"*

No one knows when the Underground Railroad finally quit running, but the Civil War marked the beginning of its end.

A month and a half after Abraham Lincoln was elected president in 1860, South Carolina seceded. As noted in the introduction, one of the grievances cited for its withdrawal from the Union was the charge that the Underground Railroad encouraged thousands of slaves "to leave their homes." Six weeks later, the six states of the Lower South also left the Union. On April 12, 1861, South Carolina militia fired cannon on Fort Sumter, a federal fort in Charleston harbor. Considering this a de facto declaration of armed insurrection, President Lincoln called up 75,000 volunteers, prompting Virginia, Arkansas, North Carolina, and Tennessee to join the Confederacy. The war was on.

Lincoln made it clear that his aim in this war was the preservation of the Union, not the emancipation of slaves. Despite his personal dislike of slavery, he believed that the president of the United States had no constitutional authority to overturn existing state and federal laws protecting human property. But he also had strategic reasons for sidestepping the issue of abolition. He rightly guessed that the typical Northern soldier would fight to preserve the Union but not to free the slaves. And he knew that if he threatened the institution of slavery, he risked driving the slaveholding border states of Missouri, Kentucky, Maryland, and Delaware into the Confederacy, a move that he believed would be disastrous for the North.

As things turned out, the same thirst for freedom that had prompted thousands of slaves to run in the years before the war sent them flooding to the North after fighting began. Henry Bibb's 1853 observation that self-emancipation was "the order of the day" was never more true. In May 1861, only a month after the attack on Fort Sumter, Virginia slaves started making their way to Fortress Monroe, the federally held garrison at the mouth of the James River, to seek asylum. Within a few days, a Confederate colonel and owner of several of the absconded slaves insisted that Fortress Monroe commander Gen. Benjamin Butler return the slaves, citing the 1850 Fugitive Slave Act as legal precedent. Butler, a lawyer in civilian life and skilled in legal duels, replied that since the law had only domestic application, and since Virginia had separated herself from the United States and declared allegiance to another government, the law no longer applied to her. The slaves, he declared, were "contraband of war" and would not be returned.

The federal government (somewhat reluctantly) backed Butler up, and the policy of accepting runaway slaves as contraband was launched. Before long, fugitives were crossing Union lines everywhere, despite their masters' attempts to convince them that the Yankees would ship them off to forced labor in Cuba or hitch them like mules to wagons and plows. In the war's first year, 15,000 slave fugitives poured into Washington, D.C., alone. And when Lincoln signed the Emancipation Proclamation on January 1, 1861, granting freedom to all slaves in the rebellious states (but not in the loyal slaveholding border states; Lincoln was still hedging his bet), flights to freedom that had been carried out surreptitiously and illegally for years could now be done with the full blessing of the federal government.[1]

The significance of this event shouldn't be overlooked. It was a stunning turnabout of policy that, although formalized by Lincoln's signature, was in part the fruit of several decades of civil disobedience to the law of the land. The resistance to unjust slave laws practiced by abolitionists and Underground Railroad workers had steadily chiseled away at the institution of slavery, sapping it of any moral standing that Southerners might try to claim for it. Racial prejudice remained strong in the North. But the untiring dedication of Railroad workers, the fugitive narratives written by its passengers, the courageous rescues of recaptured runaways, and the stalwart fidelity to "higher laws" practiced by such figures as Thomas Garrett, John Rankin, Jermain Loguen, and Harriet Tubman couldn't help but impress on many Northerners the essential wickedness of slavery. Civil disobedience to unjust laws, even when carried out by a minority of citizens, is hard to ignore owing to its moral weight and the salutary example it offers. In a fundamental sense, it wasn't only Lincoln who freed the slaves. It was also the black and white women and men who tirelessly worked the Underground Railroad.

To the extent that the Underground Railroad still operated after the Civil War began, its activity was primarily in the borderland regions of Kentucky and Missouri, two of the four slaveholding states loyal to the Union. Arnold Gragston, a young slave in Mason County, Kentucky, continued ferrying fugitives across the Ohio River and delivering them to Rev. John Rankin in Ripley until 1863, when he himself finally fled to freedom. One of the Railroad leaders in Detroit remembered after the war that the last fugitive he'd seen arrived in the city sometime in 1862. The need for the Railroad dwindled, he remarked, because "The line of freedom moved south, keeping step by step with the battle line of the union."[2]

As the southward-moving Union forces made Underground Railroad work progressively unnecessary, many Railroad workers directed their energies to the war effort. Mary Ann Shadd, John Parker, Frederick Douglass, and Harriet Tubman recruited blacks for the Union army. Tubman and Martin Delaney actually served in the army themselves, as did the sons of John Rankin, Frederick Douglass, and Josiah Henson. Levi Coffin labored for humane treatment of contrabands. William Still supplied the Union army with coal.

It's not clear when the cluster of activities associated with the Underground Railroad began, although, as mentioned in the introduction, it most likely acquired its name in 1831. As we've noted here, neither is it clear when its activities ceased. But for seasoned Railroad workers in both Cincinnati and Detroit—and, presumably, across the land—the passage of the Fifteenth Amendment in April 1870, granting voting privileges to black men, was seen as an appropriate end of the line. In Cincinnati, Levi Coffin told a jubilant crowd that he was happy to announce the closure of the Railroad. "The stock of the Underground Railroad," he said, has "gone down in the market, the business [is] spoiled, the road [is] of no further use."[3] At the other end of the line, on the same day, black Railroad stationmaster George DeBaptiste put a sign in his Detroit shop window:

> Notice to Stockholders of the Underground Railroad: This office is closed. Hereafter all stockholders will receive dividends according to their merits.[4]

One can only imagine his satisfaction.

---

## NOTES

The chapter epigraph is from the black spiritual "Go Down, Moses."

1. All fugitive slave laws were annulled by Congress on June 25, 1864, thereby relieving absconding slaves from the four loyal slaveholding states, to whom the Emancipation Proclamation didn't apply, of the risk of being returned to their masters.

2. Quoted in Fergus M. Bordewich, *Bound for Canaan* (New York: HarperCollins, 2005), 430.

3. Levi Coffin, *Reminiscences* (Cincinnati: Western Tract Society, 1876), 712.

4. Bordewich, *Bound for Canaan*, 432. A great deal of DeBaptiste's Railroad work was performed in Madison, Indiana, where from his barbershop he aided Kentucky fugitives. He relocated to Detroit in 1846 after his activities made it too dangerous for him to remain in Madison.

# Biographies: Personalities of the Underground Railroad

## HENRY BIBB (1815–1854)

Author of one of the most popular slave narratives of the antebellum period and editor of the first successful newspaper for black refugees in Canada, Henry Bibb had a life as dramatic as it was short. Born on May 10, 1815, of mixed parentage near Louisville, Kentucky—his father was rumored to have been a state senator—Bibb hated his slavery from an early age and attempted to escape twice before he was 20. He was captured and beaten each time. In an effort to settle him down, his master married Bibb to Malinda, a slave from another plantation. The two had a daughter, Mary Frances. Bibb made his third run for freedom on Christmas Day 1837, promising to return for his family. This time he was successful.

Bibb settled in Ohio, and in 1839 he returned to Kentucky to make good on his vow to rescue his wife and daughter. But the three were caught, transported south, and sold to separate owners. Bibb, who never saw his wife or daughter again, made his way to freedom in 1841 after a daring trek across prairie land and up the Mississippi River.

Bibb educated himself, moved to Detroit, remarried, and became a popular abolitionist lecturer. In 1849 he published his memoirs, *Narrative of the Life of Henry Bibb*. Realizing that his hair-raising accounts of escapes from bondage ran the risk of being dismissed as fiction, he prefaced the book with the testimony of several people, including the son of a previous owner, who attested to their truth. In addition to his memoirs, Bibb also published a pamphlet on Nat Turner's slave rebellion in Virginia and a collection of antislavery songs.

After the enactment of the 1850 Fugitive Slave Law made them feel insecure in the United States, Bibb and his second wife, Mary, crossed the border to settle in Ontario, Canada. Upon his arrival, he helped found the Fugitive Union Society, a relief organization for runaway slaves. On New Year's Day 1851, he and Mary launched the *Voice of the Fugitive*, an abolitionist newspaper. That same year he organized the North American Convention of Colored People in Toronto. Fifty-three delegates attended, and all of them signed a resolution urging blacks in the United States to immigrate to Canada.

The *Voice of the Fugitive* became a leading champion of black settlements in Canada. During Bibb's frequent lecture tours throughout the United States to raise money for the Refuge Home Society, the settlement he helped found, Mary ably supervised the newspaper. The *Voice* ran for three years, until its offices burned down in October 1853. It's unclear how the fire started, although Bibb was personally convinced it was the work of an arsonist. He died less than a year later. Free blacks throughout Canada and the United States publicly mourned his death.

## HENRY "BOX" BROWN (1815–1879?)

An ex-slave whose escape captured the nation's imagination, Henry Brown was born in Virginia and hired out at an early age to a Richmond tobacco factory owner. He married a slave belonging to a different master and paid her master out of his earnings so that she could care for their children. In 1848, the wife's master demanded more money, which Brown was unable to raise, and the very next day the man sold Brown's wife and children south.

Shortly afterward, Brown met Samuel A. Smith, a carpenter who agreed (for a price) to nail Brown up in a wooden crate and ship him to abolitionists in Philadelphia. (Smith was later arrested, convicted of slave stealing, and sentenced to prison.) The five-foot-eight Brown barely had room to move in the crate. He took with him a few crackers, a bottle of water, and an awl with which to bore breathing holes in the crate should he find himself short of oxygen. Sealed in this way, he made a 26-hour, 250-mile journey by wagon, train, and steamboat. Freighters handled the crate roughly, sometimes stacking it so that Brown was upside down. But he finally arrived at his destination. When members of the Philadelphia Vigilance Committee opened the crate, Brown joyfully greeted them and recited a line from Psalm 40: "I waited patiently for the Lord, and he inclined unto me and heard my cry." Then he fainted.

News of his escape spread quickly, and Brown became something of a celebrity. (Frederick Douglass later complained that the publicity surrounding Brown's escape precluded the use of similar strategies by future refugees.) For safety's sake, he soon left Philadelphia for Boston and then New Bedford. Over the next two years he toured the northern states for the American Anti-Slavery Society and published a narrative of his life.

After the passage of the 1850 Fugitive Slave Act, Brown worried that he would be abducted by slave catchers and returned to Virginia. His fears were well-founded: he narrowly evaded capture on one occasion. So in the fall of that same year he sailed to England, where he remained for a quarter century.

Brown was as much of a celebrity in England as in the United States. He made a living by touring the country, lecturing and displaying a panorama depicting scenes of slave life. Later in his career he billed himself as a "Prince of Africa" and a mesmerist. He married a white woman and raised a second family, returning to the United States only a few years before his death.

## WILLIAM WELLS BROWN (1814–1884)

When it comes to raw talent, Underground Railroad conductor William Wells Brown was easily the equal of Frederick Douglass. Through the written and spoken word, Brown so effectively campaigned against slavery in the United States and England that, along with Douglass, he became the public face of black abolitionism.

Brown was born into slavery in Lexington, Kentucky, though his father was white. Sold several times during his boyhood and youth, Brown eventually wound up in Saint Louis, Missouri, where his master hired him out to work on the Missouri River. He managed to escape on New Year's Day 1834 when the boat on which he was riding with his master docked in Cincinnati.

Making his way north, he worked for the next decade on a number of Lake Erie steamboats. During that time he helped dozens of fugitive slaves cross over into Canada. He also became active in the abolitionist movement, began lecturing, and published an account of his life. Its popularity among the reading public was second only to Frederick Douglass's autobiography.

In 1849, Brown sailed to England to solicit support for the abolitionist movement. Fearing to return to the United States after the 1850 Fugitive Slave Act, he remained abroad for five years. He returned only after his freedom had been purchased by the same British family that earlier had bought Douglass's freedom. While in England, Brown published what is widely recognized as the first African American novel, *Clotel, or The President's Daughter*, whose eponymous protagonist is a mulatto daughter of Thomas Jefferson. In later years he wrote plays, travel sketches, a history of blacks in America and another of blacks in the Civil War, and a second volume of memoirs. Before the Civil War and the emancipation of slaves, Brown had focused his energies on abolitionism. After the war, he redirected his efforts to ensuring that the brutality of the slave system wasn't forgotten by the white population.

## ANTHONY BURNS (1830?–1862)

In March 1854, Virginia-born slave Anthony Burns ran from his master, Charles Suttle, and hid aboard a Boston-bound ship. Once in Boston, he worked in a clothing store until, in May of that same year, he was seized by a federal marshal. Arrested under the provisions of the 1850 Fugitive Slave Act, Burns was denied bail, the right to testify in his own defense, and a trial by jury. He was locked up until he could be rendered to his master.

Word of Burns's arrest spread quickly through the city. The very next day, a mass meeting was held at Faneuil Hall in which abolitionists such as William Lloyd Garrison urged the crowd to resist Burns's return to slavery. Led by Thomas Wentworth Higginson, who later commanded a black regiment in the Civil War, an angry mob stormed the building in which Burns was being held. Fighting erupted, and one of the deputies guarding Burns was killed. But the rescue attempt was unsuccessful, and Burns remained in custody. President Franklin Pierce authorized the use of federal troops to restore peace. On June 2, after a pro forma hearing, Burns was escorted by troops to the docks, put aboard a boat, and returned to Virginia. Thousands of protesters lined the streets, and shops and houses along the route were draped in black crepe.

Burns's rendition was a crucial testing of the 1850 Fugitive Slave Act. Already flouted numerous times in northern states, the Act was in danger of becoming a mere paper law. President Pierce was determined that Burns's return to captivity would signal the government's determination to uphold it.

On his return to the South, Burns was jailed in Richmond for nearly half a year. Immediately after his release, Charles Suttle, rejecting the offer of a Boston congregation to buy Burns's freedom, sold him to a North Carolina planter. Eventually the new owner was persuaded to sell Burns to the congregation, and he returned to Boston a free man. He soon relocated to Oberlin College, where he prepared himself for the ministry. (He had been a slave preacher while still in captivity.) In 1860 he immigrated to Ontario to serve as pastor to a black congregation.

## LEVI COFFIN (1798–1877)

Longtime abolitionist and Underground Railroad stationmaster, the Quaker Levi Coffin was such an effective leader of the Railroad's western route that his Cincinnati home was often called "Grand Central Station." During his long career on the Railroad, he helped 2,000–3,000 slaves make their way to freedom.

Born near Greensboro, North Carolina, Coffin claimed that he became an abolitionist at the age of seven on encountering a slave who had been manacled to prevent him from running away to his family. By the time he was 15, Coffin was working with local Quakers, including his cousin Vestal, to feed and offer temporary shelter to runaway slaves. Eight years later, the two cousins tried to open a school to teach slaves to read the Bible, but it was closed down by angry slave owners. Soon afterward, Levi and his bride, Catherine, who shared his dislike of living in a slave state, relocated to the Free State of Indiana.

Coffin settled in Newport (now Fountain City), Indiana, where he immediately made contact with the free black community and offered his home as a hideaway for refugees. In just a few years he managed to create such an efficient network of agents and safe houses that Newport became a major hub of the western Railroad. In the meantime, Coffin prospered, running a successful general store, eventually becoming a director of the Bank of Indiana, and devoting a good part of his fortune to financing Railroad activities. Although his business ventures were often boycotted by anti-abolitionists, he felt no regret over the lost income. "If by doing my duty and endeavoring to fulfill the injunctions of the Bible, I injured my business," he wrote, "then let my business go."[1] A greater blow was the damage his Railroad activities did to his standing with the local Quaker community. Condemning Coffin's willingness to break the law in order to help slaves to freedom, the community expelled him in 1842.

In 1847, Coffin and his wife relocated to Cincinnati, where he managed a wholesale business founded and funded by the Western Free Produce Association. The association's aim was to boycott commodities produced either directly or indirectly by slave labor and to sell instead only products made by free laborers. However noble the idea, the business failed to prosper, primarily because the free-labor goods were generally inferior in quality to and more expensive than the slave-produced ones sold by Coffin's competitors.

Coffin lived in Cincinnati for the rest of his life. Between 1847 and the outbreak of the Civil War, he cooperated with black and white abolitionists to organize a system of escape that included several safe houses and dozens of conductors willing to transport fugitives to stations north of Cincinnati. Catherine Coffin and other women regularly sewed costumes to disguise fugitives as household and garden servants or as Quakers.

During and after the war, until his retirement in 1870, Coffin worked with the Freedman's Bureau to help ex-slaves establish themselves as productive and self-reliant citizens. In the year before his death, he published his *Reminiscences*, a classic in Underground Railroad literature. At his funeral, his black and white pallbearers were all fellow Railroad workers.

## ELLEN (1826–1891) AND WILLIAM (1824–1900) CRAFT

Married couple Ellen and William Craft made one of the most publicized of all slave escapes. Like most fugitives, the Crafts received no aid from

Underground Railroad resources or workers until they crossed the Mason-Dixon Line; they planned and executed their own escape.

Both Ellen and William were born in Georgia. William's appearance clearly reflected his African lineage, but Ellen, whose father was white and whose mother was mixed, was so fair-complexioned that she could pass for a white woman. Ellen was a house servant, and William was hired out by his master to various tradesmen. He was allowed to keep a small percentage of his wages.

In 1848, two years after their marriage, the Crafts conceived a plan of escape that took advantage of Ellen's light skin and the money William had saved. They would flee disguised as a young, sickly gentleman seeking medical help in the North, accompanied by his trusty manservant. Ellen bobbed her hair in a masculine style, male attire from top hat to boots was acquired, and train tickets out of Georgia were purchased.

Two problems worried the Crafts. The first was Ellen's voice; although her disguise made her look like a male youth, her voice was still feminine. The second was her illiteracy. The Crafts knew that to keep up their ruse they would have to stay at hotels along the way, and this meant that the disguised Ellen would be expected to sign hotel registers. Both problems were solved by putting Ellen's right arm in a sling and pretending that she was deaf, which prevented her from writing or speaking. William, the "manservant," would do all the talking. Ellen, the "young master," would remain mute.

The plan worked beautifully. The Crafts traveled by train and steamer through Georgia, South Carolina, North Carolina, Virginia, Maryland, and Washington, D.C., before arriving in Philadelphia. They were welcomed by leading abolitionists, including William Wells Brown and William Lloyd Garrison, and their daring escape made them instant celebrities. The Crafts soon moved to Boston and supported themselves over the next two years by traveling throughout the northern states to speak to audiences about their lives as slaves and their adventurous flight to freedom.

The passage of the 1850 Fugitive Slave Act put an end to their lecturing. Their Georgian master sent slave catchers to Boston to apprehend them and appealed directly to President Millard Fillmore to enforce the new law. Fillmore agreed to call on the military, if necessary, to return the Crafts to slavery. Getting word of the danger they faced, the couple fled first to Maine, then Canada, and finally England, where they lived for the next 19 years.

Their life in England was fruitful. They learned to read and write, published an account of their escape, threw themselves into the battle for women's rights and emancipation, and supported themselves from fees earned by public speaking. They also raised five children.

In 1869, William, Ellen, and two of their children returned to the United States. They purchased nearly 2,000 acres of land in their home state of Georgia and started a school for freedmen. But their venture was plagued by financial hardship and opposition from the local white community, and the Crafts were forced to shut the school's doors after five years. They remained on their land for a few more years, trying to eke out a living from farming, but in 1890 finally sold out and moved to Charleston, South Carolina, to live with one of their daughters. Ellen died the following year, and William a decade later.

## MARTIN DELANEY (1812–1885)

Abolitionist, journalist, physician, and novelist, Martin Delaney was an early champion of black nationalism. Although his actual participation in the Underground Railroad was limited to providing occasional refuge for runaways, the influence of his writings in the antislavery movement was immense.

Delaney was born in Charles Town, Virginia (now West Virginia) to a free mother and a slave father. When he was 10 years old, his mother relocated the family to Chambersburg, Pennsylvania (his father later purchased his freedom and joined them), where Delaney received a good education. When he was 19 he left for Pittsburgh, which remained his home for the next quarter-century. In his first years there, he taught school and apprenticed with a number of physicians. It was in Pittsburgh that he became an advocate of abolitionism and opened his home as a safe house for escaping slaves.

During his Pittsburgh years, Delaney also founded and edited *The Mystery*, an abolitionist newspaper. In 1847 he collaborated with William Lloyd Garrison and Frederick Douglass to found the *North Star*. As co-editor of the paper, Delaney's primary responsibility was fund-raising, and this meant traveling around the country speaking to antislavery groups.

During this period, Delaney continued to study medicine with Pittsburgh physicians. In 1850, he became one of the first three black men admitted to Harvard Medical School. But all three students were soon dismissed after white students complained about their presence. This bitter experience, along with the 1850 passage of the Fugitive Slave Act, convinced Delaney that blacks would never be granted equal rights or opportunities in the United States. He revived an idea he had considered as early as 1835, the formation of a free colony in Africa or South America for American blacks, and defended the idea in his 1852 book *Destiny of the Colored People in the United States*. The book's argument ran counter to the anti-immigration position held by most abolitionists, and it was condemned by many who confused it with racist-inspired colonization plans to export freed slaves to Liberia.

Delaney practiced medicine in Pittsburgh until 1856, when he moved to Chatham, Canada. In 1859, he traveled to Africa in search of an appropriate location for a black settlement. Plans continued over the next two years for the project, but nothing came of Delaney's efforts. Also in 1859, Delaney began publishing in serial form his novel *Blake; or, The Huts of America*. Delaney had been upset at Harriet Beecher Stowe's portrayal of blacks in *Uncle Tom's Cabin*, believing that she had caricatured slaves as hopelessly passive. In *Blake*, he sought to offer an alternative portrait of slave defiance and insurrection. However, he never completed the novel.

Although Delaney continued stressing the need for a free black homeland during the Civil War's first two years, by 1863 he'd thrown most of his energy into recruiting black soldiers for the Union army. Shortly before the war ended, he was commissioned the first black major in the Union Army. He served in the South with the Freedmen's Bureau until mustered out of the service in 1868.

After his return to civilian life, Delaney's career was less than stellar. He became involved in politics in South Carolina and was appointed a judge in Charleston but was impeached and briefly jailed on a corruption charge. He supported ex-Confederate general Wade Hampton's bid for the governorship in return for his reappointment to the bench. For a while in the late 1870s he was once more involved in the emigration movement, this time in response to the suppression of black privileges in the South. But he soon returned to private practice as a physician and died in obscurity in Ohio.

## FREDERICK DOUGLASS (1818–1895)

Unquestionably the most influential African American of his day, Frederick Douglass was an abolitionist leader, author, orator (his voice was described by one contemporaneous journalist as "a golden trombone"), and station-master on the Underground Railroad who opened his Rochester, New York, home to fugitives.

Born a slave in Tuckahoe, Maryland, to a slave mother and an unknown white man, Douglass was raised by his grandparents. When he was around 12 years old, a relative of his master taught him the basics of reading and writing. Although the instruction soon ended, Douglass improved his skills by secretly reading everything he could get his hands on. As he became more proficient, he started teaching other slaves to read at a weekly Sunday meeting. The school was soon discovered and broken up by white planters.

When Douglass was 16, he was hired out to Edward Covey, a poor farmer with a reputation for abusing slaves. Covey vowed to break Douglass's spirit and whipped him daily. But one day Douglass rebelled and fought Covey to a standstill. It was a turning point in Douglass's life, awakening in him a sense of dignity. "I was nothing before; I WAS A MAN NOW."[2] Shortly thereafter he made a failed run for freedom. He tried again in 1838, this time successfully, by disguising himself as a sailor, riding a train to Wilmington, Delaware, and traveling by steamboat to New York, where he was given shelter by abolitionist David Ruggles. Shortly afterward he married Anna Murray, a free black woman from Baltimore who had aided him in his escape.

Douglass and his wife settled in New Bedford, Massachusetts, where he found work as a ship caulker. He bought a subscription to William Lloyd Garrison's abolitionist weekly the *Liberator*, began attending antislavery meetings, and was soon invited to speak. His oratory was so powerful and his personal story so captivating that by 1843 he was touring northern states to speak on behalf of the American Anti-Slavery Society. Two years later, he published his *Narrative of the Life of Frederick Douglass, an American Slave*, the first of three autobiographies he would write. It was an instant success, selling thousands of copies in the United States and abroad. Its appearance both strengthened antislavery sentiment in the North and catapulted Douglass to national fame.

But the publicity also brought danger, since Douglass was still legally a slave. So in the late summer of 1845 he sailed for England, where he remained for two years, lecturing up and down the country. During his stay, sympathetic Britons collected enough money to purchase his freedom from his master. Douglass returned to the United States, settled in Rochester, and began publishing the abolitionist *North Star*, which five years later became *Frederick Douglass' Paper*. In it, Douglass published essays on the Underground Railroad, defended women's rights, argued that slavery was contrary to the spirit of the U.S. Constitution, applauded black settlements in Canada, and pressed for better educational opportunities for blacks.

In 1852, in his "Fifth of July" oration, Douglass delivered what many consider to be the single greatest speech against slavery made by an abolitionist. What does the Fourth of July matter to slaves? he asked his white audience. "Your high independence only reveals the immeasurable distance between us. . . . The rich inheritance of justice, liberty, prosperity, and independence, bequeathed by your fathers, is shared by you, not by me. The sunlight that brought life and healing to you, has brought stripes and death to me. This Fourth of July is yours, not mine. *You* may rejoice, *I* must mourn."[3]

During the Civil War, which Douglass endorsed, he publicly and privately urged President Lincoln to shift the emphasis of the conflict from a campaign to preserve the Union to a crusade to abolish slavery. After the war, he championed equal rights for blacks and land redistribution to former slaves. He accepted several political appointments, serving at various times as a federal marshal and ambassador to Haiti.

Douglass moved to Washington, D.C., in 1872 after his Rochester home burned down, possibly the work of an arsonist. Widowed 10 years later, he scandalized the nation by marrying a white woman. In his final decade, he completed work on the third version of his autobiography. He died while attending a women's rights rally in Washington, D.C.

## DANIEL DRAYTON (1802–1857)

A conductor on the eastern water route, Capt. Daniel Drayton attempted to pull off the largest single escape in U.S. slave history. It proved unsuccessful, but the publicity surrounding the attempt and Drayton's subsequent trial and imprisonment made him a hero to abolitionists.

Born in New Jersey, Drayton went to sea at an early age and by the late 1840s was master of the schooner *Pearl*. In 1847, while docked at Washington, D.C., to unload cargo, he agreed to smuggle a black family out of the city to a northern port. On earlier visits to ports around Chesapeake Bay, he had received similar requests from slaves but had refused them because, as he wrote in his memoir, he "regarded negroes as only fit to be slaves." But his views underwent a gradual change. "I knew it was asserted in the Declaration of Independence that all men are born free and equal, and I had read in the Bible that God had made of one flesh all the nations of the earth. I found out, by intercourse with the negroes, that they had the same desires, wishes, and hopes as myself. I knew very well that I should not like to be a slave even to the best of masters, and still less to such sort of masters as the greater part of slaves seems to have . . . I had never read any abolition books, nor heard any abolition lectures. . . . But, for the life of me, I could not perceive why the golden rule of doing to others as you would wish them to do to you did not apply in this case."[4]

On the evening of February 17, 1848, the *Pearl* pulled away from the dock in Washington, D.C., with 77 runaway slaves on board. Bad luck plagued the enterprise from the beginning. A black freedman informed authorities of the escape attempt, a steamboat was immediately launched in pursuit, and bad weather stalled the *Pearl* in Chesapeake Bay. Quickly overtaken, the schooner was escorted back to Washington, D.C. The slaves were paraded through the streets, jailed, and then sold south. Drayton and the *Pearl's* owner, Edwin Sayres, were charged with multiple counts of larceny.

The trial was conducted vigorously by both prosecution and defense attorneys. Despite being represented by a legal team headed by Horace Mann, Drayton was found guilty, fined the enormous sum of $10,000, and sentenced to 20 years in prison. The prison sentence was overturned on appeal, but the fine remained, with the condition that Drayton remain in prison until it was paid. Sayres received a similar punishment.

The two men languished in jail under miserable conditions for over four years until finally pardoned by President Millard Fillmore. In 1853, Drayton published a memoir of the *Pearl* rescue and his subsequent imprisonment. He died four years later. An obituary in the *Washington National Era* (July 9, 1857) stated that "Capt. Drayton's health was completely shattered by the hardships he had undergone at the hands of the kidnappers [that is, his jailers]."

## CALVIN FAIRBANK (1816–1898)

One of the best-known antebellum "abductors" of slaves, Calvin Fairbank served two separate prison terms, totaling 17 years, for helping slaves escape from bondage.

Fairbank was born in western New York. Raised in an antislavery family, he began helping slaves cross the Ohio River to freedom as early as 1837, ultimately aiding nearly 50. Ordained in the Methodist Episcopal Church when he was 26, he enrolled in Oberlin College, a hotbed of antislavery agitation, two years later. While Fairbank was at Oberlin, an escaped slave named Gilson Berry appealed to him to rescue his wife and children from slavery in Lexington, Kentucky. Fairbank agreed, and once in Lexington enlisted Delia Webster, a Vermont-born schoolteacher, in the plot. Fairbank and Webster were unable to locate Berry's family. But they did manage to get another slave family across the Ohio River and safely into the hands of Railroad stationmaster Rev. John Rankin in Ripley, Ohio.

Instead of remaining in the North, Fairbank and Webster returned to Lexington, where they were promptly arrested for "aiding and enticing slaves to leave their owners." Tried and convicted separately, Webster received two years and Fairbank five. Webster served less than two months of her sentence. Fairbank was pardoned after four years of hard labor, but only when the master of the slave he'd abducted had been paid $600 in compensation.

For the next two years, Fairbank toured northern cities and towns speaking to antislavery groups. Always more a man of action than of words, he soon returned to the business of abducting slaves from their masters. In 1851, he returned to Kentucky and conducted into Indiana a 22-year-old named Tamar who was about to be sold at auction by her Louisville master. But shortly thereafter, it was Fairbank who was abducted by Kentucky marshals, who hauled him back to Louisville on the charge of slave-stealing. Given Fairbank's notoriety in both the North and the South, the trial became something of a showcase. Fairbank was found guilty and sentenced to 15 years of hard labor. He was pardoned and released only in 1864, the last full year of the Civil War. During his 13 years in prison, he was subjected to especially harsh treatment. In his autobiography, which he published nearly a quarter-century after his release, he claimed that he'd endured more than 30,000 lashes from numerous floggings.

Fairbank's postwar years were spent in poverty, obscurity, and ill health. His autobiography sold poorly, and shortly before his death he bitterly predicted that there would not be an ex-slave or child of an ex-slave at his funeral. He was, sadly, right.

## THOMAS GARRETT (1789–1871)

A close collaborator of William Still and Harriet Tubman, Thomas Garrett was one of the leading stationmasters on the Underground Railroad's eastern route. For nearly 40 years, he used his Wilmington, Delaware, home as a depot from which he steered runaways from Delaware, Virginia, and Maryland to Philadelphia. He is credited with helping approximately 2,700 slaves to freedom.

Born in Upper Darby Township, just west of Philadelphia, Garrett was raised in a well-to-do Quaker family with abolitionist sympathies. At the age of 25, Garrett demonstrated his personal opposition to slavery by tracking down slave catchers who had snatched a family servant with the intention of selling her in the South. He caught up with the kidnappers near Philadelphia's Navy Yard and rescued the woman.

When he was in his early thirties, Garrett relocated to Wilmington, started a prosperous iron and hardware business, and became an active and open participant in Underground Railroad activities. Delaware was a slave state, and many of his neighbors were enraged by his civil disobedience. But Garrett's personal bravery and powerful physique "did not present," as William Still wrote of him, "an encouraging object for the bullying intimidation by which the pro-slavery men of that day generally overawed their opponents."[5]

In 1848, Garrett and another Wilmington Railroad worker were sued in federal court for slave stealing. Predictably, given the animosity his fellow Delawareans felt for his abolitionism, he was found guilty, and the massive fines levied by the court bankrupted him. But Garrett defiantly asserted that he hoped the trial's publicity would lead even more fugitives to his door. In fact, that is exactly what happened. Following the trial, he started a new business, which prospered as much as the old one had, and he was flooded with so many refugees that he had to build an additional story on his house to accommodate them.

Throughout the 1850s Garrett worked closely with Underground Railroad conductor Harriet Tubman, supplying her with money, clothes, shoes, food, and shelter for dozens of slaves she led to freedom. Garrett and Tubman became close friends, and he wrote glowingly of her in many letters to colleagues and acquaintances.

Unlike slave abductor Calvin Fairbank, who was all but forgotten by his contemporaries after the Civil War, Garrett was held in honor by both blacks and whites long after the Underground Railroad was a thing of the past. When the Fifteenth Amendment, giving blacks the right to vote, was ratified in 1870, jubilant Wilmington blacks saluted him as "our Moses." At his funeral the following year, his pallbearers were all ex-slaves.

## WILLIAM LLOYD GARRISON (1805–1879)

Although not directly involved in Underground Railroad activities, William Lloyd Garrison, the leading white abolitionist in the years leading up to the Civil War, was both influenced by the labors of conductors and stationmasters —particularly John Rankin of Ripley, Ohio—and in turn encouraged others to provide aid to runaway slaves. His weekly newspaper, the *Liberator*, was the best-known abolitionist publication of its day and frequently printed accounts of Railroad activity.

Garrison was born in Newburyport, Massachusetts, and raised in poverty. Apprenticed at 14 as a typesetter for the *Newburyport Herald*, he soon began writing articles under the pseudonym "Aristides." After finishing his apprenticeship, he edited a couple of papers before joining Quaker abolitionist Benjamin Lundy as co-editor of the *Genius of Universal Emancipation* in 1829. The two men took fundamentally different positions on emancipation: Lundy was a gradualist, while Garrison championed immediate and uncompensated freedom for slaves. But they worked well enough together, and their partnership ended only when Garrison was jailed for libel after accusing a Newburyport ship owner of slave-trading. Released after two months when a benefactor paid his fine, Garrison moved to Boston and in January 1831 published the first issue of the *Liberator*. In his first editorial, he memorably proclaimed his purpose: "I am aware that many object to the severity of my language; but is there not cause for severity? I will be as harsh as truth, and as uncompromising as justice. On this subject, I do not wish to think, or to speak, or write, with moderation. No! No! . . . I am in earnest—I will not equivocate—I will not excuse—I will not retreat a single inch—AND I WILL BE HEARD."[6]

A year after he launched the *Liberator*, Garrison founded the New England Anti-Slavery Society, and in the next year he co-founded the American Anti-Slavery Society. He envisioned both organizations as nonpolitical—he had come to the conclusion that the U.S. Constitution and the American political system, both of which countenanced slavery, were immoral—and open to blacks and women, not just white men. But from the beginning, these positions led to tension in both societies, eventually leading to a split in 1839 and again in 1840. One rival splinter organization refused to admit women; another focused on political action. For his part, Garrison remained an advocate of nonpolitical and nonviolent "moral suasion," believing that as the brutal facts of slavery became better known, Northern opposition to it would grow and even Southern consciences would be pricked.

Garrison's opposition to slavery continued unabated until 1865, when he published the final issue (number 1,820) of the *Liberator*. During his long career as one of the United States' most vocal abolitionists, he risked imprisonment, kidnapping, personal injury—in 1835 he was nearly lynched by an angry Boston mob—and public vilification. After the war, he devoted himself to civil rights for blacks and women and to temperance.

## JOSIAH HENSON (1789–1883)

An Underground Railroad conductor and a leader of the Dawn Settlement, one of several fugitive slave communities in Canada, Josiah Henson was born to slave parents in south central Maryland. One of his earliest memories was the brutal beating and mutilation of his father. A plantation overseer had assaulted Henson's mother, and his enraged father came to her defense. After being subdued, he was given 50 lashes with a horse-whip, his right ear was nailed to a wall and severed from his head, and he was sold south. Henson never saw him again.

As an adult, Henson became a Methodist minister. He also became a plantation manager for the man who owned him and his mother. On one occasion he was so savagely beaten by a white overseer from another plantation that both his shoulder blades were broken. Yet he believed that fleeing would be a betrayal of the trust his master showed him. Instead, he offered to purchase his freedom, and his master accepted. It was only after his master reneged on the agreement that Henson decided to run. In 1830, he fled northward with his wife and four children, enduring great hardship before they reached Canada.

Once across the border, Henson threw himself into providing for his family and building a new life. Settling originally in an old hog shed, Henson accepted any work he could find and eventually saved enough money to purchase, in 1842, the first allotment of land that eventually grew to the 1,500-acre settlement of Dawn. Ultimately attracting approximately 500 ex-slaves, Dawn operated a school of the manual arts and became famous as a producer of black walnut lumber. Throughout the settlement's existence, Henson remained one of its leaders.

In the remaining antebellum years, Henson made several tours throughout the northern states, speaking against slavery and raising money for Dawn. He also traveled twice to Kentucky, at great personal risk, to conduct slaves to freedom. He published an autobiography in 1849 (which was expanded in 1858 and again in 1876) that so impressed Harriet Beecher Stowe that the title character of her 1852 *Uncle Tom's Cabin* might have been based in part on the story of Henson's remarkable trustworthiness as a slave. At any rate, the connection between Henson and Stowe's fictional character was so established in the public mind during his lifetime that Queen Victoria insisted on meeting "Uncle Tom" when Henson visited England in 1876.

In 1878, five years before his death, Henson returned to the plantation on which he and his mother had been slaves. The plantation had become "a wilderness; the most desolate, demoralized place one can imagine." His master's daughter, now 70 and sickly, still lived in the decrepit mansion. When she met Henson, she complained of her poverty and petulantly asked whether he had brought her a gift. Henson inquired as to why she hadn't hired her ex-slaves to keep up the plantation. "'Oh,'" she replied to the man who had founded a self-sufficient colony of ex-slaves, "'they wasn't worth paying. I never could pay niggers for work.'"[7]

## WILLIAM KING (1812–1895)

An Irish-born teacher, Presbyterian minister, and former slave owner, William King was the founder of the Elgin Settlement (sometimes called Buxton, after the name of the Presbyterian mission associated with it), the most successful of the Canadian settlements of slave fugitives, and its manager for 25 years.

Educated at the University of Glasgow, King immigrated to the United States in 1833, taught school, and eventually married the daughter of a Louisiana plantation owner. In 1844 he returned to Scotland to study divinity at the University of Edinburgh. Between then and his ordination in 1846, tragedy struck: death took King's wife, two children, and father-in-law. Part of King's inheritance was 15 slaves.

Probably desiring to put as much distance between himself and Louisiana as he could, King accepted a commission as a missionary to Canada. But word soon leaked that he owned slaves, and King was censured by disapproving church authorities. King himself abominated slavery, and his reprimand by his superiors prompted his decision to free the slaves and train them in skills they would need as free men.

In 1847 King took his 15 freed slaves to Ohio, where he left them in the care of a brother while he returned to Canada and persuaded church authorities to support the founding of a settlement for ex-slaves. The Presbyterian Church, enthusiastic about the project, enlisted financial support from other denominations as well as the Canadian government. The settlement was eventually named after Lord Elgin, the governor general of Canada whose endorsement of the project was sought and gained. King was appointed managing director of the settlement, and his 15 ex-slaves, relocated from Ohio in 1849, became its founding members.

King's vision for Elgin was based on his conviction that freeing slaves wasn't enough. It was also necessary to provide them with opportunities for education, employment, and stable community that would enable them to support themselves by their own industry. The Elgin Settlement aimed to do just that. Its policy of self-sufficiency made it one of the few

Canadian communities of ex-slaves that refused to accept charitable donations from well-wishers.

King sank all of his personal fortune into Elgin, even taking out a second mortgage on a Canadian farm he owned to finance the community's activities. Although the settlement's economic situation was always precarious, it succeeded in demonstrating to the world that ex-slaves were just as capable as white men of supporting themselves and their families. As one 1864 visitor observed after visiting the settlement: "Twenty years ago, most of [the inhabitants] were slaves, who owned nothing, not even their own children. Now they own themselves; they own their houses and farms; and they have their wives and children about them."[8]

## JERMAIN LOGUEN (1813–1872)

One of the most active and open depots on the Underground Railroad was the Syracuse home of Jermain Loguen, an ex-slave, abolitionist, and minister (and, after 1868, bishop) in the African Methodist Episcopal (AME) Church. Loguen was also a leading player in the Jerry Rescue of 1851.

Born in Davidson County, Tennessee, the son of a white man (David Logue) and a slave woman, Loguen ran for freedom twice before succeeding at the age of 21. On a horse he stole from his master, he traveled the Underground Railroad to the Canadian border and settled for a while in Saint Catharines, Ontario. It was there that he appended an "n" to his last name. Learning to read, he moved to Rochester in 1837 and enrolled in the Oneida Institute, a school for free blacks that both taught manual skills and offered biblical instruction.

Ordained in the AME Church in 1840, Loguen pastored churches on both sides of the Canadian/American border but settled permanently in Syracuse toward the end of the decade. He bought real estate in the city, and by the time of his death he owned at least 13 properties. Several of them, including his own house, were used to shelter fugitives on their way to Canada. Loguen is credited with giving aid to approximately 1,500 runaways.

Throughout the 1850s, Loguen was a noted abolitionist lecturer and author. His most publicized activity was participation in the rescue of

William Henry, a fugitive slave also known as Jerry, who had settled in Syracuse. Arrested under the 1850 Fugitive Slave Act, Jerry was seized by federal marshals for deportation back to his Missouri master.

Along with Gerritt Smith, an ardent abolitionist and one of the wealthiest men in New York, Loguen led a crowd that burst into the building in which Jerry was being held, forcibly wrested him from the authorities, and secreted him away to Canada. Later indicted, Loguen fled to Canada, but he returned to Syracuse after the case fizzled out. He considered the rescue one of his finest moments.

Loguen published his account of the Jerry Rescue, as well as his own escape from bondage and subsequent career, in his 1859 memoir *The Rev. J. W. Loguen, as a Slave and as a Freeman*.

## JOHN P. PARKER (1827–1900)

For roughly 15 years before the Civil War, longtime Ripley, Ohio, resident John Parker, an ex-slave, ferried hundreds of runaways across the Ohio River from Kentucky to freedom. Although he destroyed the records he kept for fear of their discovery at the hands of slave catchers and federal officials, he estimated that during the 1850s he helped an average of one fugitive a week. Working during the night, Parker generally waited on the Kentucky side of the river until he encountered escaped slaves, whom he would then row to Ohio. But he often made forays more deeply into the Kentucky countryside to lead fugitives to the river and on more than one occasion was hotly pursued by slave catchers. His home in Ripley was frequently searched by both officers of the law and slave catchers, and he received numerous threats against his life.

Parker was born a slave in Norfolk, Virginia. While still a boy, he was sold south to a Mobile physician and forcibly marched to his new Alabama home. Despite this cruel beginning, Parker's master treated him relatively well, even allowing him to learn to read and write.

When Parker was 15, he defended a slave whom a white woman was beating by wresting the whip from her hand and striking her with it. Knowing how serious his offense was, he made a run for freedom but was caught after a few weeks of hardship and returned to his master. Apprenticed to an iron molder, he angered his superintendent, who told Parker's master that he was intractable and ought to be sold as a field hand. But

Parker managed to persuade one of his master's patients, a Mrs. Ryder, to buy him for $1,800 with the promise that he would soon purchase his freedom from her. By working several jobs and operating a pawn shop on the side, he managed to do so in a year and a half.

Parker moved first to Indiana, then Cincinnati, and finally settled in Ripley, a river town whose Underground Railroad activities made it known throughout Kentucky as the "hell hole of abolition."[9] Parker generally delivered the fugitives he ferried across the Ohio River to John Rankin, the town's leading stationmaster, who in turn sent them on to Cincinnati and other points northward. When the Civil War erupted, Parker continued aiding in the rescue of fugitives and eventually delivered, by his own estimate, more than 300 black recruits to the Union Army.

After the war, Parker operated an iron foundry in a building behind his home. He also invented a tobacco press and pulverizer for which he was granted a U.S. patent, making him one of only 55 blacks to receive patents in the 19th century. He was an omnivorous reader throughout his life, and he made sure that his children were college educated.

## JOHN RANKIN (1793–1886)

There are few participants in the Underground Railroad more influential than John Rankin, a Tennessee-born Presbyterian minister who wrote a seminal antislavery tract and also served as an active conductor for nearly 40 years. William Lloyd Garrison claimed that his reading of Rankin's book "was the cause of my entering the anti-slavery conflict,"[10] and preacher and abolitionist Henry Ward Beecher once said that Rankin and his sons "abolished slavery."[11]

Rankin was born and raised in northeastern Tennessee and ordained in 1814. Early on, he grew convinced that slavery was sinful and began preaching against it from the pulpit. Denouncing slavery was a risky thing for a clergyman to do in Tennessee, and before long Rankin's congregation let him know of their dissatisfaction. He relocated to a church in Kentucky, joined the Kentucky Abolition Society, and helped start a school for slaves, which soon closed due to public opposition.

In early 1822 Rankin crossed the Ohio River to settle in the river town of Ripley. He and his large family initially lived in a house next to the river. Seven years later, he built a home on a hill high above the town and erected a flagpole from which he hung a lit lantern every night as a beacon for fugitive slaves crossing the river from Kentucky. An estimated 2,000 runaways found shelter in the Rankin home before following Underground Railroad routes northward. Ex-slave and Ripley resident John Parker, who regularly ferried fugitives across the Ohio to freedom, worked closely with Rankin. Both men were often threatened by slave catchers searching for runaways. A bounty of $3,000 was offered for Rankin's seizure and rendition to Kentucky.

Soon after moving to Ripley, Rankin began publishing a series of antislavery essays in the local newspaper. Rankin had learned that his brother Thomas, a Virginia merchant, was a slave owner. The ostensible purpose of the essays was to convince Thomas of the error of his ways. But more broadly, they attacked the institution of slavery in general by arguing that no sound moral, scriptural, biological, or economic defense of slaveowning was possible. The essays were published in book form in 1826 as *Letters on American Slavery*. Rankin's brother, who freed his slaves the following year, was just one of many readers who found the book's antislavery arguments persuasive.

Although Ripley under Rankin's influence grew in abolitionist sentiment—when he first settled there it was a rough river town—some in his congregation were uncomfortable with his commitment to the Underground Railroad. The tension came to a head in 1846, when Rankin resigned as pastor of his church after nearly a quarter-century of ministry and founded another one for abolitionist-minded worshippers. His Railroad activities ended with the advent of the Civil War. Although he was grateful for that conflict's abolition of slavery, he regretted its carnage until the end of his days.

## DAVID RUGGLES (1810–1849)

Described by his friend Frederick Douglass as "a whole-souled man, fully imbued with a love of his afflicted and hunted people,"[12] David Ruggles aided approximately 1,000 fugitive slaves during his short life. He was one of the leading black abolitionists in the United States before his health broke when he was in his early thirties.

Ruggles was born in Connecticut to free parents. His father was a blacksmith and his mother a caterer. Both were ardent Methodists. Ruggles was well educated at free schools, and he set off for New York City when he was 16.

He worked as a mariner before opening a grocery store in which he sold only goods produced by free labor. Increasingly active in the abolitionist movement, he became a road agent for abolitionist newspapers and traveled the lecture circuit. He also started writing occasional pieces for the abolitionist press, including an 1835 essay in which he indicted white wives who turned a blind eye to their husbands' slave mistresses.

In 1834, Ruggles opened a bookstore and lending library in New York City, perhaps the first one owned by a black man. He also began publishing abolitionist pamphlets, which may be one of the reasons the store was torched by an arsonist a year later. In 1835, as a tribute to his growing presence in the abolitionist movement, Ruggles was elected secretary of the New York Committee of Vigilance.

Like vigilance committees in other northern cities, the one Ruggles headed was charged with offering assistance—food, clothing, shelter, medical treatment, sometimes money, and contacts helpful in finding employment—to fugitive slaves. Ruggles's job was to coordinate the efforts of the committee, but he also frequently offered his own home to runaways. One of them, in 1838, was Frederick Douglass. Douglass and his wife were also married in Ruggles's home. As secretary of the vigilance committee, Ruggles compiled a directory of New York City officials indicating which ones were sympathetic to fugitive slaves and which ones were hostile.

Ruggles's antislavery activity got him into trouble with local officials on several occasions. The same year he assisted Douglass, he was arrested on charges of harboring a fugitive slave from Arkansas. The charges were eventually dropped, but Ruggles spent months in jail, which seriously undermined his health. He was also sued for libel by a sea captain whom he accused of running slaves. Ruggles was exonerated, but the long-drawn-out trial exhausted him physically and emotionally, and it also bankrupted him. He resigned from the vigilance committee in 1839.

The next few years were hard. His health was broken, his eyesight was almost gone, and he lived in penury. Eventually, with the aid of other abolitionists, he moved to Massachusetts and underwent a series of hydrotherapeutic sessions, which he believed restored his health. He was so impressed by the water cure that he opened a spa himself in 1846. But his health remained fragile, and he died three years later, not having reached his 40th birthday.

## MARY ANN SHADD (1823–1893)

One of the most influential voices in the black refugee community in Canada, Mary Ann Shadd was the eldest child of free parents in Wilmington, Delaware. Her father Abraham, a shoemaker, was an active member of the Underground Railroad and the American Anti-Slavery Society and an agent in Delaware for William Lloyd's Garrison's *Liberator*. So from an early age, his daughter absorbed the spirit of abolitionism.

When she was 10 years old, Shadd's parents moved the family to West Chester, Pennsylvania, which offered better educational opportunities for their children. For the next six years, Shadd studied at a Quaker boarding school. Afterward, between 1839 and 1850, she taught in several schools for black children in Delaware, New York, and Pennsylvania.

When the 1850 Fugitive Slave Act was signed into law, Shadd, her father, and her brother Isaac joined the flood of black migration to Canada. Settling in Windsor, she opened an integrated school with the assistance of the American Missionary Association and began lecturing in the northern states in support of black emigration to Canada. She was convinced that the only chance blacks had for genuine prosperity and freedom was settlement in Canada.

In 1853, Shadd and ex-slave and Underground Railroad worker Samuel Ringgold Ward launched the *Provincial Freeman*, a newspaper that would run, with one interruption, until 1858. It was the second black newspaper in Canada, following Henry Bibb's *Voice of the Fugitive* founded two years earlier. In the pages of her newspaper, Shadd soon engaged in a bitter feud with Bibb about black immigrants in Canada. Bibb argued that blacks should live in black settlements and send their children to black schools. He also defended the solicitation of funds from white charities and individuals to found and support black settlements. Shadd, on the other hand, was a fierce proponent of integration and a withering foe of white charity to blacks. "Self reliance," she insisted, "is the fine road to independence." She criticized black clergymen who failed to defend education and self-sufficiency when preaching to their flocks. And hers was also one of the earliest voices for women's rights. Frederick Douglass called her a woman of "unceasing industry" and "unconquerable zeal." "We do not know her equal," he concluded, "among the colored ladies of the United States."[13]

In 1856, Shadd married Thomas Cary, a barber from Toronto. When Cary died in 1860, leaving her a widow with two children, she closed down the *Provincial Freeman* and returned to the United States. During the Civil War she recruited black soldiers for the Union Army and taught school in Washington, D.C. Four years after the war's end, she enrolled in Howard University's law school, receiving her degree in 1883. Just as she had been the first African American woman to edit a newspaper, she became the second one to be admitted to the bar.

In her later years, Shadd worked closely with Susan B. Anthony and Elizabeth Cady for women's suffrage.

## WILLIAM STILL (1819 or 1821–1902)

Along with Thomas Garrett, William Still was the leading stationmaster on the eastern route of the Underground Railroad. Located in Philadelphia, he was particularly active in assisting fugitives in the decade leading up to the Civil War.

Still was born in New Jersey to Levin and Charity Still. His father, an ex-slave from Maryland's eastern shore, had purchased his freedom and moved north. Afterward, his mother escaped to freedom with their four children and joined him. Captured and returned to slavery, she escaped a second time, but had to leave her two sons behind. In retaliation for her escape, her sons were sold south. Still was born after his mother's second successful escape.

Settling in Philadelphia in 1844, Still took a position three years later as janitor and clerk with the Pennsylvania Society for the Abolition of Slavery. He also began a stove and coal business that eventually proved quite lucrative. When a vigilance committee to aid runaways was organized in Philadelphia following the passage of the 1850 Fugitive Slave Act, Still was elected secretary and for the next 10 years supervised the Underground Railroad in Philadelphia, working closely with Garrett and Harriet Tubman. Frequently offering fugitive slaves refuge in his own home, Still more typically coordinated efforts that ensured that fugitives were fed, clothed, medically treated, and properly sheltered until they could be moved northward on the Railroad.

Still also kept meticulous records of many of the slaves that passed through his station, noting their names, origins, escape stories and, in many cases, their destinations. Fearing that these documents would wind up in the hands of slave catchers or federal authorities, Still hid them until after the Civil War ended. Then he retrieved them, wrote them up into a narrative, added to them sketches of Railroad conductors and station-masters, and published them in 1872 as *The Underground Rail Road.* The book is one of the few contemporaneous records of the Underground Railroad written by a black man. Curiously, one of the refugees Still wound up helping was a brother whom he didn't know he had—one of the two youths Chastity left behind when she fled slavery a second time.

In 1855, largely in response to Southern insistence that free blacks lacked the skills, intelligence, and initiative to be self-supporting, Still traveled to Ontario to observe firsthand and report on the condition of refugee slaves living there in the black settlements. Beginning in 1861 and continuing for the next several years, Still lobbied for equal access and treatment of black passengers on Philadelphia's street and rail cars.

After the war, his business thriving, Still turned his energy to philan-thropy and social reform in the Philadelphia area. He was instrumental in the establishment of a YMCA for black men, a mission school, and an orphanage for the children of black soldiers and sailors.


## HARRIET BEECHER STOWE (1811–1896)

Although she wasn't directly involved with the Underground Railroad, Harriet Beecher Stowe heard the stories of many slave refugees through her acquaintance with stationmasters like Levi Coffin. She included some of them in her best-known work, *Uncle Tom's Cabin*—a novel, Abraham Lincoln later quipped, that started the Civil War—and thereby exerted a powerful influence on antislavery sentiment in the northern states (not to mention anti-Northern sentiment in the South).

Born in Connecticut to Congregational minister and abolitionist Lyman Beecher, Stowe moved with him to Cincinnati when he was ap-pointed president of a theological seminary there in 1832. She married Calvin Stowe, a professor at the seminary, and began raising a family. It was during her years in Cincinnati, a town separated from the slave state of Kentucky by the Ohio River, that Stowe, already an abolitionist, heard accounts of bondage and escape from both Underground Railroad agents and runaways.

Stowe began writing shortly before her marriage. Afterward, in order to supplement her husband's small income, she became a regular contributor to several magazines. Her first book, a collection of short stories, appeared in 1843. But her reputation soared in 1851 when she began serializing *Uncle Tom's Cabin* in the abolitionist periodical *National Era*. The entire novel was published the following year and became an instant best seller. Readers snatched up more than 3,000 copies the first day and 300,000 by the end of the year. Eventually the book was translated into 22 languages.

Southern readers, who for the most part were outraged by Stowe's depiction of slave owners and overseers, claimed the book was a crude caricature. In response, Stowe published *A Key to Uncle Tom's Cabin* in 1852, a compendium of all the factual documents she had consulted in writing the book. As she described her novel in *A Key*, "This work, more, perhaps, than any other work of fiction that ever was written, has been a collection and arrangement of real incidents, of actions really performed, of words and expressions really uttered, grouped together with reference to a general result, in the same manner that the mosaic artist groups his fragments of various stones into one general picture. His is a mosaic of gems—this is a mosaic of facts."[14] Even though *Uncle Tom's Cabin* may not appeal to modern literary tastes, Stowe's *Key* remains an interesting historical resource.

After the success of *Uncle Tom's Cabin*, Stowe discovered that she was in great demand as an author. In subsequent years she published several more novels as well as travelogues and numerous articles on social issues. Her later years were plagued by misfortune, however. Two of her children died under miserable circumstances, and in the 1870s a beloved brother, the well-known preacher Henry Ward Beecher, was embroiled in a nationally publicized adultery scandal. The hubbub was so relentless that Stowe retreated to Florida for a while to escape it. While there, she published the travelogue *Palmetto Leaves*. In later years she returned north, and she died in Connecticut.

## HARRIET TUBMAN (1822–1913)

The most famous of all Underground Railroad agents, Harriet Tubman was both a conductor and an abductor. By most accounts, she made

19 trips below the Mason-Dixon Line to lead more than 300 slaves to freedom. Many of them were her relatives. A close collaborator with other Underground Railroad leaders such as William Still and Thomas Garrett, Tubman was admired by abolitionists as much as she was reviled by slave owners. John Brown referred to her as a "general," and slaves and freedmen alike called her "Moses."

Tubman was born a slave in Maryland and set to work as a maid while still a child. When she was 12 she was sent to the fields and regularly beaten. At the age of 13 she was hit over the head with a lead weight, lay unconscious for several days, and suffered periodic blackouts for the rest of her life. An intensely religious woman, Tubman thought of the episodes as experiences of the divine.

She married in 1844 and made a run for freedom five years later. Her husband refused to accompany her. Making her way to Philadelphia, she worked several jobs for the next couple of years until she had sufficient funds to return south. Although her husband, who had remarried, still refused to follow her to the North, Tubman began taking away her immediate family members as well as acquaintances and strangers. In 1857, she succeeded in leading her elderly parents to freedom—a particularly difficult task, given their age.

Tubman was a disciplined and no-nonsense conductor. She regularly carried a firearm on her excursions, not only to protect herself from slave catchers but also to threaten the faint-hearted among the fugitives she was leading northward. She gave sleeping potions to infants whose crying might alert slave patrols, and she was adept at locating well-hidden, obscure routes of travel. When she went to the South seeking slaves who wished to run, she often disguised herself as an old man or woman; as she walked, she sang hymns with revealing lyrics to let slaves know who she was. Her tactics paid off. As Tubman was fond of boasting, she never lost a passenger the whole time she was conducting on the Underground Railroad.

In the 1850s, Tubman's home base was Saint Catharines, Ontario. She lived there out of fear of the 1850 Fugitive Slave Act, and as the decade progressed she began to lead fugitives all the way to Canada instead of settling them in any northern state. Her usual method was to work jobs between journeys to the South, saving up money to fund her trips. When she returned with fugitives, she frequently requested material aid from the many antislavery societies in the northern states. Delaware's Thomas Garrett was especially helpful.

Tubman bought a home in Auburn, New York, shortly before the Civil War. During the conflict, she joined the Union Army in South Carolina as a scout and nurse. On one excursion, known as the Combahee River Raid, Tubman guided three steamboats around Confederate mines she had scouted out earlier to rescue more than 700 slaves. She received no salary for her service and was granted a governmental pension only in 1899.

Tubman returned to her Auburn home after the war. In 1869, she married a second time, and the same year saw the publication of *Scenes from the Life of Harriet Tubman*, an autobiography narrated by Tubman and transcribed by her friend Sarah Bradford. Tubman was active in the women's suffrage movement, traveling at various times to New York, Boston, and Washington, D.C., to advocate for it. After the death of her husband she converted her home into a facility for elderly and indigent black men and women, where she herself died.

## DAVID WALKER (1785–1830)

One of the enduring myths about the Underground Railroad in particular and American slavery in general is that slaves were for the most part passive, too cowed by bondage to initiate rebellion or to escape, and that the abolitionist movement was largely a white affair. The several slave insurrections in the South, the number of runaways to the North, and the existence of some 50 black abolitionist groups before whites even began organizing in the 1830s testify to the contrary.

One of the most eloquent exemplars of antebellum black initiative was David Walker, author of the 1829 *Appeal to the Colored Citizens of the World*. Walker was born in North Carolina to a free mother and an enslaved father. He traveled widely as a young man, moving from Charleston to Philadelphia and eventually to Boston, where he settled in the 1820s. He ran a used clothing store there and soon made a local name for himself as an eloquent abolitionist spokesman.

Walker's *Appeal* was cleverly modeled after the U.S. Constitution. He called its Introduction a "Preamble" and its four chapters "Articles." His intention was to suggest that the Constitution, given its support of slavery, was in need of legal and moral supplementation. In the pamphlet he argued for immediate, universal, and uncompensated emancipation. He criticized slavery-endorsing churches for their abandonment of Christian values and criticized patriots for their hypocrisy in touting American freedom while either embracing or tolerating slavery. Most notoriously, he called upon blacks, free as well as enslaved, to take their destiny into their own hands. To his black readers, he wrote: "There is a great work for you to do, as trifling as some of you may think of it. You have to prove to the Americans and the world, that we are MEN, and not *brutes*, as we have been represented, and by millions treated."[15] To whites, he issued a warning: "Remember Americans, that we must and shall be free and enlightened as you are, will you wait until we shall, under God, obtain our liberty by the crushing arm of power? Will it not be dreadful for you? I speak Americans for your good. We must and shall be free I say, in spite of you. . . . And woe, woe, will be to you if we have to obtain our freedom by fighting."[16]

Three editions of Walker's *Appeal* were printed within a year. He urged literate blacks to discuss its contents with freedmen and slaves who couldn't read. He gave copies of the book to black sailors traveling to southern ports, and there are reports that he even sewed copies inside the lining of clothes he sold in his shop. The *Appeal* energized black abolitionists, even though some white ones found it too radical. But, unsurprisingly, it enraged and frightened Southerners. Copies were banned throughout the southern states and very soon a bounty, funded by planters, was placed on Walker's head.

Walker died in 1830. His friends and defenders rumored that he'd been poisoned, but in all probability he died of tuberculosis.

## JONATHAN WALKER (1799–1878)

A water route conductor who was, notoriously, branded on orders of a Florida court for attempting to sail slaves to freedom, Jonathan Walker was born in Cape Cod, Massachusetts, and relocated to Florida in 1836. But five years later he returned to the North because, he wrote, he couldn't bear to expose his children to the "poisonous influences of slavery."

In early summer 1844, Walker returned to Florida with the intention of salvaging copper from a wrecked ship. But while in Pensacola, he agreed to pilot seven runaways in a small boat from Florida to the Bahamas. En route, Walker fell ill with sunstroke and the boat drifted until discovered by a sloop. The slaves and Walker were returned to Florida, and Walker was imprisoned in a Pensacola jail, chained to the floor, verbally abused by guards, and poorly and infrequently fed. He endured this treatment for four months before coming to trial.

No one was surprised when Walker was found guilty of "slave stealing." But what shocked many throughout the nation was that the judge ordered Walker's right hand branded with the letters "S.S." for "Slave Stealer." The Quaker poet and abolitionist John Greenleaf Whittier would later write that the "S.S." properly stood for "Slave Savior." After the branding, Walker was pilloried for an hour, during which Pensacola citizens pelted him with rotten eggs. Finally, he was heavily fined and remanded to prison until the fine was paid. He languished in jail, suffering mistreatment and malnutrition, for nearly a year before Northern well-wishers collected enough money to pay off his debt.

After his release, Walker toured the northern states for a few years describing his ordeal and speaking against slavery. He published an account of his imprisonment in 1854. Hundreds of copies of a daguerreotype of his branded hand circulated throughout the nation. Walker eventually moved to Michigan, where he resided until his death.

## SAMUEL RINGGOLD WARD (1817–1866)

Known as "the black Daniel Webster" because of his oratorical skills, Samuel Ringgold Ward was a Congregational minister, a vice-presidential nominee of the emancipationist Liberty Party, and a zealous abolitionist who worked at various times for the American Anti-Slavery Society and the Anti-Slavery Society of Canada.

Born to slave parents in Maryland—his father claimed descent from an African prince—his family fled to freedom when he was three years old, first to New Jersey and then New York City. Ward attended the famous African Free School, established in 1787 by the New York Manumission Society for the education of black children. He was licensed to preach by the New York Congregational Association in 1839 but spent the next two years as a travelling representative of the American and New York Anti-Slavery Societies. He was ordained in 1841 and served churches in

New York state, interrupted by a brief trip abroad for his health, for the next 10 years.

In addition to his pastoral work, Ward became involved in politics. Unlike abolitionists influenced by William Lloyd Garrison, who rejected all political activity under the assumption that the U.S. Constitution was inherently tainted because of its defense of slavery, Ward believed that emancipation of slaves was ultimately a question of legislation rather than moral suasion. Throughout the 1840s he was active in both the Liberty Party and the Free Soil Party and spoke against slavery from both political lectern and church pulpit.

Ward moved his family to Syracuse with the intention, he writes in his memoir, to settle his affairs and migrate to Canada. Along with hundreds of other ex-slaves, he feared that the passage of the 1850 Fugitive Slave Act put him in jeopardy. But his departure from the United States was accelerated by his participation in the Jerry Rescue in October 1851. Fearing arrest, he and his family fled to Canada immediately after the rescue.

In Canada, he co-edited the *Provincial Freeman* with Mary Ann Shadd and worked for the Anti-Slavery Society of Canada, which soon sent him to England to raise funds for the relief of American slaves migrating to Canada. He stayed there two years, and his success in securing financial support for the Anti-Slavery Society exceeded all expectations. While in England he also published his *Autobiography of a Fugitive Slave* (1855).

Unwilling to return to the United States, Ward used the royalties from the publication of his memoir to relocate to Jamaica, where he farmed and ministered to a small congregation until his death.

## DELIA WEBSTER (1817–1904)

Abolitionist and Underground Railroad conductor Delia Webster is best known for her abduction, in collaboration with Calvin Fairbank, of a Kentucky family of slaves. Although the family was safely delivered to Ohio, both Fairbank and Webster were subsequently captured by authorities, tried, convicted, and imprisoned.

Webster was born in Vermont, studied for a while at Oberlin College, and moved to Lexington, Kentucky, when she was 25. Two years later, in

1844, she assumed the leadership of an exclusive school for girls when the owners and founders, long suspected of aiding slave fugitives, fled to the North.

Fairbank, who had already guided more than 40 slaves to freedom, was asked by fugitive Gilson Berry, whom he'd met in Oberlin, to travel to Kentucky in order to rescue the family Berry had left behind when he fled slavery. Fairbank agreed, and when he arrived in Lexington asked Webster, whom he also knew from Oberlin, to help. The Berry rescue fell through for a number of reasons. But in the meantime, Fairbank and Webster conspired to abduct Lewis Hayden, his wife, and their son. In late September 1844, they hired a carriage, drove to Hayden's residence, hid the son on the carriage floor, whitened Hayden's and his wife's faces with flour, and transported the three of them to the Ohio River. Once there, they were ferried across and delivered to John Rankin in Ripley, who sent them on their way northward, first to Oberlin, then to Sandusky, and finally to Canada.

Webster and Fairbank were arrested on their way back to Lexington. In separate trials, they were convicted and sentenced to prison. Webster received two years. But public outrage over the incarceration of a woman—even though her time in jail seems to have been relatively comfortable—prompted the governor of Kentucky to pardon her in February 1845. She served less than two months.

Webster returned to Vermont and wrote a short account of her trial and conviction sardonically entitled *Kentucky Jurisprudence*. She taught school in the North for a few years and associated with abolitionist societies. But in 1852 she bought a 600-acre farm in Kentucky, not far from the Ohio River. Webster's publicly stated plan was to open a school and hire free black labor to work the farm, but it's clear that her real purpose in purchasing the land was to establish a station for the Underground Railroad on the Kentucky side of the Ohio River. Her efforts were stymied from the start by hostility from local whites who correctly suspected her complicity in the disappearance of several slaves. She was actually arrested and jailed for several weeks, but in 1854 she slipped away and settled in a town in Ohio.

In later life, Webster suffered from poverty and, like her colleague Calvin Fairbank, was all but forgotten by the public and the press.

## NOTES

1. Levi Coffin, *Reminiscences* (Cincinnati: Western Tract Society, 1876), 109.

2. Frederick Douglass, *My Bondage and My Freedom*, ed. John Stauffer (New York: Modern Library, 2003), 140.

3. Frederick Douglass, "Extract from an Oration, at Rochester, July 5, 1852," in ibid., 273.

4. Daniel Drayton, *Personal Memoir of Daniel Drayton, for Four Years and Four Months a Prisoner (for charity's sake) in Washington Jail* (Boston: Bela Marsh and New York: American and Foreign Anti-Slavery Society, 1853), 20–21.

5. William Still, *The Underground Rail Road* (Philadelphia: Porter & Coates, 1872), 649.

6. William Lloyd Garrison, "To the Public," January 1, 1831, in *William Lloyd Garrison and the Fight against Slavery: Selections from the Liberator*, ed. William E. Cain (New York: Bedford/St. Martin's, 1994), 70.

7. Josiah Henson, *Autobiography of Josiah Henson* (Mineola, NY: Dover, 1969), 160–61.

8. Fred Landon, "The Buxton Settlement in Canada," *Journal of Negro History* 3 (1918): 366.

9. Stuart Seely Sprague, ed., *His Promised Land: The Autobiography of John P. Parker* (New York: W.W. Norton, 1996), 87.

10. Quoted in Ann Hagedorn, *Beyond the River: The Untold Story of the Heroes of the Underground Railroad* (New York: Simon & Schuster, 2002), 58.

11. William Birney, *James G. Birney and His Times* (New York: Appleton, 1890), 168.

12. Douglass, *My Bondage and My Freedom*, 202.

13. Quoted in Jane Rhodes, *Mary Ann Shadd Cary: The Black Press and Protest in the Nineteenth Century* (Bloomington: Indiana University Press, 1999), xi.

14. Harriet Beecher Stowe, *A Key to Uncle Tom's Cabin* (Boston: John P. Jewett, 1854), 5.

15. David Walker, *Appeal to the Colored Citizens of the World*, ed. Peter P. Hinks (University Park: Pennsylvania State University Press, 2006), 32.

16. Ibid., 72–73.

# Appendix:
# Primary Documents
# of the Underground
# Railroad

## Fugitive Slave Clause, Northwest Ordinance (1787)

Enacted by the Continental Congress, the Northwest Ordinance established land north of the Ohio and east of the Mississippi rivers as official U.S. territory. The land was ceded by the British after the War of Independence. The ordinance forbade slavery in the Northwest Territory but permitted rendering fugitive slaves to their owners.

> Article VI. There shall be neither slavery nor involuntary servitude in the said Territory, otherwise than in the punishment of crimes, whereof the party shall have been duly convicted; provided, always, that any person escaping into the same, from whom labor or service is lawfully claimed in any one of the original States, such fugitive may be lawfully reclaimed and conveyed to the person claiming his or her labor or service aforesaid. Approved 13 July 1787.

> **Source:** *Supplement to the First Volume of the Columbian Magazine* (Philadelphia, 1787), 855.

## Fugitive Slave Clause, U.S. Constitution (1787)

Submitted by South Carolina's two delegates to the Constitutional Convention, this clause extended Article VI of the Northwest Ordinance to the 13 and all future states. The two documents made all activities of the future Underground Railroad de facto illegal. The Fugitive Slave Clause was superseded by the Thirteenth Amendment, ratified in 1865.

> Article IV, Section 2. No person held to service or labor in one State, under the laws thereof, escaping into another, shall, in consequence of any law or regulation therein, be discharged from such service or labor, but shall be delivered up on claim of the party to whom such service or labor may be due. Approved 13 September 1787.
>
> **Source:** National Archives (http://www.archives.gov/exhibits/charters/constitution_transcript.html)

## Fugitive Slave Act of 1793

Both the Northwest Ordinance and the U.S. Constitution mandated the return of runaway slaves to their masters. But neither document prescribed the means for doing so. The Fugitive Slave Act of 1793 attempted to fill that gap.

> An Act respecting fugitives from justice, and persons escaping from the service of their masters.
>
> *Be it enacted,* That, whenever the Executive authority of any State in the Union, or of either of the Territories Northwest or South of the river Ohio, shall demand any person as a fugitive from justice, of the Executive authority of any such State or Territory to which such person shall have fled, and shall moreover produce the copy of an indictment found, or an affidavit made before a magistrate of any State or Territory as aforesaid, charging the person so demanded with having committed treason, felony, or other crime, certified as authentic by the Governor or Chief Magistrate of the State or Territory from whence the person so charged fled, it shall be the duty of the executive authority of the State or Territory to which such person shall have fled, to cause his or her arrest to be given to the Executive authority making such demand, or to the agent when he shall appear. . . .
>
> Section 2. *And be it further enacted,* That any agent appointed as aforesaid, who shall receive the fugitive into his custody, shall be empowered to transport him or her to the State or Territory from which he or she shall have fled. And if any person or persons shall, by force, set at liberty, or rescue the fugitive from such agent while transporting, as aforesaid, the person or persons so offending shall, on convic-

tion, be fined not exceeding five hundred dollars, and be imprisoned not exceeding one year.

Section 3. *And be it also enacted,* That when a person held to labour . . . shall escape into any other part of the said States or Territory, the person to whom such labor or service may be due, his agent or attorney, is hereby empowered to seize or arrest such fugitive from labor, and to take him or her before any Judge of the Circuit or District Courts of the United States, residing or being within the State, or before any magistrate of a county, city, or town corporate, wherein such seizure or arrest shall be made, and upon proof to the satisfaction of such Judge or magistrate, either by oral testimony or affidavit taken before and certified by a magistrate of any such State or Territory, that the person so seized or arrested, doth, under the laws of the State or Territory from which he or she fled, owe service or labor to the person claiming him or her, it shall be the duty of such Judge or magistrate to give a certificate thereof to such claimant, his agent, or attorney, which shall be sufficient warrant for removing the said fugitive from labor to the State or Territory from which he or she fled.

Section 4. *And be it further enacted,* That any person who shall knowingly and willingly obstruct or hinder such claimant, his agent, or attorney, in so seizing or arresting such fugitive from labor, or shall rescue such fugitive from such claimant, his agent or attorney, when so arrested pursuant to the authority herein given and declared; or shall harbor or conceal such person after notice that he or she was a fugitive from labor, as aforesaid, shall, for either of the said offences, forfeit and pay the sum of five hundred dollars. Which penalty may be recovered by and for the benefit of such claimant, by action of debt, in any Court proper to try the same, saving moreover to the person claiming such labor or service his right of action for or on account of the said injuries, or either of them. Approved, February 12, 1793.

**Source:** "Annals of Congress, 2nd Congress, 2nd Session (November 5, 1792 to March 2, 1793)," in *Proceedings and Debates of the House of Representatives of the United States at the Second Session of the Second Congress, Begun at the City of Philadelphia, November 5, 1791,* pp. 1414–15.

## Fugitive Slave Act of 1850

States opposed to slavery ignored or undermined the Fugitive Slave Act of 1793. Many of them passed "Personal Liberty" laws to protect fugitives, forbade local officials to cooperate with federal authorities in the pursuit of runaways, and turned a blind eye to Underground Railroad rescues. Under pressure from angry slaveholders, Congress passed a new Act in 1850 that incorporated the first one's provisions and added harsh penalties for noncompliance.

> . . . Section 5. And be it further enacted, That it shall be the duty of all marshals and deputy marshals to obey and execute all warrants and precepts issued under the provisions of this act, when to them directed; and should any marshal or deputy marshal refuse to receive such warrant, or other process, when tendered, or to use all proper means diligently to execute the same, he shall, on conviction thereof, be fined in the sum of one thousand dollars, to the use of such claimant . . . ; and after arrest of such fugitive, by such marshal or his deputy, or whilst at any time in his custody under the provisions of this act, should such fugitive escape, whether with or without the assent of such marshal or his deputy, such marshal shall be liable, on his official bond, to be prosecuted for the benefit of such claimant, for the full value of the service or labor of said fugitive . . . : and the better to enable the said commissioners, when thus appointed, to execute their duties faithfully and efficiently, . . . they are hereby authorized and empowered . . . to summon and call to their aid the bystanders, or *posse comitatus* of the proper county, when necessary to ensure a faithful observance of the clause of the Constitution referred to, in conformity with the provisions of this act; and all good citizens are hereby commanded to aid and assist in the prompt and efficient execution of this law, whenever their services may be required, as aforesaid, for that purpose; and said warrants shall run, and be executed by said officers, anywhere in the State within which they are issued.
>
> Section 6. And be it further enacted, That when a person held to service or labor in any State or Territory of the United States, has heretofore or shall hereafter escape into another State or Territory of the United States, the person or persons to whom such service or labor may be due, or his, her, or their agent or attorney, duly authorized, by power of attorney, in writing, acknowledged and certified under the seal of some legal officer or court of the State or Territory in which the same may be executed, may pursue and reclaim such fugitive person, either by procuring a warrant from some one of the courts, judges, or commissioners aforesaid, of the proper circuit, district, or county, for

the apprehension of such fugitive from service or labor, or by seizing and arresting such fugitive, where the same can be done without
process, and by taking, or causing such person to be taken, forthwith
before such court, judge, or commissioner, whose duty it shall be to
hear and determine the case of such claimant in a summary manner. . . . In no trial or hearing under this act shall the testimony of
such alleged fugitive be admitted in evidence. . . .

Section 7. And be it further enacted, That any person who shall
knowingly and willingly obstruct, hinder, or prevent such claimant,
his agent or attorney, or any person or persons lawfully assisting him,
her, or them, from arresting such a fugitive from service or labor, either with or without process as aforesaid, or shall rescue, or attempt
to rescue, such fugitive from service or labor, from the custody of such
claimant, his or her agent or attorney, or other person or persons lawfully assisting as aforesaid, when so arrested, pursuant to the authority
herein given and declared; or shall aid, abet, or assist such person so
owing service or labor as aforesaid, directly or indirectly, to escape from
such claimant, his agent or attorney, or other person or persons legally
authorized as aforesaid; or shall harbor or conceal such fugitive, so as
to prevent the discovery and arrest of such person, after notice or
knowledge of the fact that such person was a fugitive from service or
labor as aforesaid, shall, for either of said offences, be subject to a fine
not exceeding one thousand dollars, and imprisonment not exceeding six months . . . ; and shall moreover forfeit and pay, by way of civil
damages to the party injured by such illegal conduct, the sum of one
thousand dollars for each fugitive so lost. . . .

Section 8. And be it further enacted, That the marshals, their deputies, and the clerks of the said District and Territorial Courts, shall be
paid, for their services, the like fees as may be allowed for similar services in other cases; and where such services are rendered exclusively
in the arrest, custody, and delivery of the fugitive to the claimant, his
or her agent or attorney, or where such supposed fugitive may be dis-
charged out of custody for the want of sufficient proof as aforesaid,
then such fees are to be paid in whole by such claimant, his or her
agent or attorney; and in all cases where the proceedings are before a
commissioner, he shall be entitled to a fee of ten dollars in full for his
services in each case, upon the delivery of the said certificate to the
claimant, his agent or attorney; or a fee of five dollars in cases where
the proof shall not, in the opinion of such commissioner, warrant such
certificate and delivery, inclusive of all services incident to such

arrest and examination, to be paid, in either case, by the claimant, his or her agent or attorney. . . .

Section 9. And be it further enacted, That, upon affidavit made by the claimant of such fugitive, his agent or attorney, after such certificate has been issued, that he has reason to apprehend that such fugitive will he rescued by force from his or their possession before he can be taken beyond the limits of the State in which the arrest is made, it shall be the duty of the officer making the arrest to retain such fugitive in his custody, and to remove him to the State whence he fled, and there to deliver him to said claimant, his agent, or attorney. And to this end, the officer aforesaid is hereby authorized and required to employ so many persons as he may deem necessary to overcome such force, and to retain them in his service so long as circumstances may require. . . .

Section 10. And be it further enacted, That when any person held to service or labor in any State or Territory, or in the District of Columbia, shall escape therefrom, the party to whom such service or labor shall be due, his, her, or their agent or attorney, may apply to any court of record therein, or judge thereof in vacation, and make satisfactory proof to such court, or judge in vacation, of the escape aforesaid, and that the person escaping owed service or labor to such party . . . And the said court, commissioner, judge, or other person authorized by this act to grant certificates to claimants or fugitives, shall, upon the production of the record and other evidences aforesaid, grant to such claimant a certificate of his right to take any such person identified and proved to be owing service or labor as aforesaid, which certificate shall authorize such claimant to seize or arrest and transport such person to the State or Territory from which he escaped. . . . Approved, September 18, 1850.

**Source:** Fugitive Slave Act. U.S. Statutes at Large, 9 (1850): 462–65.

## Two Abductions of Fugitive Slaves (1836, 1844)

Slave catchers hired by the owners of fugitive slaves frequently traveled north in pursuit of their quarry. Although abductions of Northern blacks increased after the 1850 Fugitive Slave Act, they also occurred in the decades preceding it. Neither fugitives nor free blacks, especially those in the border states, were entirely safe. These two newspaper accounts, the first written by black abolitionist David Ruggles and the second by ex-slave

William Wells Brown, tell of kidnappings in New York City and the District of Columbia.

## THE KIDNAPPING OF GEORGE JONES, 1836

It is too bad to be told, much less to be endured!—On Saturday, 23 August, about 12 o'clock, Mr. George Jones, a respectable free colored man, was arrested at 21 Broadway, by certain police officers, upon the pretext of his having "committed assault and battery." Mr. Jones, being conscious that no such charge could be sustained against him, refused to go with the officers. His employers, placing high confidence in his integrity, advised him to go and answer to the charge, promising that any assistance should be afforded to satisfy the end of justice. He proceeded with the officers, accompanied with a gentleman who would have stood his bail—he was locked up in Bridewell [Prison]—his friend was told that "when he was wanted he could be sent for." Between the hours of 1 and 2 o'clock, Mr. Jones was carried before the Hon. Richard Riker, Recorder of the City of New York. In the absence of his friends, and in the presence of several notorious kidnappers, who preferred and by oath sustained that he was a runaway slave, poor Jones, having no one to utter a word in his behalf but a boy, in the absence of numerous friends who could have borne testimony to his freedom, was by the Recorder pronounced to be a SLAVE!

In less than three hours after his arrest, he was bound in chains, dragged through the streets, like a beast to the shambles! My depressed countrymen, we are all liable; your wives and children are at the mercy of merciless kidnappers. We have no protection in law, because the legislators withhold justice. We must no longer depend on the interposition of Manumission or Anti-Slavery Societies, in the hope of peaceable and just protection; where such outrages are committed, peace and justice cannot dwell. While we are subject to be thusly inhumanly practiced upon, no man is safe; we must look to our own safety and protection from kidnappers, remembering that self-defense is the first law of nature.

Let a meeting be called—let every man who has sympathy in his heart to feel when bleeding inhumanity is thus stabbed afresh, attend the meeting; let a remedy be prescribed to protect us from slavery. Whenever necessity requires, let that remedy be applied. Come what will, anything is better than slavery.

**Source:** *Liberator*, August 6, 1836.

# THE KIDNAPPING OF YOUNG WILKINSON, 1844

I left Cadiz this morning at four o'clock, on my way for Mount Pleasant. Passing through Georgetown at about five o'clock, I found the citizens standing upon the corners of the streets, talking as though something had occurred during the night. Upon inquiry I learned that about ten o'clock at night, five or six men went to the house of a colored man by the name of John Wilkinson, broke open the door, knocked down the man and his wife, and beat them severely, and seized their boy, aged fourteen years, and carried him off into slavery. After the father of the boy had recovered himself, he raised the alarm, and with the aid of some of the neighbors, put out in pursuit of the kidnappers, and followed them to the river; but they were too late. The villains crossed the river, and passed into Virginia. I visited the afflicted family this morning. When I entered the house, I found the mother seated with her face buried in her hands, weeping for the loss of her child. The mother was much bruised, and the floor was covered in several places in blood. I had been in the house but a short time, when the father returned from the chase of the kidnappers. When he entered the house, and told the wife that their child was lost forever, the mother wrung her hands and screamed out, "Oh, my boy! Oh my boy! I want to see my child!" and raved as though she was a maniac. I was compelled to turn aside and weep for the first time I came into the State. I would that every Northern apologist for slavery could have been present to have beheld that scene. I hope to God that it may never be my lot to behold another such. One of the villains was recognized, but it was by a colored man, and the colored people have not the right of their oath in this State. This villain will go unwhipped by Justice. What have the North to do with Slavery?

**Source:** *National Anti-Slavery Standard* (New York), November 7, 1844.

# The Underground Railroad in Indiana (1826–1847)

Quaker Levi Coffin was one of the most important Underground Railroad stationmasters of his day. Originally from North Carolina, he relocated to Newport, Indiana, in 1826 before settling in Ohio nearly 20 years later. This passage from his memoirs describes his Railroad work during the Indiana period.

Soon after we located at Newport, I found that we were on a line of the U.G.R.R. [Underground Railroad]. Fugitives [who] often passed through that place were often pursued and captured . . . I was pained to hear of the capture of these fugitives, and inquired of some of the Friends [Quakers] in our village why they did not take them in and secrete them, when they were pursued, and then aid them on their way to Canada? I found that they were afraid of the penalty of the law. I told them that I read in the Bible when I was a boy that it was right to take in the stranger and administer to those in distress, and that I thought it was always safe to do right. The Bible, in bidding us to feed the hungry and clothe the naked, said nothing about color, and I should try to follow out the teachings of that good book. I was willing to receive and aid as many fugitives as were disposed to come to my house. I knew that my wife's feelings and sympathies regarding this matter were the same as mine, and that she was willing to do her part. It soon became known to the colored people in our neighborhood and others, that our house was a depot where the hunted and harassed fugitive journeying northward, on the Underground Railroad, could find succor and sympathy. It also became known at other depots on the various lines that converged at Newport.

In the winter of 1826–27, fugitives began to come to our house, and as it became more widely known on different routes that the slaves fleeing from bondage would find a welcome and shelter at our house, and be forwarded safely on their journey, the number increased. Friends in the neighborhood, who had formerly stood aloof from the work, fearful of the penalty of the law, were encouraged to engage in it when they saw the fearless manner in which I acted, and the success that attended my efforts. They would contribute to clothe the fugitives, and would aid in forwarding them on their way, but were timid about sheltering them under their roof; so that part of the work devolved on us. Some seemed really glad to see the work go on, if somebody else would do it. Other doubted the propriety of it, and tried to discourage me, and dissuade me from running such risks. They manifested great concern for my safety and pecuniary interests, telling me that such a course of action would injure my business and perhaps ruin me; that I ought to consider the welfare of my family; and warning me that my life was in danger, as there were many threats made against me by the slave-hunters and those who sympathized with them. . . .

The Underground Railroad business increased as time advanced, and it was attended with heavy expenses, which I could not have borne had not my affairs been prosperous. I found it necessary to keep a team and a wagon always at command, to convey the fugitive slaves on their journey. Sometimes, when we had large companies, one or two other teams and wagons were required. These journeys had to be made at night, often through deep mud and bad roads, and along by-ways that were seldom traveled. Every precaution to evade pursuit had to be used, as the hunters were often on the track, and sometimes ahead of the slaves. We had different routes for sending the fugitives to depots, ten, fifteen, or twenty miles distant, and when we heard of slave-hunters having passed on one road, we forwarded our passengers by another.

In some instances where we learned that the pursuers were ahead of them, we sent a messenger and had the fugitives brought back to my house to remain in concealment until the bloodhounds in human shape had lost the trail and given up the pursuit.

I soon became extensively known to the friends of the slaves, at different points on the Ohio River. . . . Seldom a week passed without our receiving passengers. We found it necessary to be always prepared to receive such company and properly care for them. We knew not what night or what hour of the night we would be roused from slumber by a gentle rap at the door. That was the signal announcing the arrival of a train of the Underground Railroad, for the locomotive did not whistle, nor make any unnecessary noise. I have often been awakened by this signal, and sprang out of bed in the dark and opened the door. Outside in the cold or rain, there would be a two-horse wagon loaded with fugitives, perhaps the greater part of them women and children. I would invite them, in a low tone, to come in, and they would follow me into the darkened house without a word, for we knew not who might be watching and listening. When they were all safely inside and the door fastened, I would cover the windows, strike a light and build a good fire. By this time my wife would be up and preparing victuals for them, and in a short time the cold and hungry fugitives would be made comfortable. I would accompany the conductor of the train to the stable, and care for the horses, that had, perhaps, been driven twenty-five or thirty miles that night, through the cold and rain. The fugitives would rest on pallets before the fire the rest of the night. Frequently, wagon-loads of passengers from the different lines have met at our house, having no previous knowledge of each other. The companies varied in number, from two or three fugitives to seventeen. . . .

The number of fugitives varied considerably in different years, but the annual average was more than one hundred. They generally came to us destitute of clothing, and were often barefooted. Clothing must be collected and kept on hand, if possible, and money must be raised to buy shoes, and purchase goods to make garments for women and children. The young ladies of the neighborhood organized a sewing society, and met at our house frequently, to make clothes for the fugitives.

Sometimes when the fugitives came to us destitute, we kept them several days, until they could be provided with comfortable clothes. This depended on the circumstances of danger. If they had come a long distance and had been out several weeks or months—as was sometimes the case—and it was not probable that hunters were on their track, we thought it safe for them to remain with us until fitted for traveling through the thinly settled country to the North. Sometimes fugitives have come to our house in rags, footsore, and toil-worn, and almost wild, having been out for several months traveling at night, hiding in canebrakes or thickets during the day, often being lost and making little headway at night, particularly in cloudy weather, when the north star could not be seen, sometimes almost perishing for want of food, and afraid of every white person they saw, even after they came into a free State, knowing that slaves were often captured and taken back after crossing the Ohio River.

**Source:** Levi Coffin, *Reminiscences* (Cincinnati: Western Tract Society, 1876), 107–9, 110–14.

## The Escape of William Wells Brown (1834)

Born into slavery in Kentucky, William Wells Brown was sold to several masters before escaping from his final one, a Captain Price, who made the mistake of taking Brown with him on a steamboat journey to Cincinnati, where Brown absconded. In this selection from his autobiography, which was second in popularity among slave narratives only to Frederick Douglass's, Brown describes his escape and how he acquired a new name as a free man.

At last the time for action arrived. The boat landed at a point which appeared to me the place of all others to start from. I found that it would be impossible to carry anything with me, but what was upon my person. I had some provisions, and a single suit of clothes, about half worn. When the boat was discharging her cargo, and the passengers engaged carrying their baggage on and off shore, I improved the opportunity to convey myself with my little effects on land. Taking up a trunk, I went up the wharf, and was soon out of the crowd. I made directly for the woods, where I remained until night, knowing well that I could not travel, even in the State of Ohio, during the day, without danger of being arrested.

I had long since made up my mind that I would not trust myself in the hands of any man, white or colored. The slave is brought up to look upon every white man as an enemy to him and his race; and twenty-one years in slavery had taught me that there were traitors, even among colored people. After dark, I emerged from the woods into a narrow path, which led me into the main travelled road. But I knew not which way to go. I did not know North from South, East from West. I looked in vain for the North Star; a heavy cloud hid it from my view. I walked up and down the road until near midnight, when the clouds disappeared, and I welcomed the sight of my friend—truly the slave's friend—the North Star!

As soon as I saw it, I knew my course, and before daylight I travelled twenty or twenty-five miles. It being in the winter, I suffered intensely from the cold; being without an overcoat, and my other clothes rather thin for the season. I was provided with a tinder-box, so that I could make up a fire when necessary. And but for this, I should certainly have frozen to death; for I was determined not to go to any house for shelter. I knew of a man . . . who had run away near Cincinnati, on the way to Washington, but had been caught and carried back into slavery; and I felt that a similar fate awaited me, should I be seen by anyone. I travelled at night, and lay by during the day.

On the fourth day, my provisions gave out, and then what to do I could not tell. Have something to eat, I must; but how to get it was the question! On the first night after my food was gone, I went to a barn on the roadside, and there found some ears of corn. I took ten or twelve of them, and kept on my journey. During the next day, while in the woods, I roasted my corn and feasted upon it, thanking God that I was so well provided for.

My escape to a land of freedom now appeared certain, and the prospects of the future occupied a great part of my thoughts. What should be my occupation, was a subject of much anxiety to me; and the next thing [was] what should be my name? [Although named William by his mother, one of his masters, whose own son was also named William, had insisted he be called Sandford. Brown loathed the name.]

So I was not only hunting for my liberty, but also hunting for a name; though I regarded the latter as of little consequence, if I could but gain the former. Travelling along the road, I would sometimes speak to myself, sounding my name [William] over, by way of getting used to it, before I should arrive among civilized human beings. On the fifth or sixth day, it rained very fast, and it froze about as fast as it fell, so that my clothes were one glare of ice. I travelled on at night until I became so chilled and benumbed—the wind blowing into my face—that I found it impossible to go any further, and accordingly took shelter in a barn, where I was obliged to walk to keep from freezing.

I have ever looked upon that night as the most eventful part of my escape from slavery. Nothing but the providence of God, and that old barn, saved me from freezing to death. I received a very severe cold, which settled upon my lungs, and from time to time my feet had been frost bitten, so that it was with difficulty I could walk. In this situation I travelled two days, when I found that I must seek shelter somewhere, or die.

The thought of death was nothing frightful to me, compared with that of being caught, and again carried back into slavery. Nothing but the prospect of enjoying liberty could have induced me to undergo such trials. . . . This, and this alone, cheered me onward. But I at last resolved to seek protection from the inclemency of the weather, and therefore I secured myself behind some logs and brush, intending to wait there until someone should pass by; for I thought it probable that I might see some colored person, or, if not, someone who was not a slaveholder; for I had an idea that I should know a slaveholder as far as I could see him.

The first person that passed was a man in a buggy wagon. He looked too genteel for me to hail him. Very soon, another passed by on horseback. I attempted speaking to him, but fear made my voice fail me. As he passed, I left my hiding place, and was approaching the road, when I observed an old man walking towards me, leading a white horse.

He had on a broad brimmed hat and a very long coat, and was evidently walking for exercise. As soon as I saw him, and observed his dress, I thought to myself, "You are the man that I have been looking for!" Nor was I mistaken. He was the very man!

On approaching me, he asked me, "if I was not a slave." I looked at him some time, and then asked him "if he knew of anyone who would help me, as I was sick." He answered that he would; but again asked, if I was not a slave. I told him I was. He then said that I was in a very pro-slavery neighborhood, and if I would wait until he went home, he would get a covered wagon for me. I promised to remain. He mounted his horse, and was soon out of sight.

After he was gone, I meditated whether to wait or not; being apprehensive that he had gone for someone to arrest me. But I finally concluded to remain until he should return; removing some few rods to watch his movements. After a suspense of an hour and a half or more, he returned with a two-horse covered wagon, such as are usually seen under the shed of a Quaker meeting house on Sundays; for the old man proved to be a Quaker.

He took me to his house, but it was some time before I could be induced to enter it; not until the old lady came out, did I venture into the house. . . . The only fault I found with them was their being too kind. I had never had a white man to treat me as an equal, and the idea of a white lady waiting on me at the table was still worse! . . . The fact that I was a free man—could walk, talk, eat and sleep as a man, and no one to stand over me with the blood-clotted cowhide—all this made me feel that I was not myself.

The kind friend that had taken me in was named Wells Brown. He was a devoted friend of the slave; but was very old, and not in the enjoyment of good health. After being by the fire awhile, I found that my feet had been very much frozen. I was seized with a fever which threatened to confine me to my bed. But my friends soon raised me, treating me as kindly as if I had been one of their children. I remained with them twelve or fifteen days, during which time they made me some clothing, and the old gentleman purchased me a pair of boots.

I found that I was about fifty or sixty miles from Dayton, in the State of Ohio, and between one and two hundred miles from Cleveland, on Lake Erie, a place I was desirous of reaching on my way to Canada. This I know will sound strangely to the ears of people in foreign lands, but it is nevertheless true. An American citizen was fleeing from a Democratic, Republican, Christian government, to receive protection under the monarchy of Great Britain. While the people of the United States boast of their freedom, they at the same time keep three millions of their own citizens in chains. . . .

Before leaving this good Quaker friend, he inquired what my name was besides William. I told him that I had no other name. "Well," said he, "thee must have another name. Since thee has got out of slavery, thee has become a man, and men always have two names."

I told him that he was the first man to extend the hand of friendship to me, and I would give him the privilege of naming me.

"If I name thee," said he, "I shall call thee Wells Brown, after myself."

"But," said I, "I am not willing to lose my name of William. As it was taken from me once against my will, I am not willing to part with it again upon any terms."

"Then," said he, "I will call thee William Wells Brown."

"So be it," said I; and I have been known by that name ever since I left the house of my first white friend, Wells Brown.

**Source:** William Wells Brown, *Narrative of William W. Brown, An American Slave* (London: Charles Gilpin, 1849), 94–104.

## Journey on the Underground Railroad (1849)

Josiah Henson, ex-slave and one of the leaders of the black Canadian settlement of Dawn, returned to Kentucky on two separate occasions to lead slaves to freedom. In this selection from his autobiography, he describes the second trip, in which he conducted brothers from the Lightfoot family to Canada.

In order to prevent the bloodhounds from following on our trail, we seized a skiff, a little below the city, and made our way down the river. It was not the shortest way, but it was the surest.

It was sixty-five miles from Maysville to Cincinnati, and we thought we could reach that city before daylight, and then take the stage for Sandusky. Our boat sprung a leak before we had got half way, and we narrowly escaped being drowned; providentially, however, we got to the shore before the boat sunk. We then took another boat, but this detention prevented us from arriving in Cincinnati in time for the stage. Day broke upon us when we were about ten miles above the city, and we were compelled to leave our boat from fear of being apprehended.

This was an anxious time. However, we had got so far away that we knew there was no danger of being discovered by the hounds, and we thought we would go on foot. When we got within seven miles of Cincinnati, we came to the Miami River, and we could not reach the city without crossing it.

This was a great barrier to us, for the water appeared to be deep, and we were afraid to ask the loan of a boat, being apprehensive it might lead to our detection. We went first up and then down the river, trying to find a convenient crossing-place, but failed. I then said to my company, "Boys, let us go up the river and try again." We started, and after going about a mile we saw a cow coming out of a wood, and going to the river as though she intended to drink. Then said I, "Boys, let us go and see what the cow is about, it may be that she will tell us some news." I said this in order to cheer them up. One of them replied, in rather a peevish way, "Oh, that cow can't talk"; but I again urged them to come on. The cow remained until we approached her within a rod or two; she then walked into the river, and went straight across without swimming, which caused me to remark, "The Lord sent that cow to show us where to cross the river!" This has always seemed to me to be a very wonderful event.

Having urged our way with considerable haste, we were literally saturated with perspiration, though it was snowing at the time, and my companions thought that it would be highly dangerous for us to proceed through the water, especially as there was a large quantity of ice in the river. But as it was a question of life or death with us, there was no time left for reasoning; I therefore advanced—they reluctantly following. The youngest of the Lightfoots, ere we reached halfway over the river, was seized with violent contraction of the limbs, which prevented further self-exertion on his part; he was, therefore, carried the remainder of the distance. After resorting to continued friction, he partially recovered, and we proceeded on our journey.

We reached Cincinnati about eleven on Sunday morning, too late for the stage that day; but having found some friends, we hid ourselves until Monday evening, when we recommenced our long and toilsome journey, through mud, rain, and snow, towards Canada. We had increased our distance about one hundred miles, by going out of our road to get among the Quakers. During our passage through the woods, the boy before referred to was taken alarmingly ill, and we were compelled to proceed with him on our backs; but finding this mode of conveying him exceedingly irksome, we constructed a kind of litter with our shirts and handkerchiefs laid across poles. By this time we got into the State of Indiana, so that we could travel by day so long as we kept to the woods. Our patient continued to get worse, and it appeared, both to himself and to us, that death would soon release him from his sufferings. He therefore begged to be left in some secluded spot, to die alone, as he feared that the delay occasioned by his having to be carried through the bush, might lead to the capture of the whole company. With very considerable reluctance we acceded to his request, and laid him in a sheltered place, with a full expectation that death would soon put an end to his sufferings. The poor fellow expressed his readiness to meet the last struggle in hope of eternal life. Sad, indeed, was the parting; and it was with difficulty we tore ourselves away.

We had not, however, proceeded more than two miles on our journey, when one of the brothers of the dying man made a sudden stop, and expressed his inability to proceed whilst he had the consciousness that he had left his brother to perish, in all probability, a prey to the devouring wolves. His grief was so great that we determined to return, and at length reached the spot, where we found the poor fellow apparently dying, moaning out with every breath a prayer to heaven. Words cannot describe the joyousness experienced by the Lightfoots when they saw their poor afflicted brother once more; they literally danced for joy. We at once prepared to resume our journey as we best could, and once more penetrated the bush. After making some progress, we saw, at a little distance on the road, a wagon approaching, and I immediately determined to ascertain whether some assistance could not be obtained.

I at length circumvented the road, so as to make it appear that I had been journeying in an opposite direction to that which the wagon was taking. When I came up with the driver, I bade him good day. He said, "Where is thee going?" "To Canada." I saw his coat, heard his *thee* and *thou*, and set him down for a Quaker. I therefore plainly told him our circumstances. He at once stopped his horses, and expressed his willingness to assist us. I returned to the place where my companions were in waiting for me, and soon had them in the presence of the Quaker. Immediately on viewing the sufferer he was moved to tears, and without delay turned his horses' heads, to proceed in the direction of his home, although he had intended to go to a distant market with a load of produce to sale. The reception we met with from the Quaker's family overjoyed our hearts, and the transports with which the poor men looked upon their brother, now so favorably circumstanced, cannot be described.

We remained with this happy family for the night, and received from them every kindness. It was arranged that the boy should remain behind, until, through the blessing of God, he should recover. We were kindly provided with a sack of biscuit and a joint of meat, and once more set our faces in the direction of Lake Erie.

After proceeding some distance on our road, we perceived a white man approaching, but as he was traveling alone, and on foot, we were not alarmed at his presence. It turned out that he had been residing for some time in the South, and although a free white man, his employers had attempted to castigate him, in return for which he had used violence, which made it necessary that he should at once escape. We traveled in company, and found that his presence was of signal service to us in delivering us out of the hands of the slave-hunters who were now on our track, and eagerly grasping after their prey. We had resolved on reaching the lake, a distance of forty miles, by the following morning; we, therefore, walked all night.

Just as the day was breaking, we reached a wayside tavern, immediately contiguous to the lake, and our white companion having knocked up the landlord, ordered breakfast for six. Whilst our breakfast was in course of preparation, we dozed off into slumber, wearied with our long continued exertion.

Just as our breakfast was ready, whilst half-asleep and half-awake, an impression came forcibly upon me that danger was nigh, and that I must at once leave the house. I immediately urged my companions to follow me out, which they were exceedingly unwilling to do; but as they had promised me submission, they at length yielded to my request. We retired to the yard at the side of the house, and commenced washing ourselves with the snow, which was now up to our knees. Presently we heard the tramping of horses, and were at once warned of the necessity of secreting ourselves. We crept beneath a pile of bushes, close at hand, which permitted a full view of the road. The horsemen came to a dead stop at the door of the house, and commenced their inquiries; my companions at once recognized the parties on horseback, and whispered their names to me. This was a critical moment, and the loud beatings of their hearts testified the dreadful alarm with which they viewed the scene. Had we been within doors, we should have been inevitably sacrificed. Our white friend proceeded to the door in advance of the landlord, and maintained his position. He was at once interrogated by the slave-hunters whether he had seen any negroes pass that way. He said, yes, he thought he had. Their number was demanded, and they were told about six, and that they were proceeding in the direction of Detroit; and that they might be some few miles on the road. They at once reined their horses, which were greatly fatigued, through having been ridden all night, and were soon out of sight. We at length ventured into the house, and devoured breakfast in an incredibly short space of time. After what had transpired, the landlord became acquainted with our circumstances, and at once offered to sail us in his boat across to Canada. We were happy enough to have such an offer, and soon the white sail of our little bark was laying to the wind, and we were gliding along on our way, with the land of liberty in full view. Words cannot describe the feelings experienced by my companions as they neared the shore—their bosoms were swelling with inexpressible joy as they mounted the seats of the boat, ready, eagerly, to spring forward, that they might touch the soil of the freeman. And when they reached the shore, they danced and wept for joy, and kissed the earth on which they first stepped, no longer the SLAVE—but the FREE.

After the lapse of a few months, on one joyous Sabbath morning, I had the happiness of clasping the poor boy we had left in the kind care of the Quaker, no longer attenuated in frame, but robust and healthy, and surrounded by his family. Thus my joy was consummated. It is one of the greatest sources of my happiness to know, that by similar means to those above narrated, I have been instrumental in delivering one hundred and eighteen human beings out of the cruel and merciless grasp of the slaveholder.

**Source:** *The Autobiography of the Rev. Josiah Henson,* ed. John Lobb (London: Christian Age Office, 1878), 112–19.

## The Case of Margaret Garner (1856)

Margaret Garner was a fugitive slave who fled from Kentucky across the frozen Ohio River with her husband and four children. When cornered by slave catchers in Cincinnati, she tried to kill her children rather than see them returned to slavery. She killed one but the slave catchers prevented her from harming the rest, all of whom were returned south with her. This account is by stationmaster Levi Coffin, who lived in Cincinnati at the time.

Perhaps no case that came under my notice, while engaged in aiding fugitive slaves, attracted more attention and aroused deeper interest and sympathy than the case of Margaret Garner, the slave mother who killed her child rather than see it taken back to slavery. This happened in the latter part of January 1856. The Ohio River was frozen over at the time, and the opportunity thus offered for escaping to a free State was embraced by a number of slaves living in Kentucky, several miles back from the river. A party of seventeen, belonging to different masters in the same neighborhood, made arrangements to escape together. There was snow on the ground and the roads were smooth, so the plan of going to the river on a sled naturally suggested itself. The time fixed for their flight was Sabbath night, and having managed to get a large sled and two good horses, belonging to one of their masters, the party of seventeen crowded into the sled and started on their hazardous journey in the latter part of the night. They drove the horses at full speed, and at daylight reached the River below Covington, opposite Wester Row. They left the sled and horses here, and as quickly as possible crossed the river on foot. It was now broad daylight, and people were beginning to pass about the streets and the fugitives divided their company that they might not attract so much notice.

An old slave named Simon and his wife Mary, together with their son Robert and his wife Margaret Garner and four children, made their way to the house of a colored man named Kite, who had formerly lived in their neighborhood and had been purchased from slavery by his father, Joe Kite. They had to make several inquiries in order to find Kite's house, which was below Mill Creek, in the lower part of the city. This afterward led to their discovery; they had been seen by a number of persons on their way to Kite's, and were easily traced by pursuers. The other nine fugitives were more fortunate. They made their way up town and found friends who conducted them to safe hiding-places, where they remained until night. They were put on the Underground Railroad, and went safely through to Canada. . . .

In a few minutes . . . [Kite's] house was surrounded by pursuers—the masters of the fugitives, with officers and a posse of men. The door and windows were barred, and those inside refused to give admittance. The fugitives were determined to fight, and to die, rather than to be taken back to slavery. Margaret, the mother of the four children, declared that she would kill herself and her children before she would return to bondage. The slave men were armed and fought bravely. The window was first battered down with a stick of wood, and one of the deputy marshals attempted to enter, but a pistol shot from within made a flesh wound on his arm and caused him to abandon the attempt. The pursuers then battered down the door with some timber and rushed in. The husband of Margaret fired several shots, and wounded one of the officers, but was soon overpowered and dragged out of the house. At this moment, Margaret Garner, seeing that their hopes of freedom were in vain, seized a butcher knife that lay on the table, and with one stroke cut the throat of her little daughter, whom she probably loved the best. She then attempted to take the life of the other children and to kill herself, but she was overpowered and hampered before she could complete her desperate work. The whole party was then arrested and lodged in jail.

The trial lasted two weeks, drawing crowds to the courtroom every day. . . . The counsel for the defense brought witnesses to prove that the fugitives had been permitted to visit the city at various times previously. It was claimed that Margaret Garner had been brought here by her owners a number of years before, to act as nurse girl, and according to the law which liberated slaves who were brought into free States by the consent of their masters, she had been free from that time, and her children, all of whom had been born since then—following the condition of the mother—were likewise free.

The Commissioner decided that a voluntary return to slavery, after a visit to a free State, re-attached the conditions of slavery, and that the fugitives were legally slaves at the time of their escape. . . .

[I]n spite of touching appeals, of eloquent pleadings, the Commissioner remanded the fugitives back to slavery. He said that it was not a question of feeling to be decided by the chance current of his sympathies; the law of Kentucky and the United States made it a question of property.

**Source:** Levi Coffin, *Reminiscences* (Cincinnati: Western Tract Society, 1876), 557–60, 566.

## Escape of Henry "Box" Brown (1849)

Few escapes on the Underground Railroad were as dramatic as the one made by Richmond slave Henry Brown, who had himself nailed up in a wooden crate and shipped to abolitionists in Philadelphia. Underground Railroad stationmaster and chronicler William Still tells his story.

Brown was a man of invention as well as a hero. In point of interest, however, his case is no more remarkable than many others. Indeed, neither before nor after escaping did he suffer one-half what many others have experienced.

He was decidedly an unhappy piece of property in the city of Richmond, Va. In the condition of a slave he felt that it would be impossible for him to remain. Full well did he know, however, that it was no holiday task to escape the vigilance of Virginia slave-hunters, or the wrath of an enraged master for committing the unpardonable sin of attempting to escape to a land of liberty. So Brown counted well the cost before venturing upon this hazardous undertaking. Ordinary modes of travel he concluded might prove disastrous to his hopes; he, therefore, hit upon a new invention altogether, which was to have himself boxed up and forwarded to Philadelphia direct by express. The size of the box and how it was to be made to fit him most comfortably, was of his own ordering. Two feet eight inches deep, two feet wide, and three feet long were the exact dimensions of the box, lined with baize. His resources with regard to food and water consisted of the following: One bladder of water and a few small biscuits. His mechanical implement to meet the death-struggle for fresh air, all told, was one large gimlet. Satisfied that it would be far better to peril his life for freedom in this way than to remain under the galling yoke of slavery, he entered his box, which was safely nailed up and hooped with five hickory hoops, and was then addressed by his next friend, James A. Smith, a shoe dealer, to Wm. H. Johnson, Arch Street, Philadelphia, marked, "This side up with care." In this condition he was sent to Adams' Express office in a dray, and thence by overland express to Philadelphia. It was twenty-six hours from the time he left Richmond until his arrival in the City of Brotherly Love. The notice, "This side up, etc.," did not avail with the different expressmen, who hesitated not to handle the box in the usual rough manner common to this class of men. For a while they actually had the box upside down, and had him on his head for miles.

A few days before he was expected, certain intimation was conveyed to a member of the [Philadelphia] Vigilance Committee [probably Still himself] that a box might be expected by the three o'clock morning train from the South, which might contain a man. One of the most serious walks he ever took—and they had not been a few—to meet and accompany passengers, he took at half past two o'clock that morning to the depot. Not once, but for more than a score of times, he fancied the slave would be dead. He anxiously looked while the freight was being unloaded from the cars, to see if he could recognize a box that might contain a man; one alone had that appearance, and he confessed it really seemed as if there was the scent of death about it. But on inquiry, he soon learned that it was not the one he was looking after, and he was free to say he experienced a marked sense of relief. That same afternoon, however, he received from Richmond a telegram, which read thus, "Your case of goods is shipped and will arrive tomorrow morning."

. . . Next morning, according to arrangement, the box was at the Anti-Slavery office in due time. The witnesses present to behold the resurrection were J.M. McKim, Professor C.D. Cleveland, Lewis Thompson, and the writer. . . .

All was quiet. The door had been safely locked. The proceedings commenced. Mr. McKim rapped quietly on the lid of the box and called out, "All right!" Instantly came the answer from within, "All right, sir!"

The witnesses will never forget that moment. Saw and hatchet quickly had the five hickory hoops cut and the lid off, and the marvelous resurrection of Brown ensued. Rising up in his box, he reached out his hand, saying, "How do you do, gentlemen?" The little assemblage hardly knew what to think or do at the moment. He was about as wet as if he had come up out of the Delaware. Very soon he remarked that, before leaving Richmond he had selected for his arrival-hymn (if he lived) the Psalm [40] beginning with these words: "I waited patiently for the Lord, and He heard my prayer." And most touchingly did he sing the psalm, much to his own relief, as well as to the relief of his small audience.

**Source:** William Still, *The Underground Rail Road* (Philadelphia: Porter & Coates, 1872), 69–70.

## Escape of William and Ellen Craft (1848)

One of the most daring escapes was pulled off by the Crafts, husband and wife slaves who disguised themselves as an invalid planter (Ellen) seeking medical attention in the north and "his" loyal manservant (William). They rode trains and steamers all the way to freedom in Philadelphia. Once again, the narrator is William Still.

A quarter of a century ago, William and Ellen Craft were slaves in the State of Georgia. With them, as with thousands of others, the desire to be free was very strong. For this jewel they were willing to make any sacrifice, or to endure any amount of suffering. In this state of mind they commenced planning. After thinking of various ways that might be tried, it occurred to William and Ellen, that one might act the part of master and the other the part of servant.

Ellen being fair enough to pass for white, of necessity would have to be transformed into a young planter for the time being. All that was needed, however, to make this important change was that she should be dressed elegantly in a fashionable suit of male attire, and have her hair cut in the style usually worn by young planters. Her profusion of dark hair offered a fine opportunity for the change. So far this plan looked very tempting. But it occurred to them that Ellen was beardless. After some mature reflection, they came to the conclusion that this difficulty could be very readily obviated by having the face muffled up as though the young planter was suffering badly with the face or toothache; thus they got rid of this trouble. Straightway, upon further reflection, several other very serious difficulties stared them in the face. For instance, in traveling, they knew that they would be under the necessity of stopping repeatedly at hotels, and that the custom of registering would have to be conformed to, unless some very good excuse could be given for not doing so.

Here they again thought much over matters, and wisely concluded that the young man had better assume the attitude of a gentleman very much indisposed. He must have his right arm placed carefully in a sling; that would be a sufficient excuse for not registering, etc. Then he must be a little lame, with a nice cane in the left hand; he must have large green spectacles over his eyes, and withal he must be very hard of hearing and dependent on his faithful servant (as was no uncommon thing with slaveholders), to look after all his wants.

William was just the man to act this part. To begin with, he was very "likely-looking"; smart, active and exceedingly attentive to his young master—indeed, he was almost eyes, ears, hands and feet for him. William knew that this would please the slave-holders. The young planter would have nothing to do but hold himself subject to his ailments and put on a bold air of superiority; he was not to deign to notice anybody. If, while traveling, gentlemen, either politely or rudely, should venture to scrape acquaintance with the young planter, in his deafness he was to remain mute; the servant was to explain. In every instance when this occurred, as it actually did, the servant was fully equal to the emergency—none dreaming of the disguises in which the Underground Rail Road passengers were traveling.

They stopped at a first-class hotel in Charleston, where the young planter and his body servant were treated, as the house was wont to treat the chivalry. They stopped also at a similar hotel in Richmond, and with like results.

They knew that they must pass through Baltimore, but they did not know the obstacles that they would have to surmount in the Monumental City. They proceeded to the depot in the usual manner, and the servant asked for tickets for his master and self. Of course the master could have a ticket, but "bonds will have to be entered before you can get a ticket," said the ticket master. "It is the rule of this office to require bonds for all negroes applying for tickets to go North, and none but gentlemen of well-known responsibility will be taken," further explained the ticket master.

The servant replied, that he knew "nothing about that"—that he was "simply traveling with his young master to take care of him—he being in a very delicate state of health, so much so, that fears were entertained that he might not be able to hold out to reach Philadelphia, where he was hastening for medical treatment," and ended his reply by saying, "my master can't be detained." Without further parley, the ticket master very obligingly waived the old "rule," and furnished the requisite tickets. The mountain being thus removed, the young planter and his faithful servant were safely in the cars for the city of Brotherly Love.

Scarcely had they arrived on free soil when the rheumatism departed—the right arm was unslung—the toothache was gone—the beardless face was unmuffled—the deaf heard and spoke—the blind saw—and the lame leaped as an hart, and in the presence of a few astonished friends of the slave, the facts of this unparalleled Underground Rail Road feat were fully established by the most unquestionable evidence.

**Source:** William Still, *The Underground Rail Road* (Philadelphia: Porter & Coates, 1872), 382–84.

# Scenes in the Life of Harriet Tubman (1851–1860)

Harriet Tubman is the most famous of all the conductors and abductors of the Underground Railroad. Between 1851 and 1860, she made 19 trips below the Mason-Dixon Line to lead more than 300 slaves to freedom. In 1869, author Sarah Bradford recorded conversations with the illiterate Tubman and published them as *Scenes in the Life of Harriet Tubman.* In this selection from it, Tubman discusses her methods as a conductor.

It will be impossible to give any connected account of the journeys taken by Harriet for the rescue of her people, as she herself has no idea of the dates connected with them, or of the order in which they were made. She thinks she was about 25 when she made her own escape, and this was in the last year of James K. Polk's administration. From that time until the beginning of the war, her years were spent in these journeyings back and forth, with intervals between, in which she worked only to spend the avails of her labor in providing for the wants of her next party of fugitives. By night she traveled, many times on foot, over mountains, through forests, across rivers, mid perils by land, perils by water, perils from enemies, perils among false brethren. Sometimes members of her party would become exhausted, foot-sore, and bleeding, and declare they could not go on, they must stay where they dropped down, and die; others would think a voluntary return to slavery better than being overtaken and carried back, and would insist upon returning; then there was no remedy but force; the revolver carried by this bold and daring pioneer would be pointed at their heads. "Dead niggers tell no tales," said Harriet; "Go on or die"; so she compelled them to drag their weary limbs on their northward journey.

At one time she collected and sent on a gang of thirty-nine fugitives in the care of others, as from some cause she was prevented from accompanying them. Sometimes, when she and her party were concealed in the woods, they saw their pursuers pass, on their horses, down the high road, tacking up the advertisements for them on the fences and trees.

"And den how we laughed," said she. "*We* was the fools, and *dey* was the wise men; but we wasn't fools enough to go down de high road in de broad daylight." At one time she left her party in the woods, and went by a long and roundabout way to one of the "stations of the Underground Railroad," as she called them. Here she procured food for her famished party, often paying out of her hard-gained earnings, five dollars a day for food for them. But she dared not go back to them till night, for fear of being watched, and thus revealing their hiding place. After nightfall, the sound of a hymn sung at a distance comes upon the ears of the concealed and famished fugitives in the woods, and they know that their deliverer is at hand. They listen eagerly for the words she sings, for by them they are to be warned of danger, or informed of safety. . . .

And so by night travel, by hiding, by signals, by threatening, she brought the people safely to the land of liberty. But after the passage of the [1850] Fugitive Slave Law, she said, "I wouldn't trust Uncle Sam wid my people no longer; I brought 'em all clar off to Canada."

**Source:** Sarah H. Bradford, *Scenes in the Life of Harriet Tubman* (Auburn, NY: W. J. Moses, 1869), 24–27.

## The Christiana Riot (1851)

In September 1851, Maryland slaveholder Edward Gorsuch traveled to Christiana, a town in southern Pennsylvania, to reclaim runaway slaves. He was accompanied by an officer of the law, one Marshal Kline, his son Dickinson, his nephew Joshua, and several men. The town's vigilance committee, led by ex-slave William Parker, refused to give the fugitives up, and an armed conflict that came to be known as the Christiana Riot erupted. Gorsuch was killed in the fray, and several of the blacks involved were subsequently charged with treason. All were acquitted. This account was dictated by William Parker shortly after the end of the Civil War. It has the feel of a story told many times.

Mr. Gorsuch then said, "You have my property."

To which I replied, "Go in the room down there, and see if there is anything there belonging to you. There are beds and a bureau, chairs, and other things. Then go out to the barn; there you will find a cow and some hogs. See if any of them are yours."

He said, "They are not mine; I want my men. They are here, and I am bound to have them."

Thus we parleyed for a time, all because of the pusillanimity of the Marshal [Kline], when he, at last, said, "I am tired waiting on you; I see you are not going to give up. Go to the barn and fetch some straw," said he to one of his men. "I will set the house on fire, and burn them up."

"Burn us up and welcome," said I. "None but a coward would say the like. You can burn us, but you can't take us; before I give up, you will see my ashes scattered on the earth."

By this time day had begun to dawn; and then my wife came to me and asked if she should blow the horn, to bring friends to our assistance. I assented, and she went to the garret for the purpose. When the horn sounded from the garret window, one of the ruffians asked the others what it meant; and Kline said to me, "What do you mean by blowing that horn?"

I did not answer. It was a custom with us, when a horn was blown at an unusual hour, to proceed to the spot promptly to see what was the matter. Kline ordered his men to shoot any one they saw blowing the horn. There was a peach-tree at that end of the house. Up it two of the men climbed; and when my wife went a second time to the window, they fired as soon as they heard the blast, but missed their aim. My wife then went down on her knees, and, drawing her head and body below the range of the window, the horn resting on the sill, blew blast after blast, while the shots poured thick and fast around her. They must have fired ten or twelve times. The house was of stone, and the windows were deep, which alone preserved her life.

They were evidently disconcerted by the blowing of the horn. Gorsuch said again, "I want my property, and I will have it."

"Old man," said I, "you look as if you belonged to some persuasion."

"Never mind," he answered, "what persuasion I belong to; I want my property."

While I was leaning out of the window, Kline fired a pistol at me, but the shot went too high; the ball broke the glass just above my head. I was talking to Gorsuch at the time. I seized a gun and aimed it at Gorsuch's breast for he evidently had instigated Kline to fire; but Pinckney caught my arm and said, "Don't shoot." The gun went off, just grazing Gorsuch's shoulder. Another conversation then ensued between Gorsuch, Kline, and myself, when another one of the party fired at me but missed. Dickinson Gorsuch, I then saw, was preparing to shoot; and I told him if he missed, I would show him where shooting first came from.

I asked them to consider what they would have done, had they been in our position. "I know you want to kill us," I said, "for you have shot at us time and again. We have only fired twice, although we have guns and ammunition, and could kill you all if we would, but we do not want to shed blood."

"If you do not shoot any more," then said Kline, "I will stop my men from firing."

They then ceased for a time. This was about sunrise.

Mr. Gorsuch now said, "Give up and let me have my property. Hear what the Marshal says; the Marshal is your friend. He advises you to give up without more fuss, for my property I will have."

I denied that I had his property, when he replied, "You have my men."

"Am I your man?" I asked.

"No."

I then called Pinckney forward.

"Is that your man?"

"No."

Abraham Johnson I called next, but Gorsuch said he was not his man.

The only plan left was to call both Pinckney and Johnson again; for had I called the others, he would have recognized them, for they were his slaves.

Abraham Johnson said, "Does such a shrivelled up old slaveholder as you own such a nice, genteel young man as I am?"

At this Gorsuch took offence, and charged me with dictating his language. I then told him there were but five of us, which he denied, and still insisted that I had his property. One of the party then [verbally] attacked the Abolitionists, affirming that, although they declared there could not be property in man, the Bible was conclusive authority in favor of property in human flesh.

"Yes," said Gorsuch, "does not the Bible say, 'Servants, obey your masters'?"

I said that it did, but the same Bible said, "Give unto your servants that which is just and equal."

At this stage of the proceedings, we went into a mutual Scripture inquiry, and bandied views in the manner of garrulous old wives.

When I spoke of duty to servants, Gorsuch said, "Do you know that?"

"Where," I asked, "do you see it in Scripture, that a man should traffic in his brother's blood?"

"Do you call a nigger my brother?" said Gorsuch.

"Yes," said I.

"William," said Samuel Thompson, "he has been a [Sunday School] class-leader."

When Gorsuch heard that, he hung his head, but said nothing. We then all joined in singing,

"Leader, what do you say
About the judgment day?
I will die on the field of battle,
Die on the field of battle,
With glory in my soul."

Then we all began to shout, singing meantime, and shouted for a long while. Gorsuch, who was standing head bowed, said, "What are you doing now?"

Samuel Thompson replied, "Preaching a sinner's funeral sermon."

"You had better give up, and come down."

I then said to Gorsuch, "'If a brother see a sword coming, and he warn not his brother, then the brother's blood is required at his hands; but if the other see the sword coming, and warn his brother, and his brother flee then his brother's blood is required at his own hand.' I see the sword coming, and, old man, I warn you to flee; if you flee not, your blood be upon your own hand."

It was now about seven o'clock.

"You had better give up," said old Mr. Gorsuch, after another while, "and come down, for I have come a long way this morning, and want my breakfast; for my property I will have, or I'll breakfast in hell. I will go up and get it."

He then started upstairs, and came far enough to see us all plainly. We were just about to fire upon him, when Dickinson Gorsuch, who was standing on the old oven, before the door, and could see into the upstairs room through the window, jumped down and caught his father, saying, "O father, do come down! do come down! They have guns, swords, and all kinds of weapons! They'll kill you! Do come down!"

The old man turned and left. When down with him, young Gorsuch could scarce draw breath, and the father looked more like a dead than a living man, so frightened were they at their supposed danger. The old man stood some time without saying anything; at last he said, as if soliloquizing, "I want my property, and I will have it."

Kline broke forth, "If you don't give up by fair means, you will have to by foul."

I told him we would not surrender on any conditions.

Young Gorsuch then said, "Don't ask them to give up—*make* them do it. We have money, and can call men to take them. What is it that money won't buy?"

Then said Kline, "I am getting tired waiting on you; I see you are not going to give up."

He then wrote a note and handed it to Joshua Gorsuch, saying at the same time, "Take it, and bring a hundred men from Lancaster."

As he started, I said, "See here! When you go to Lancaster, don't bring a hundred men—bring five hundred. It will take all the men in Lancaster to change our purpose or take us alive."

He stopped to confer with Kline, when Pinckney said, "We had better give up."

"You are getting afraid," said I.

"Yes," said Kline, "give up like men. The rest would give up if it were not for you."

"I am not afraid," said Pinckney; "but where is the sense in fighting against so many men, and only five of us?"

The whites, at this time, were coming from all quarters, and Kline was enrolling them as fast as they came. Their numbers alarmed Pinckney, and I told him to go and sit down; but he said, "No, I will go down stairs."

I told him, if he attempted it, I should be compelled to blow out his brains. "Don't believe, that any living man can take you," I said. "Don't give up to any slaveholder."

To Abraham Johnson, who was near me, I then turned. He declared he was not afraid. "I will fight till I die," he said.

At this time, Hannah, Pinckney's wife, had become impatient of our persistent course; and my wife, who brought me her message urging us to surrender, seized a corn-cutter, and declared she would cut off the head of the first one who should attempt to give up.

Another one of Gorsuch's slaves was coming along the highroad at this time, and I beckoned to him to go around. Pinckney saw him, and soon became more inspirited. Elijah Lewis, a Quaker, also came along about this time; I beckoned to him, likewise; but he came straight on, and was met by Kline, who ordered him to assist him. Lewis asked for his authority, and Kline handed him the warrant. While Lewis was reading, Castner Hanway came up, and Lewis handed the warrant to him. Lewis asked Kline what Parker said.

Kline replied, "He won't give up."

Then Lewis and Hanway both said to the Marshal, "If Parker says they will not give up, you had better let them alone, for he will kill some of you. We are not going to risk our lives"; and they turned to go away.

While they were talking, I came down and stood in the doorway, my men following behind.

Old Mr. Gorsuch said, when I appeared, "They'll come out, and get away!" and he came back to the gate.

I then said to him, "You said you could and would take us. Now you have the chance."

They were a cowardly-looking set of men.

Mr. Gorsuch said, "You can't come out here."

"Why?" said I. "This is my place. I pay rent for it. I'll let you see if I can't come out."

"I don't care if you do pay rent for it," said he. "If you come out, I will give you the contents of these"—presenting, at the same time, two revolvers, one in each hand.

I said, "Old man, if you don't go away, I will break your neck."

I then walked up to where he stood, his arms resting on the gate, trembling as if afflicted with palsy, and laid my hand on his shoulder, saying, "I have seen pistols before today."

Kline now came running up, and entreated Gorsuch to come away.

"No," said the latter, "I will have my property, or go to hell."

"What do you intend to do?" said Kline to me.

"I intend to fight," said I. "I intend to try your strength."

"If you will withdraw your men," he replied, "I will withdraw mine."

I told him it was too late. "You would not withdraw when you had the chance, you shall not now."

Kline then went back to Hanway and Lewis. Gorsuch made a signal to his men, and they all fell into line. I followed his example as well as I could; but as we were not more than ten paces apart, it was difficult to do so. At this time we numbered but ten, while there were between thirty and forty of the white men.

While I was talking to Gorsuch, his son said, "Father, will you take all this from a nigger?"

I answered him by saying that I respected old age; but that, if he would repeat that, I should knock his teeth down his throat. At this he fired upon me, and I ran up to him and knocked the pistol out of his hand, when he let the other one fall and ran in the field.

My brother-in-law, who was standing near, then said, "I can stop him"; and with his double-barrel gun he fired.

Young Gorsuch fell, but rose and ran on again. Pinckney fired a second time, and again Gorsuch fell, but was soon up again, and, running into the cornfield, lay down in the fence corner.

I returned to my men, and found Samuel Thompson talking to old Mr. Gorsuch, his master. They were both angry.

"Old man, you had better go home to Maryland," said Samuel.

"You had better give up, and come home with me," said the old man.

Thompson took Pinckney's gun and struck Gorsuch, and brought him to his knees. Gorsuch rose and signaled to his men. Thompson then knocked him down again, and he again rose. At this time all the white men opened fire, and we rushed upon them; when they turned, threw down their guns, and ran away. We, being closely engaged, clubbed our rifles. We were too closely pressed to fire, but we found a good deal could be done with empty guns.

Old Mr. Gorsuch was the bravest of his party; he held on to his pistols until the last, while all the others threw away their weapons. I saw as many as three at a time fighting with him. Sometimes he was on his knees, then on his back, and again his feet would be where his head should be. He was a fine soldier and a brave man. Whenever he saw the least opportunity, he would take aim. While in close quarters with the whites, we could load and fire but two or three times. Our guns got bent and out of order. So damaged did they become, that we could shoot with but two or three of them. Samuel Thompson bent his gun on old Mr. Gorsuch so badly, that it was of no use to us.

When the white men ran, they scattered. I ran after Nathan Nelson, but could not catch him. I never saw a man run faster. Returning, I saw Joshua Gorsuch coming, and Pinckney behind him. I reminded him that he would like "to take hold of a nigger," told him that now was his "chance," and struck him a blow on the side of the head, which stopped him. Pinckney came up behind, and gave him a blow which brought him to the ground; as the others passed, they gave him a kick or jumped upon him, until the blood oozed out at his ears.

Nicholas Hutchings, and Nathan Nelson of Baltimore County, Maryland, could outrun any men I ever saw. They and Kline were not brave, like the Gorsuches. Could our men have got them, they would have been satisfied.

One of our men ran after Dr. Pierce, as he richly deserved attention; but Pierce caught up with Castner Hanway, who rode between the fugitive and the Doctor, to shield him and some others. Hanway was told to get out of the way, or he would forfeit his life; he went aside quickly, and the man fired at the Marylander, but missed him—he was too far off. I do not know whether he was wounded or not; but I do know, that, if it had not been for Hanway, he would have been killed.

Having driven the slavocrats off in every direction, our party now turned towards their several homes. Some of us, however, went back to my house, where we found several of the neighbors.

The scene at the house beggars description. Old Mr. Gorsuch was lying in the yard in a pool of blood, and confusion reigned both inside and outside of the house.

Levi Pownell said to me, "The weather is so hot and the flies are so bad, will you give me a sheet to put over the corpse?"

In reply, I gave him permission to get anything he needed from the house.

"Dickinson Gorsuch is lying in the fence-corner, and I believe he is dying. Give me something for him to drink," said Pownell, who seemed to be acting the part of the Good Samaritan.

When he returned from ministering to Dickinson, he told me he could not live.

The riot, so called, was now entirely ended. The elder Gorsuch was dead; his son and nephew were both wounded, and I have reason to believe others were—how many, it would be difficult to say. Of our party, only two were wounded. One received a ball in his hand, near the wrist; but it only entered the skin, and he pushed it out with his thumb. Another received a ball in the fleshy part of his thigh, which had to be extracted; but neither of them were sick or crippled by the wounds. When young Gorsuch fired at me in the early part of the battle, both balls passed through my hat, cutting off my hair close to the skin, but they drew no blood. The marks were not more than an inch apart.

A story was afterwards circulated that Mr. Gorsuch shot his own slave, and in retaliation his slave shot him; but it was without foundation. His slave struck him the first and second blows; then three or four sprang upon him, and, when he became helpless, left him to pursue others. *The women put an end to him.* His slaves, so far from meeting death at his hands, are all still living.

**Source:** William Parker, "The Freedman's Story: In Two Parts," *Atlantic Monthly* 17 (February and March 1866), Part 2, 283–88.

## Voices from the Canadian Settlements (1855)

After the 1850 Fugitive Slave Act, migration of fugitive slaves to Canada increased. Most integrated into white communities, but several all black settlements were founded as experiments in black self-sufficiency. The Elgin settlement, sometimes called Buxton, and the Dawn settlement, were the most successful of them all. Probably the least successful was the Refugee Home Society.

In 1855, journalist Benjamin Drew traveled to Canada to interview residents in the settlements and subsequently published his findings in a book entitled *The Refugee*. Included here are statements from four of the settlers.

## MR. AND MRS. ISAAC RILEY, ELGIN

*Mr. Riley:* In Perry County, Missouri, where I was raised, I never saw an overseer, nor a negro trader, nor driver, nor any abuse, such as is practiced in other places. I've never seen any separations of families. I always from a small boy meant to be free at some day. After I had a son, it grieved me to see some small boys in the neighborhood, who were hired out to work twenty miles from home. I looked at my boy, and thought if he remained, he would have to leave us in the same way, and grow up in ignorance. It appeared to me cruel to keep him ignorant.

I escaped with my wife and child to Canada. Among the French near Windsor, I got small wages, . . . and morning and night up to my knees in water. Still, I preferred this to abundance in slavery. I crossed over and got work and better pay in Michigan. They would have liked to have me remain, and offered to build a house for me. But I did not feel free in Michigan, and did not remain. I went to St. Catharines [Canada], and got fifty cents a day. By and by, I heard of Mr. [Rev. William] King's settlement [Elgin]. I came here, and have got along well. My children can get good learning here.

*Mrs. Riley:* I was born in Maryland and raised in Perry County, Mo. Where I was raised, the treatment was kind. I used to hear of separations of families, but never saw any. I never saw the lash used, nor the paddle, nor ever heard of the abuse of slaves until I came into Canada. I see many here, who have suffered from hard treatment, and who have seen it practiced on others, but I never saw an overseer, nor a negro trader in my life; if I did, I didn't know it. I never knew anything about places they call "the quarters" in my life. I could not go when I pleased, but was sometimes allowed to go out without a pass ten or twelve miles from home. I was never stopped on my way by patrols—never heard about such things where I was raised. I was never sent to school; but my master, who had owned my mother, and raised me from the cradle, was very kind, and taught me to read and spell some, but not to write.

I used often to think that I would like to be as free as the white people were. I often told them, when they made me angry, that they had no more business with me, than I had with them.

My master was very particular about my having clothing and food enough. When I first came to Canada, the colored people seemed cold and indifferent to each other; and so it was with the white people and the colored. It seemed as if the white people did not want to speak to us. I took this very much to heart, for where I grew up, the white people talk freely to their neighbors' colored people. I felt so about it, that if they had come for me, I would have gone back willingly. . . .

For two years before I left, my husband talked of coming to Canada. I felt no desire for leaving. But a young man, a relative of my master, often persuaded me to leave for Canada, and he talked with a great deal of reason. He said he would not, if he were I, bring my boy up to be a slave: "you don't know," he would say, "how long the master may live, and when he dies, you may come under altogether different treatment." At last, when there was a camp meeting, I told my husband we had better leave, as it might be so by and by, that we could not leave at all. We left, and made a long camp meeting of it.

We crossed over at Windsor, and had rather hard times about Potico, among the French—there's where the people seemed so distant. I thought if Canada was all like that place, it was a hard place. We stayed there a few months, and went to St. Catharines, where we did better. After a while, we heard that Mr. King was buying a place to settle the colored people. We came up here before it was surveyed, and Mr. Riley helped the surveyors. He took one hundred acres of land, and we are well contented. If I do not live to see it, perhaps my children will, that this will one day be a great place.

My two oldest children go to school. The oldest is well along, and studies Latin and Greek. The other three are not old enough to go to school. We have good schools here—music and needlework are taught.

I think my present condition here far preferable to what it would have been in slavery. There we were in darkness. Here we are in light. My children also would have grown up, had I remained there, in ignorance and darkness.

# WILLIAM HENRY BRADLEY, DAWN

This is my name since I left slavery: in slavery I was known as Abram Young. I left Maryland with my wife and two children in 1851.

I look at slavery as the most horrid thing on earth. It is awful to think of the poor slaves panting for a place of refuge, and so few able to find it. There is not a day or night that I don't think about them, and wish that slavery might be abolished, and every man have his God-given rights.

I have prospered well in freedom. I thank the Lord for my success here. I own fifty acres of land, bought and paid for by my own energy and exertions, and I have the deed in my house.

If there were a law to abolish the use of liquor as a beverage, it would be a good thing for Canada.

I own two span of horses, twelve head of hogs, six sheep, two milk cows, and am putting up a farm barn.

There is a great deal of prejudice here. Statements have been made that colored people wished for separate schools: some did ask for them, and so these have been established, although many colored people have prayed against them as an infringement of their rights. Still, we have more freedom here than in the United States, as far as the government law guarantees. In consequence of the ignorance of the colored men, who come here unlearned out of slavery, the white people have an overpowering chance. There are many respectable colored people moving in, but I have not much hope of a better state of things. Public sentiment will move mountains of laws.

Steam engines don't work harder than a man's heart and veins, when he starts from his master, and fears being overtaken. I don't understand how an honest man can partake of any principle to carry him back.

If a man could make slaves of mud or block, and have them work for him, it would be wrong. All men came of the hand of the Almighty: every man ought to have life, and his own method of pursuing happiness.

# WILLIAM A. HALL, DAWN

I was born seven miles from Nashville, Tenn., Davidson County. I lived one year in Mississippi, I saw there a great deal of cotton growing and persecution of slaves by men who had used them well in Tennessee. No man would have thought there could have been such a difference in treatment, when the masters got where they could make money. They drove the hands severely. My mother and brothers and sisters, when they changed their country, changed their position from good to bad. They were in Mississippi the last I heard of them, and I suppose they are there yet. It makes me miserable to consider that they are there: for their condition has been kept fresh in my memory, by seeing so much suffering and enduring so much. I went from Mississippi to Bedford County, Tenn. My master died here, and I was in hopes to go to see my mother. The doctor who attended my master had me sold at auction, and bought me himself, and promised he would never sell me to anybody; but in six months he tried to sell me. Not making out, he sent me to his father's farm in Tennessee, where I was treated tolerably well.

I remained there one year, then he took me horse-driving to Louisiana and back.

I saw some of the dreadfulest treatment on the sugar farms in the sugar-making season. The mill did not stop only to gear horses. People would come to my master and beg money to buy a loaf of bread. I saw them chained. I saw twelve men chained together, working on the levees. I saw three hundred that speculators had, dressing them up for sale. The overseers were about the mills, carrying their long whips all the time and using them occasionally. When they wanted to whip severely, they put the head and hands in stocks in a stooping posture.

The last two years I was in Tennessee, I saw nine persons at different times, made fast to four stakes, and whipped with a leather strap from their neck to their heels and on the bottoms of their feet, raising blisters: then the blisters broken with a platted whip, the overseer standing off and fetching hard blows. I have seen a man faint under this treatment. I saw one about eighteen years old, as smart as you would see on the foot, used in this way: seven weeks after he fainted in consequence; his nerves were so shattered that he seemed like a man of fifty.

The overseer tied me to a tree, and flogged me with the whip. Afterwards he said he would stake me down, and give me a farewell whipping, that I would always remember. While he was eating supper, I got off my shoe, and slipped off a chain and ran: I ran, I suppose, some six hundred yards: then hearing a dog, which alarmed me, I climbed a hill, where I sat down to rest. Then I heard a shouting, hallooing, for dogs to hunt me up. I tried to understand, and made out they were after me. I went through the woods to a road on a ridge. I came to a guide-board—in order to read it, I pulled it up, and read it in the moonlight, and found I was going wrong—turned about and went back, travelling all night: lay by all day, travelled at night till I came where Duck River and Tennessee come together. Here I found I was wrong—went back to a road that led down Tennessee River, the way I wanted to go. This was Monday night—the day before they had been there for me. I got something to eat, and went on down the river, and travelled until Saturday night at ten, living on green corn and watermelons. Then I came to a house where an old colored man gave me a supper: another kept me with him three days. My clothes were now very dirty: I got some soap of a woman, and went to a wash-place, and washed my clothes and dried them. A heavy rain came on at daybreak, and I went down to the river for a canoe—found none—and went back for the day—got some bread, and at night went on down the river; but here were so many roads, I could not make out how to go. I laid all day in a corn field. At night I found a canoe, 12 feet long, and travelled down the river several days, to its mouth. There I got on an island, the river being low. I took my canoe across a tongue of land—a sandbar—into the Ohio, which I crossed into Illinois. I travelled three nights, not daring to travel days, until I came to Golconda, which I recognized by a description I had given on a previous attempt, for this last time when I got away was my fourth effort. I went on to three forks in the road, took the left, travelled through the night, and lay by. At two, I ventured to go on, the road not being travelled much. But it seemed to go too far west: I struck through the woods, and went on till so tired I could walk no further. I got into a tobacco-pen, and stayed till morning. Then I went through the woods, and came to where a fire had been burning—I kindled it up, roasted a lot of corn, then travelled on about three miles completely lost. I now came to a house, and revolved in my mind some hours whether to go or not, to ask. At last I ventured, and asked the road— got the information—reached Marion: got bewildered, and went wrong again, and travelled back for Golconda—but I was set right by some children. At dark I went on, and at daybreak got to Frankfort— 13 miles all night long, being weak for want of food. A few miles further on I found an old friend, who was backward about letting me in, having been troubled at night by white children. At last he let me in, and gave me some food, which I much needed. The next night he gave me as much as I could carry with me.

I went on to within five miles of Mount Vernon. At 4 A.M., I lay down, and slept till about noon. I got up and tried to walk, but every time I tried to stoop under the bushes, I would fall down. I was close to a house, but did not dare to go to it; so I laid there and was sick—vomited, and wanted water very bad. At night I was so badly off that I was obliged to go to the house for water. The man gave me some, and said, "Are you a runaway?" I said, "No—I am walking away." "Where do you live?" "I live here now." "Are you a free man?" "Why should I be here, if I am not a free man?—this is a free country." "Where do you live, anyhow?" "I live here, don't you understand me?" "You are a free man, are you?" "Don't you see he is a free man, who walks in a free country?" "Show me your pass—I s'pose you've got one." "Do you suppose men need a pass in a free country: this is a free country." "I suppose you run away—a good many fugitives go through here, and do mischief." Said I, "I am doing no mischief—I am a man peaceable, going about my own business; when I am doing mischief, persecute me—while I'm peaceable, let no man trouble me." Said he, "I'll go with you to Mount Vernon." "You may go, if you have a mind to: I am going, if it is the Lord's will that I shall get there. Good evening;" and I started out of the gate. He said, "Stop!" Said I, "Man, don't bother me—I'm sick, and don't feel like being bothered." I kept on: he followed me. "Stop, or I'll make you stop!" "Man, didn't I tell you I was sick, and don't want to be bothered." I kept on, he picked up a little maul at a wood pile, and came with me, his little son following, to see what was going on.

He walked a mile and a quarter with me, to a neighbor of his—called—there came out three men. He stated to them, "Here's a runaway going to Mount Vernon: I think it would be right to go with him." I made no reply. He said, "We'll go in with him, and if he be correct, we'll not injure him—we'll not do him no harm, nohow." I stood consulting with myself, whether to fight or run; I concluded to run first, and fight afterward. I ran a hundred yards: one ran after me to the edge of the woods, and turned back. I sat down to rest—say, an hour. They had gone on ahead of me on horses. I took a back track, and found another road which led to Mount Vernon, which I did not reach until daybreak, although he said 'twas only five miles.

I hastened on very quick through town, and so got off the track again: but I found a colored friend who harbored me three days, and fulfilled the Scriptures in one sense to perfection. I was hungry, and he fed me; thirsty, and he gave me drink; weary, and he ministered to my necessities; sick, and he cared for me till I got relieved: he took me on his own beast, and carried me ten miles, and his wife gave me food for four days' travel. His name was Y_____.

I travelled on three nights, and every morning found myself close to a town. One was a large one. I got into it early—I was scared, for people was stirring—but I got through it by turning to my right, which led me thirty miles out of my way. I was trying to get to Springfield. Then I went on to Taylorville. I lay out all day, two miles out, and while there, a man came riding on horseback within two feet of me. I thought he *would* see me, but he wheeled his horse, and away he went. At dark I got up and started on. It rained heavily. I went on to the town. I could discover nothing—the ground was black, the sky was cloudy. I travelled a while by the lights in the windows; at last ventured to ask the way, and got a direction for Springfield. After the rain the wind blew cold; I was chilled: I went into a calf lot, and scared up the calves, and lay where they had been lying, to warm myself. It was dark yet. I stayed there half an hour, trying to get warm, then got up, and travelled on till daybreak. It being in a prairie, I had to travel very fast to get a place to hide myself. I came to a drain between two plantations, and got into it to hide. At sundown I went on, and reached Springfield, as near as I could guess, at 3 o'clock. I got into a stable, and lay on some boards in the loft.

When I awoke, the sun was up, and people were feeding horses in the stable. I found there was no chance to get out, without being discovered, and I went down and told them that I was a stranger, knowing no one there; that I was out until late, and so went into the stable. I asked them if there was any harm. They said "No." I thanked them and pursued my way. I walked out a little and found a friend who gave me breakfast. Then I was taken sick, and could not get a step from there for ten days: then I could walk a little, and had to start.

I took direction for Bloomington—but the directions were wrong, and I got thirty miles out of my way again: so that when I reached Bloomington, I was too tired to go another step. I begged for a carriage, and if they had not got one, the Lord only knows what would have happened. I was conveyed to Ottawa [Michigan], where I found an abolitionist who helped me to Chicago. From about the middle of August to the middle of November, I dwelt in no house except in Springfield, sick—had no bed till I got to Bloomington. In February, I cut wood in Indiana—I went to Wisconsin, and stayed till harvest was over; then came to a particular friend, who offered me books.

I had no money for books: he gave me a Testament, and gave me good instruction. I had worn out two Testaments in slavery, carrying them with me trying to get some instruction to carry me through life. "Now," said he, "square up your business and go to the lake, for there are men here now, even here where you are living, who would betray you for half a dollar if they knew where your master is. Cross the lake: get into Canada." I thanked him for the book, which I have now; settled up and came to Canada.

I like Canada. If the United States were as free as Canada, I would still prefer to live here. I can do as much toward a living here in three days, as there in six.

## THOMAS JONES, THE REFUGEE HOME SOCIETY

I was a slave in Kentucky, and made my escape five years ago, at the age of thirty. The usage in Kentucky on the front part of the State is pretty good—back, it is rather tight.

I came here without anything. I had no money or aid of any kind. I went right into the bush chopping wood. I brought my lady with me, and we were married on the way. I have one child. With what I earned by hard licks, I bought land and have built me a frame house. I now follow plastering and anything I can find to do. I am worth three or four thousand dollars, and pay about thirty dollars a year tax.

If a man have aid furnished him, he does not have so much satisfaction in what he has—he feels dependent and beholden, and does not make out so well. I have seen this, ever since I have been here—the bad effects of this giving. I have seen men waiting, doing nothing, expecting something to come over to them. Besides, it makes a division among the colored people. The industrious are against it, the other class favor it; and so they fall out. My opinion is, that the fugitive on the road should be assisted, but not after he gets here. If people have money to give, they had better give it to those who suffer in trying to help them here. For those who come sick, or actually stand in need, there is a society here among ourselves to take care of them.

In regard to aid from societies on the other side, there are many who know that money is raised for the poor travelling fugitive, and they take advantage of it: free people of color from the States come over pretending to be fugitives, who never were fugitives. They come in a miserable condition, often drinking men, worthless, to get the money that is raised. I have known six or seven such cases.

The colored people are doing very well. They are poor, some of them, but are all able to have enough to eat and wear, and they have comfortable homes, with few exceptions—and some of these are in a way to have them. Some few don't seem to care whether they have good houses or not, as is the case among all people.

In the Refugees Home they are not doing very well. Land was to be sold to the refugees at cost, giving them five acres, and they to buy twenty. Some dissatisfaction exists because there has been an advance made of four shillings an acre for surveying, although the land had been surveyed once. The refugees all refused to pay it. They were to clear up the five acres in three years. Some had not been on three years, but went with that understanding. Alterations were made, too, enlarging the size of the houses. One of them has left the lands in consequence, and more talk of doing so. They doubt about getting deeds, and they begin to think 'tis a humbug. The restrictions in regard to liquor, and not selling under so many years, nor the power to will his property to his friends, only to his children, if he have any, make them dissatisfied. They want to do as they please. If they want to exchange and get a bigger place, they want to do it without being cramped.

In addition, the men who have settled there, have been a bother to the society. As they were dependent, smart men would not go, and it has been occupied by men who expected aid from the other side.

The colored men must rely on their own two hands, or they'll never be anything.

The colored people are temperate and moral.

**Source:** Benjamin Drew, *The Refugee; or, The Narratives of Slaves in Canada, Related by Themselves* (Boston: John P. Jewett, 1856), 298–301, 312–13, 314–20, 326–28.

## "Stealing the Livery of Heaven to Serve the Devil" (1857)

Mary Ann Shadd, a black freeborn woman from Delaware, migrated with her family to Canada in the wake of the 1850 Fugitive Slave Act. Settling in Ontario, she founded the *Provincial Freeman*, a newspaper for slaves seeking asylum in Canada. In opposition to Henry Bibb's editorial position in the *Voice of the Fugitive*, the other Canadian paper for refugees, Shadd argued that black settlements that relied on charity from white abolitionist groups lent credence to those proslavery voices that claimed that blacks were incapable of self-sufficiency. In this editorial she refers to two settle-ments, Buxton (or the Elgin Settlement) and the Refugee Home Society; the former refused outside contributions, and the latter, founded by Henry Bibb, accepted them. Her criticism of the Refugee Home Society is similar to that made by settler Thomas Jones (above).

> The Rev. S. Ewer, an agent of the Free Mission Baptists, has lately written a letter to the *American Baptist*, in which the refugees in Can-ada are represented as "needing aid in order to live." The Canadian whites are charged with being not only deficient in sympathy, but as "not wanting our slaves" to come to the Provinces; and free colored men are said to be indifferent to their fugitive brethren, &c. We can-not conceive of a more untruthful, contradictory, and injurious letter than this same, in part, and in the whole! A new impulse is, by this means, to be given to wholesale begging, we suppose.
>
> Mr. Ewer said when in London, during the winter, that after hav-ing traveled to the settlements, and among the colored people, ex-tensively, he was of opinion from observation and testimony that there was no need for the begging for fugitives—that as a few of their churches (Free Mission Baptists) needed aid in their erection, &c.—instance the Dawn Church—their society would help them; but the begging for food, clothes, &c., for the people at large, was wrong. This was said after a visit to the admirable settlement of Buxton, into which such aid *is not permitted to be sent*; and after having been among some of the most destitute settlements.
>
> But the reverend gentleman has neared the region of the Refugees Home, that moral pest of Canadian Refugees, and of a sudden, his optics become clearer. 'Tis an insult to the Elgin settlement to be put in such a degrading juxtaposition, for the Home is clearly sought to be introduced into favorable notice by the association, although so daintily handled. . . .
>
> The religious body known as the Free Mission Baptists, we respect highly; they are right on the slavery question, they are right in sym-pathy to the slave. But they are wrong in so far as they impose upon us and support their superannuated ministers, and give heed to their messages to revivify the almost defunct begging degradation.

What despotism was ever equal to that of pushing and hounding on to further debasement, the men who would be self-reliant and loyal to this free land? But we cannot believe that such a respectable body will countenance this great wrong, even in so old a man as Mr. Ewer.

**Source:** *Provincial Freeman*, April 4, 1857.

## An Anti-Underground Railroad Polemic (1860)

Printed polemics for and against slavery became common in the decades leading up to the Civil War. One of the most unusual was a "memoir" purportedly written by a white Underground Railroad conductor named Frank Wilmot. Wilmot's narrative melodramatically defends the Southern claim that slaves were happy with their lot and that fugitives were usually seduced or forced into running by zealous Northern abolitionists.

I became the head of a company of four conductors, who desired me to aid them in carrying off three Creole girls, owned by a man in one of the southern counties of Kentucky. For the part I was to perform, I was to receive $3000. These girls had just been purchased from a slave dealer in New Orleans, and were considered by my comrades to be very handsome. Their object in obtaining the girls was a dishonorable one. Although I had seen them, I was not smitten with their beauty, and only looked upon the enterprise as one of profit, money being, during these ten horrid years of my life, an idol which I worshipped.

On the night we selected for our foray on the house of the planter, we repaired to the spot. One of our party, rapping at the door, the planter opened it, and remarked, that if we were benighted, he took pleasure in affording us a shelter. We entered, with seeming gratitude, and partook of a pleasant supper, which was already on the table. Conversation being opened, he alluded to the recent purchase he had made of the three girls, stating that they were sisters. They were intended, he remarked, as house servants, to wait upon his daughters and wife, the latter being in delicate health.

At a given signal, we seized and bound him hand and foot. The females screamed, and several of the negroes from the slave quarters rushed in. Seeing their master bound, and learning from what we said, that we wished to take them north, a scene followed, the recollection of which thrills me with horror. Every one seized upon the first thing at hand, and making at us, a terrible combat commenced. Knives were freely used, pistols fired, and it was with the greatest difficulty we made our escape out of the windows and doors. I really thought my time had come, for we were hotly pursued by the excited negroes, only keeping them at bay by occasionally firing a shot from our pistols. They lighted pine torches and followed in our wake, shouting after us with demoniac yells. Our ammunition began to run short, and we were determining whether to separate or remain together, when we struck upon a cow path. This we rapidly followed, but it shortly led us into a rugged defile; a number of trees had here fallen across it, and stopped our further progress. The blacks, with their blazing brands, rushed upon us, whooping like so many devils, the crackling and blazing of the torches rendering the scene the most awful and terrific I had ever witnessed. Horrid thoughts of approaching death crowded on my excited and fevered brain; and when I saw my three companions slaughtered in the most dreadful manner by my side, I sank into a state of utter unconsciousness.

When I awoke it was dark, and no one was visible. The cold and stiff arm of one of my dead comrades was lying across my breast. The blood from his wounds had run down my bosom, and was now thick and clotty. My feelings were awful. My heart almost ceased to beat, but with a great effort I arose to my feet. The moon was just rising, and shed her soft, ambient rays on the scene of carnage. I seemed to have escaped any serious wound, except what appeared to be the cut of a knife on my right arm. It was painful and stiffened. I gazed upon the bodies of my dead comrades, and then turned away with a sickening sensation.

I slowly made my way through the brushwood, and over the trunks of the fallen trees, and after walking a few miles, came to the Mississippi river. Here I bathed myself, and by the moon's light washed my bloody garments as well as I could. Discarding my shirt and vest, I buttoned my coat close to my neck, listening patiently for the puff of a steamboat. One of these, the *Signet*, in a short time made its appearance, and as soon as she was near enough to hear me, I hailed her. A boat was sent ashore, and I took passage for St. Louis. . . .

The boat sped along very swiftly. It was just the dawn of the day, when one of the firemen darted past me like an arrow, shouting "fire! fire! fire!" In a moment all was bustle and confusion. The pilot seemed seized with a panic, and instead of running the boat on shore, he kept her in the middle of the river. Ultimately, wrapped in flames, she was run on the foot of an island. But few reached the shore at that time, as she swung round and floated off. At this instant the boilers exploded, tearing away all the forward part of the cabin. The yawl was soon filled with terrified people, leaving myself almost alone on the deck. The flames were wrapping everything in their destructive embrace; and there seemed nothing but certain death for me. The explosion of the boilers had scattered around a thousand fragments, and many torn and mangled human beings lay about. The scene was appalling, and even now as I write, it makes me shudder.

There I stood on the deck, almost alone. I could not swim, and I felt my fate fast closing around me. In a moment I was seized in the arms by a sturdy negro, who leaping into the boiling, muddy water, gallantly battled among the floating fragments and reached the shore in safety. I was as helpless as an infant, and when I turned my eyes to my preserver, what was my surprise and astonishment, to see old black Sam and his master, Mr. Moreland, standing over me. [Wilmot had met Alabama planter Moreland and his slave Sam earlier in the narrative. At that time, Moreland had explained to Wilmot that slaves were content and loyal, that slave owners were compassionate, and that abolitionists, either gullibly or duplicitously, misrepresented the institution of slavery.]

I arose to my feet, and undertook to thank them. Words failed me, and I burst into tears.

"I will give you, Mr. Moreland, any price you may demand for Sam," said I, after I had somewhat composed myself, "so that I can set him free."

"Ah!" replied he, "Mr. Wilmot, Sam wouldn't leave me for the world. If he had wanted his freedom he would have long since had it. I have offered repeatedly to set him free, but he would never accept the boon."

Another packet approaching our now burnt boat, the saved passengers were taken aboard; and without anything occurring worthy of record, we reached Cairo in the course of the following day. Here I parted company with Mr. Moreland and the noble slave Sam, on whom I lavished several hundred dollars as a present. From Cairo I journeyed to Cincinnati, and from that city to Boston, where I tendered my resignation as a conductor on the Underground Railroad, which was received graciously, after my taking a solemn oath that I would not, on pain of death, disclose the names of the parties who

# ANNOTATED BIBLIOGRAPHY

American Experience. *Roots of Resistance: The Story of the Underground Railroad*. Time-Life Video, 1995. Videocassette (VHS), 60 min. A documentary on the Underground Railroad that includes interviews with descendants of both fugitives and slave owners.

Aptheker, Herbert. *American Negro Slave Revolts*. New York: International Publishers, 1993. Explores the white South's deep fear of slave insurrection and chronicles insurrection attempts from 1791 to 1860.

Aptheker, Herbert, ed. *A Documentary History of the Negro People in the United States*. Vol. 1, *From Colonial Times through the Civil War*. New York: Citadel Press, 1965. Section Three, "The Abolitionist Era," collects dozens of documents related to the Underground Railroad.

Bibb, Henry. *The Life and Adventures of Henry Bibb: An American Slave*. Madison: University of Wisconsin Press, 2001. First published 1849. One of the widest-read slave narratives of its day, offers an acute psychological analysis of the ways slaves coped with their bondage.

Bland, Sterling Lecater, Jr. *Voices of the Fugitives: Runaway Slave Stories and Their Fictions of Self-Creation*. Westport, CT: Greenwood, 2000. Argues that the typical slave narrative is a combination of fact and identity-construction on the part of the author.

Blight, David W., ed. *Passages to Freedom: The Underground Railroad in History and Memory*. New York: Smithsonian Books/HarperCollins, 2004. A superb collection of articles by leaders in the field. Lavishly illustrated.

Blockson, Charles L. *Hippocrene Guide to the Underground Railroad*. New York: Hippocrene, 1994. Offers detailed information, organized by state, of specific Underground Railroad stations and routes.

Blockson, Charles L., ed. *The Underground Railroad.* New York: Prentice Hall, 1987. A collection of first-person narratives from fugitive slaves, organized by state. Many of the stories are taken from Levi Coffin's and William Stills's contemporaneous accounts.

Bordewich, Fergus M. *Bound for Canaan.* New York: HarperCollins, 2005. A sweeping narrative history of the Underground Railroad. Well documented.

*The Boston Slave Riot, and Trial of Anthony Burns.* Boston: Fetridge, 1854. A pamphlet that appeared shortly after Burns's rendition to Virginia. Includes eyewitness accounts of the "riotous" events following Burns's arrest as well as transcripts from his trial.

Bradford, Sarah H. *Scenes in the Life of Harriet Tubman.* Auburn, NY: W.J. Moses, 1869. An "autobiography" of Tubman, compiled from interviews with her.

Brown, Henry. *Narrative of the Life of Henry "Box" Brown.* Edited by John Ernest. Chapel Hill: University of North Carolina Press, 2008. A memoir first published in 1851 of the slave who made a well-known escape from servitude by mailing himself from Richmond to Philadelphia.

Buckmaster, Henrietta. *Let My People Go: The Story of the Underground Railroad and the Growth of the Abolition Movement.* Columbia: University of South Carolina Press, 1992. A well-written and comprehensive history with a rich bibliography up to 1941, the book's original publication date. Lacks specific citations throughout the text, however.

Calarco, Tom. *People of the Underground Railroad: A Biographical Dictionary.* Westport, CT: Greenwood, 2008. Offers the profiles of 100 people—abolitionists, fugitives, rescuers, and so on—associated with the Underground Railroad.

Calarco, Tom. *Places of the Underground Railroad: A Geographical Guide.* With Cynthia Vogel, Kathryn Grover, Rae Hallstrom, Sharron L. Pope, and Melissa Waddy-Thibodeaux. Santa Barbara, CA: Greenwood, 2010. An encyclopedia of locations associated with the Underground Railroad in the United States and Canada. Contains illustrations and maps.

Campbell, Stanley W. *Slave Catchers: Enforcement of the Fugitive Slave Law, 1850–1860.* Chapel Hill: University of North Carolina Press, 1970. An exhaustive study of the 1850 Fugitive Slave Law, covering its inception, constitutionality, public reception, and enforcement.

Chadwick, Bruce. *Traveling the Underground Railroad: A Visitor's Guide to More Than 300 Sites.* Secaucus, NJ: Carol Publishing Group, 1999. A state-by-state guide prefaced with an 80-page history of the Underground Railroad. Maps and illustrations.

Clinton, Catherine. *Harriet Tubman: The Road to Freedom*. New York: Back Bay Books, 2004. A well-documented biography of Tubman, with a focus on her Underground Railroad activities.

Coffin, Levi. *Reminiscences*. Cincinnati: Western Tract Society, 1876. A memoir of one of the leading Underground Railroad stationmasters on the western route.

Craft, William, and Ellen Craft. *Running a Thousand Miles for Freedom; or, The Escape of William and Ellen Craft from Slavery*. New York: Arno Press, 1969. A chronicle first published in 1860 of one of the most famous escapes by the husband-and-wife team who disguised themselves as an invalid planter and "his" manservant.

Douglass, Frederick. *My Bondage and My Freedom*. Edited by John Stauffer. New York: Modern Library, 2003. First published 1855. The second and perhaps the best of Douglass's three autobiographies, written 10 years after the *Narrative* that established him as a leader of the abolitionist movement.

Drayton, Daniel. *Personal Memoir of Daniel Drayton, for Four Years and Four Months a Prisoner (for charity's sake) in Washington Jail*. Boston: Bela Marsh and New York: American and Foreign Anti-Slavery Society, 1853. A memoir of the man who captained the *Pearl* during the unsuccessful escape attempt of nearly 80 slaves in 1848.

Drew, Benjamin. *The Refugee: A North-Side View of Slavery*. Reading, MA: Addison-Wesley, 1969. Antebellum interviews with ex-slaves who settled in cities or black settlements in Canada first published in 1855.

Fairbank, Calvin. *Rev. Calvin Fairbank during Slavery Times*. New York: Negro Universities Press, 1969. The memoir first published in 1890 of the "abductor" who spent nearly two decades in jail for slave stealing.

Ferrell, Claudine L. *The Abolitionist Movement*. Westport, CT: Greenwood, 2006. A concise history of antebellum abolitionism. Good introductory text.

Forbes, Ella. *But We Have No Country: The 1851 Christiana Resistance*. Cherry Hill, NJ: Africana Homestead Legacy Publishers, 1998. An account of the Christiana Riot, with special emphasis on the clash between the rhetoric of freedom and the reality of slavery in the antebellum United States.

Franklin, John Hope, and Loren Schweninger. *Runaway Slaves: Rebels on the Plantation*. New York: Oxford University Press, 1999. An excellent history of slave runaways, offering a profile of the typical fugitive, methods of escape, and perils of recapture.

Frost, Karolyn Smardz. *I've Got a Home in Glory: A Lost Tale of the Underground Railroad*. New York: Farrar, Straus and Giroux, 2007. A history of Thomas and Lucie Blackburn's 1831 escape from servitude, their migration to Canada, and the Canadian government's protection of them from rendition.

Gara, Larry. *The Liberty Line: The Legend of the Underground Railroad*. Lexington: University Press of Kentucky, 1996. A groundbreaking history first published in 1961 that dispels many myths about the Underground Railroad, especially the claim that fugitive slaves were merely passive passengers.

Genovese, Eugene D. *Roll, Jordan, Roll: The World the Slaves Made*. New York: Vintage, 1971. A cultural history of slavery from the slave's perspective. Part Four, "Whom God Hath Hedged In," offers a good overview of everyday slave resistance.

Greenspan, Ezra, ed. *William Wells Brown: A Reader*. Athens: University of Georgia Press, 2008. An anthology of the ex-slave and Underground Railroad conductor's many works. Includes selections from his autobiography, his abolitionist writings, and his fiction.

Griffler, Keith P. *Frontline of Freedom: African Americans and the Forging of the Underground Railroad in the Ohio Valley*. Lexington: University Press of Kentucky, 2004. Examines the crucial role of blacks along the Ohio River's Railroad routes.

Hadden, Sally E. *Slave Patrols: Law and Violence in Virginia and the Carolinas*. Cambridge, MA: Harvard University Press, 2001. A study of slave patrols from the late 18th century to the end of the Civil War. Argues that the brutality of slave patrols was transferred to postwar Southern social institutions.

Hagedorn, Ann. *Beyond the River: The Untold Story of the Heroes of the Underground Railroad*. New York: Simon & Schuster, 2002. Focuses on the Underground Railroad in Ripley, Ohio, and the work of agents John Rankin and John Parker.

Henson, Josiah. *Autobiography of Josiah Henson*. Mineola, NY: Dover, 2003. A memoir first published in 1881 of the ex-slave who helped found the Canadian settlement of Dawn and was the inspiration for Harriet Beecher Stowe's character of Uncle Tom.

History Channel. *Underground Railroad.* A&E Home Video, 2002. DVD, 95 min. A documentary on the Underground Railroad that styles it as "the first civil rights movement."

Hudson, J. Blaine. *Encyclopedia of the Underground Railroad.* Jefferson, NC: McFarland, 2006. Includes a timeline as well as several appendices, the most useful of which are a bibliography of slave autobiographies and a list of antislavery and Underground Railroad songs. However, the entries contain many factual errors.

Hudson, J. Blaine. *Fugitive Slaves and the Underground Railroad in the Kentucky Borderland.* Jefferson, NC: McFarland, 2011. An examination of Underground Railroad activity in northern Kentucky.

Jackson, Ruby West, and Walter T. McDonald. *Finding Freedom: The Untold Story of Joshua Glover, Runaway Slave.* Madison: Wisconsin Historical Society Press, 2007. A biography of the fugitive who was rescued from slave catchers in Milwaukee in 1954.

*Journal of Negro History* (1916–2001). Renamed the *Journal of African American History* in 2002, an invaluable source of articles, many of them pioneering, on the Underground Railroad.

Kashatus, William C. *In Pursuit of Freedom: Teaching the Underground Railroad.* Portsmouth, NH: Heinemann, 2005. Offers a good overview of the Underground Railroad. Especially useful for teachers at the secondary level.

Klees, Emerson. *Underground Railroad Tales: With Routes through the Finger Lakes Region.* Rochester, NY: Friends of the Finger Lakes, 1997. Somewhat misleadingly titled, this volume culls stories of slave escapes on the Underground Railroad from Midwest, mid-Atlantic, and New England lines, along with a chapter on Railroad activity in the New York Finger Lakes district.

Loguen, Jermain. *The Rev. J.W. Loguen as a Slave and a Freeman.* Syracuse, NY: J.G.K. Truair, 1859. The autobiography of an ex-slave, Underground Railroad stationmaster in Syracuse, and participant in the 1851 Jerry rescue.

McFeely, William S. *Frederick Douglass.* New York: W.W. Norton, 1991. An excellent biography of Douglass by a Pulitzer Prize–winning historian.

McGowan, James A. *Station Master on the Underground Railroad: The Life and Letters of Thomas Garrett.* Rev. ed. Jefferson, NC: McFarland, 2005. A biography of the Wilmington, Delaware, stationmaster, with generous passages from his letters.

Morgans, James Patrick. *The Underground Railroad on the Western Frontier: Escapes from Missouri, Arkansas, Iowa and the Territories of Kansas, Nebraska and the Indian Nations, 1840–1865*. Jefferson, NC: McFarland, 2010. The title says it all.

Mull, Carol E. *The Underground Railroad in Michigan*. Jefferson, NC: McFarland, 2010. Offers an account of abolitionist and Underground Railroad activities in Michigan.

National Park Service. *Underground Railroad*. Washington, D.C.: U.S. Department of the Interior, 1998. Collects essays by three Underground Railroad scholars: Larry Gara's "Myth and Reality," Brenda Stevenson's "Slavery in America," and C. Peter Ripley's "The Underground Railroad."

Osofsky, Gilbert, ed. *Puttin' On Ole Massa: The Slave Narratives of Henry Bibb, William Wells Brown, and Solomon Northup*. New York: Harper Torchbooks, 1969. A convenient compilation of three slave memoirs written by two Underground Railroad workers and of one free black kidnapped and sold into slavery.

Pickard, Kate E. R. *The Kidnapped and the Ransomed: The Narrative of Peter and Vina Still after Forty Years of Slavery*. Lincoln: University of Nebraska Press, 1995. An account of Peter Still's life as a slave and a free man, written from interviews with him, first published in 1856. Peter was the long-lost brother of Underground Railroad stationmaster William Still.

Pirtle, Carol. *Escape Betwixt Two Suns: A True Tale of the Underground Railroad*. Carbondale: Southern Illinois University Press, 2000. A study of the Underground Railroad in southern Illinois that focuses on stationmaster and conductor William Hayes.

Power, Michael, and Nancy Butler. *Slavery and Freedom in Niagara*. Niagara-on-the-Lake, ON: Niagara Historical Society, 1993. A short treatise that explores the history of Canada's 1793 antislavery act, John Graves Simcoe's advocacy of it, and the community of ex-slaves that subsequently emerged in the Niagara region.

Quarles, Benjamin. *Black Abolitionists*. New York: Oxford University Press, 1969. Argues that in the abolitionist and Underground Railroad movements, blacks were protagonists rather than passive recipients of aid.

Rankin, John. *Letters on American Slavery*. Boston: Garrison & Knapp, 1833. William Lloyd Garrison claimed that this book made him an abolitionist.

A repudiation of antebellum moral, economic, and theological defenses of slavery first published in 1826 by a leading figure in the Underground Railroad.

Reinhardt, Mark. *Who Speaks for Margaret Garner?* Minneapolis: University of Minnesota Press, 2010. A compilation of contemporaneous legal and journalistic documents pertaining to Margaret Garner's escape, capture, and trial for the murder of her daughter.

Rhodes, Jane. *Mary Ann Shadd Cary: The Black Press and Protest in the Nineteenth Century.* Bloomington: Indiana University Press, 1998. A groundbreaking biography of the abolitionist who edited the second black newspaper in Canada.

Ricks, Mary Kay. *Escape on the* Pearl. New York: HarperCollins, 2007. A well-documented account of Capt. Daniel Drayton's unsuccessful attempt in 1848 to transport nearly 80 slaves to freedom aboard the schooner *Pearl*.

Runyon, Randolph Paul. *Delia Webster and the Underground Railroad.* Lexington: University Press of Kentucky, 1996. A biography of the abolitionist slave abductor who, along with Calvin Fairbank, was sentenced to a Kentucky prison for "slave stealing."

Shadd, Adrienne, Afua Cooper, and Karolyn Smardz Frost. *The Underground Railroad: Next Stop, Toronto!* Toronto: Natural Heritage Books, 2002. A generously illustrated history of the Underground Railroad terminal in Toronto and of the black community there.

Siebert, Wilbur H. *The Underground Railroad from Slavery to Freedom.* Mineola, NY: Dover, 2006. A classic history of the Underground Railroad first published in 1898. Although criticized for relying too heavily on anecdotal information and for downplaying the active role of blacks, it remains a valuable resource.

Slaughter, Thomas P. *Bloody Dawn: The Christiana Riot and Racial Violence in the Antebellum North.* New York: Oxford University Press, 1991. Analysis of the Christiana Riot. Especially insightful in chapters on the trial and its aftermath.

Smedley, R. C. *History of the Underground Railroad in Chester and the Neighboring Counties of Pennsylvania.* Mechanicsburg, PA: Stackpole Books, 2005. A history of the Underground Railroad in southeastern Pennsylvania first published in 1883. Based on eyewitness accounts from participants.

Somewhat implausibly claims that Railroad activity stretched back to the late 18th century.

Snodgrass, Mary Ellen. *The Underground Railroad: An Encyclopedia of People, Places, and Operations*. 2 vols. Armonk, NY: M.E. Sharpe, 2008. An indispensible resource, replete with cross-indexed entries, illustrations, and maps.

Sprague, Stuart Seely, ed. *His Promised Land: The Autobiography of John P. Parker*. New York: W.W. Norton, 1996. Transcripts of interviews given by Parker, an Underground Railroad leader in Ripley, Ohio. Only recently discovered, the manuscript is an illuminating portrait of the clandestine activity of a conductor.

Stauffer, John. *Giants: The Parallel Lives of Frederick Douglass and Abraham Lincoln*. New York: Twelve, 2008. Offers revealing biographical portraits of Douglass and Lincoln and explores their respective views on slavery, blacks, and emancipation.

Stewart, James Brewer. *Holy Warriors: The Abolitionists and American Slavery*. Rev. ed. New York: Hill and Wang, 1997. One of the best histories of the American abolitionist movement. Omits footnoted documentation, although it provides a good bibliography.

Still, William. *The Underground Rail Road*. Philadelphia: Porter & Coates, 1872. One of the few contemporaneous records of the Underground Railroad by an African American, Still's book is a record of over 600 fugitive slaves who made their way to Philadelphia from the South.

Switala, William J. *Underground Railroad in Delaware, Maryland, and West Virginia*. Mechanicsburg, PA: Stackpole Books, 2004. A well-documented history of Underground Railroad activities in the border states.

Switala, William J. *Underground Railroad in New York and New Jersey*. Mechanicsburg, PA: Stackpole Books, 2006. Especially helpful in tracing water routes over Lakes Erie and Ontario.

Switala, William J. *Underground Railroad in Pennsylvania*. 2nd ed. Mechanicsburg, PA: Stackpole Books, 2008. Pennsylvania was one of the busiest Underground Railroad states. This book focuses on not merely the often-discussed eastern connections, but also central and western ones.

Tobin, Jacqueline L. *From Midnight to Dawn: The Last Tracks of the Underground Railroad*. New York: Random House, 2007. A narrative history of Underground Railroad activity in the proximity of Detroit (often called "midnight" by conductors and slaves) and nearby Canada ("dawn"). Also a good survey of black settlements in Canada. Lacks footnoted documentation, but provides a good bibliography.

Tobin, Jacqueline L., and Raymond G. Dobard. *Hidden in Plain View: A Secret History of Quilts and the Underground Railroad*. New York: Anchor Books, 1999. Defends the controversial thesis that slave quilts coded navigational messages to help fugitives on their way.

Turner, Glennette Tilley. *The Underground Railroad in Illinois*. Glen Ellyn, IL: Newman Educational Publishing, 2001. Explores Underground Railroad activities, routes, and stations in Illinois. Illustrations and map.

Ullman, Victor. *Look to the North Star: A Life of William King*. Toronto: Umbrella Press, 1969. A biography of the founder of the Elgin Settlement.

Walker, David. *Appeal to the Colored Citizens of the World*. Edited by Peter P. Hinks. University Park: Pennsylvania State University Press, 2006. An incendiary condemnation of slavery first published in 1829 by a free black urging slaves to resist their bondage and warning whites that they risked insurrection if slavery continued.

Walker, Jonathan. *The Branded Hand: Trial and Imprisonment of Jonathan Walker*. New York: Arno Press, 1969. A memoir first published in 1845 of the Underground Railroad conductor whose right hand was branded by Florida officials with "S.S." for "Slave Stealer."

Ward, Samuel Ringgold. *Autobiography of a Fugitive Slave*. Chicago: Johnson, 1970. A memoir first published in 1855 of an ex-slave, Baptist minister, abolitionist, and Underground Railroad worker who was one of the leaders in the 1851 Jerry Rescue in Syracuse, New York.

Webster, Delia. *Kentucky Jurisprudence: A History of the Trial of Miss Delia A. Webster*. Vergennes, VT: E.W. Blaisdell, 1845. An account of Delia Webster's trial and conviction for abducting a family of Kentucky slaves and leading them to freedom in Ohio.

Weisenburger, Steven. *Modern Medea: A Family Story of Slavery and Child-Murder from the Old South*. New York: Hill and Wang, 1998. An account of the capture and trial of fugitive Margaret Garner, who killed one of her children rather than see her returned to slavery.

Wilmot, Frank A. *Disclosures and Confessions of Frank A. Wilmot, the Slave Thief and Negro Runner*. Philadelphia: Barclay, 1860. One of a number of proslavery "confessions" (fictional) from former Underground Railroad conductors who renounced their activities as immoral and detrimental to the well-being of slaves.

Winks, Robin W. *The Blacks in Canada: A History*. 2nd ed. Montreal & Kingston: McGill-Queen's University Press, 2008. Chapters 4–7 explore the migration and settlement of slave fugitives in Canada.

Wish, Harvey, ed. *Antebellum: Writings of George Fitzhugh and Hinton Rowan Helper on Slavery*. New York: Capricorn Books, 1960. Antebellum contributions to the slave debate, two by Fitzhugh arguing for slavery on "humanitarian" grounds, one by Helper arguing against it on economic grounds.

# INDEX

**About the Author**

KERRY WALTERS is the William Bittinger Professor of Philosophy and Professor of Peace and Justice Studies at Gettysburg College (PA), near the site of the historic Civil War battle. Walters is the author or editor of more than 20 books, including *Benjamin Franklin and His Gods*, *Revolutionary Deists: Early America's Rational Infidels*, and a critical edition of Thomas Paine's *The Age of Reason*.